Theoharis departs not only from current trends in criticism that stress the discontinuities and fragmentation of *Ulysses*, but he also restores neglected, significant sources to Joyce studies. This original study shows how Joyce found form in what his literary and philosophical contemporaries, and so many of his subsequent critics, have viewed as modernism's disarray.

Theoharis Constantine Theoharis is associate professor of literature at the Massachusetts Institute of Technology.

Joyce's *Ulysses*

J o y c e' s

ULYSSES

An Anatomy of the Soul

by Theoharis Constantine Theoharis

The University of North Carolina Press

Chapel Hill & London

© 1988 The University of North Carolina Press

The paper in this book meets the guidelines for permanence and durability
of the Committee on Production Guidelines for Book Longevity of the Council
on Library Resources.

Printed in the United States of America

92 91 90 89 88   5 4 3 2 1

The author is grateful for permission to reproduce passages from the following:

Selections from Dante's *Vita Nuova* and *De Vulgari Eloquentia* are reprinted from
The Literary Criticism of Dante Alighieri, translated and edited by Robert S. Haller.
Copyright © 1973 the University of Nebraska Press.

From F. S. L. Lyons, *Charles Stewart Parnell*. Copyright © 1977 by Oxford
University Press.

From Dante Alighieri, *The Divine Comedy*, translated with a commentary by
Charles Singleton, Bollingen Series 80. Vol. 1, *Inferno*. Copyright © 1973 by
Princeton University Press. Vol. 2, *Purgatorio*. Copyright © 1973 by Princeton
University Press. Vol. 3, *Paradiso*. Copyright © 1975 by Princeton University Press.

Library of Congress Cataloging-in-Publication Data

Theoharis, Theoharis Constantine.
Joyce's Ulysses.

Bibliography: p.
Includes index.
1. Joyce, James, 1882–1941. Ulysses—Sources.
I. Title.
PR6019.O9U746   1988   823'.912   87-35839
ISBN 0-8078-1795-3 (alk. paper)

For John Hunt

contents

viii
Contents

a c k n o w l e d g m e n t s

Leopold Bloom sadly lacks companions, but his story has created a large company of happy men and women. As I take my public place there I have many thanks to make. I am grateful to the Mabelle MacLeod Lewis Foundation for material assistance. John Henry Raleigh and Philip Damon of the University of California, Berkeley gave this work rigorous attention. John Bishop, also at Berkeley, has tried to protect me from my extravagances, and given this project the full benefit of his extraordinary knowledge and uncanny literary intuition of Joyce's mind and art. Guy Davenport, of the University of Kentucky, read the book with great keenness and generosity. Don Gifford, of Williams College, has spent twelve years educating me in the ways of Joyce's comedy and craft, with learning and patience that make any gratitude pale. Cynthia Wolff, at MIT, has been Athena to this book—protector, enabler, and ever-mindful advocate. Since John Hunt had to spend his superior intelligence and literary sense reading every word of every attempt to get this book right, I have dedicated it to him.

Joyce held no mean conception of the artist's function. Nothing less than truth, nothing short of reality qualified as an artist's subjects. To these a writer was entirely responsible; revealing these in his art, he made himself eternal. The young Joyce construed the relations of art, truth, and reality as follows:

Human society is the embodiment of changeless laws which the whimsicalities and circumstances of men and women involve and overwrap. The realm of literature is the realm of these accidental manners and humours—a spacious realm; and the true literary artist concerns himself mainly with them. Drama has to do with the underlying laws first, in all their nakedness and divine severity, and only secondarily with the motley agents who bear them out. . . .

. . . Still I think out of the dreary sameness of existence, a measure of dramatic life may be drawn. Even the most commonplace, the deadest among the living, may play a part in a great drama. It is a sinful foolishness to sigh back for the good old times, to feed the hunger of us with the cold stones they afford. Life we must accept as we see it before our eyes, men and women as we meet them in the real world, not as we apprehend them in the world of faery. The great human comedy in which each has share, gives limitless scope to the true artist, today as yesterday and as in years gone. The forms of things, as the earth's crust, are changed. The timbers of the ship of Tarshish are falling asunder or eaten by the wanton sea; time has broken into the fastnesses of the mighty; the gardens of Armida are become as treeless wilds. But the deathless passions, the human verities which so found expression then, are indeed deathless, in the heroic cycle, or in the scientific age, Lohengrin, the drama of which unfolds itself in a scene of seclusion, amid half-lights, is not an Antwerp legend but a world drama.[1]

Fourteen years elapsed from the twentieth of January, 1900, when Joyce, the college student, made these pronouncements in "Drama and Life," until the time he began *Ulysses*, and in the interim he dropped the high idealistic rhetoric of that essay and other youthful pieces. Flight from Ireland, life with Nora Barnacle, difficulties with publishers, and penury brought him face-to-face with the prized human verities, and the encounter withered the untried boldness of his messianic posing. In 1902, with the world still before him, Joyce, writing on James Clarence Mangan, presented an oblique view of his own aspirations and beliefs as a literary artist.

> Beauty, the splendour of truth, is a gracious presence when the imagination contemplates intensely the truth of its own being or the visible world, and the spirit which proceeds out of truth and beauty is the holy spirit of joy. These are realities and these alone give and sustain life. . . . In those vast courses which enfold us and in that great memory which is greater and more generous than our memory, no life, no moment of exaltation is ever lost; and all those who have written nobly have not written in vain, though the desperate and weary have never heard the silver laughter of wisdom. Nay, shall not such as these have part, because of that high, original purpose which remembering painfully or by way of prophecy they would make clear, in the continual affirmation of the spirit?   [*CW*, p. 83]

By 1914 Joyce had stopped presenting his artistic destiny so voluptuously, partly because he was no longer twenty-two years old, partly because hard experience had made him secretive about his cherished ambitions, and partly because such expression was unnecessary when he was actually accomplishing his artistic purpose. However, the mature writer preserved, I believe, the heroic visionary stamina of the young man, even though he stopped proclaiming it. The philosophical and religious vocabulary of the latter quotation, bloated as it may be by decorative exuberance, indicates an ambition on Joyce's part to write on a grand scale in the tradition that had produced Dante, Blake, and Ibsen, among others: the tradition of renegade moralists, of messianic truth-tellers. Joyce was not a man who forgot things. The "spirit" so incoherently glorified as literature's subject here is one subject of *Ulysses*, transformed there through comedy, and through a technically philosophical exactitude that gave coherent intellectual design to Joyce's genius.

Considered together, the two quotations present Joyce's earliest formulation of an inherited distinction in literary theory and practice between the novel and the epic. Although theories and histories of the novel proceed from many different axioms to many different ends, most have in common some version of the claim that the novel deals with immediately observed social reality, with what Joyce called the realm of "motley agents" and their "accidental manners and humours." From Virgil through Dante, Milton, and Joyce, the epic has had as its object of imitation the eternal nature of the created cosmos, and humanity's struggle to discover and achieve its essential identity as a rational and moral agent in that cosmos. Joyce's aspiring praise of the "holy spirit of joy" that proceeds out of the beautiful truth imagination discovers in the contemplation of its being and the world's, and his ontological revery of the "vast courses" and "great memory" that order life mark the earliest limits of his epic ambition.

To a great extent, this generic distinction between realistic representation of historical circumstances and symbolic representation of philosophical truth, between story and myth, fact and idea, derives from classical theoretical debate about the nature of Homer's poems. The question, focused most famously in Plato's opposition to Homer's moral authority, was: did Homer have secret knowledge of the nature of the soul and its place in the cosmos, which he represented allegorically in his epics, or was he simply an anthologist of legends, histories, geographies, folktales, and war memoirs who presented his material for interpretation at face value? For the most part, the debate in Greece was won by the realists, but a stubborn tradition of allegorical reading of the *Odyssey* and *Iliad*, in which the adventures of heroes were held to be moralized codes describing the struggles of the soul in the world, persisted into the Middle Ages and Renaissance.[2]

When Joyce made *Ulysses* an epic novel he worked in both traditions of Homeric interpretation at once, comically transfiguring both but not substantially flouting either. He made a story out of "whimsicalities and circumstances" in the life of a man well acquainted with the "dreary" and the "commonplace." That narrative of immediately observed social reality, dense with meaning at face value, is at the same time a form presenting the inspired imagination's contemplative, sacred, and joyous discovery of the truth and beauty of Being in the world. The fusion of the novel's and the epic's objects of imitation in *Ulysses* displays Joyce's development of his conception, expressed in "Drama and Life," that the changeless can be embodied in the changing, that the universal and particular can be presented at once.

From Virgil forward, Homer's epics have been persistently thought of as stories universally representative. Samuel Johnson's famous remark from *A Preface to Shakespeare* expresses the traditional conviction about Homer's eternal value, which Joyce shared: "but the poems of *Homer* we yet know not to transcend the common limits of human intelligence, but by remarking, that nation after nation, and century after century, has been able to do little more than transpose his incidents, new name his characters, and paraphrase his sentiments."[3] Transposition, renaming, and paraphrasing, all species of parody, make up the bulk of Joyce's analogical art in *Ulysses*, but they are not his only mode of universalizing Bloom's story. The logic of analogy and allusion in *Ulysses* is not only a logic of synoptic comparison of stories and cultures, but a philosophically constructed account of cosmological order, and humanity's place in it.

Joyce expressed his idea of the narrative universality of Homer's *Odyssey* often. Two of his clearest statements came when he started work on *Ulysses*. To Georges Borach he remarked: "The most beautiful, all-embracing theme is that of the *Odyssey*. It is greater, more human than that of *Hamlet*, *Don Quixote*, Dante, *Faust*"; and to Frank Budgen he said: "No-age Faust isn't a man. But you mentioned Hamlet. Hamlet is a human being, but he is a son only. Ulysses is son to Laertes, but he is father to Telemachus, husband to Penelope, lover of Calypso, companion in arms of the Greek warriors around Troy, and King of Ithaca. He was subjected to many trials, but with wisdom and courage came through them all. . . . I see him from all sides . . . he is a complete man as well—a good man. At any rate, that is what I intend he shall be."[4]

Introduction

Concerning the philosophical universality of *Ulysses*, its ontological scope, Joyce remained silent throughout his life. For the
most part, literary scholars have followed his example, treating
Ulysses as a work exclusively concerned with life in society, treating it as the novel it clearly is, relegating the epic structure to
ironic parody or merely arrogant technical display on Joyce's part. I
have turned my attention in this study to the ontological order
Joyce set inside and around the social and psychological reality of
Bloom's day. In the narrative one story is made many stories, any
story, by citations of topical and structural similarity. Hence the
*Odyssey, Hamlet, Don Giovanni, The Marriage of Figaro, The Wife
of Scarli*, each an adultery revenge plot in one way or another, figure more or less prominently in the telling of Bloom's Dublin journey. Working up from the story, this symbolic magnification of
Bloom's marriage plot unifies many discrete artistic particulars into
a general story. Working down from the allusive symbolic order,
Bloom's marriage plot and all its analogues in other artworks are
embodiments of what Joyce called "changeless laws," of what I
have called the ontological subject of the epic—the nature of the
cosmos and humanity's place in it.

Ulysses presents reality at any and all levels of consideration as
the constant interflux of oppositions, either opposite forces or contrary states of being. The physics of that interchange are identical
in any and all instances, and appear most clearly in *Ulysses* as the
narrative struggle of one man and one woman to find satisfying
lives together. While Homer supplied topical and stylistic elements
for Joyce's physics of interchanging states and coalescing forces, the
tradition of rational humanism which located that dynamic preeminently in the human soul supplied Joyce with a philosophical
model for construing all lives as one life, all states and forces as
one, in Bloom's.

In *Ulysses* Joyce cites many luminaries who might be included in
any definition of a rationalist, humanist tradition. I have concentrated on Aristotle, Bruno, Dante, and Arnold because those writers, appearing in many contrarily organized relationships in *Ulysses*, all saw the soul's power to unite opposites as the force by
which humanity takes its proper place in the cosmos. And they all
saw that force as a constant, normal function of life, instead of an
intermittently transcendental flash in which people leapt out of the

realm of bodily experience. In fact, all of them thought of the soul and body as unified rather than separable. That urge to unify made them most relevant to Joyce's design in *Ulysses*. Readers curious to discover how all this may be true are here invited to turn the page.

abbreviations

The following books are cited in the text by the abbreviations given below.

A   Aristotle. *De Anima*. Translated by W. S. Hett. Cambridge: Harvard University Press, Loeb Classical Library, 1975.

C   Giordano Bruno. *Five Dialogues by Giordano Bruno: Cause, Principle, and Unity*. Translated with an Introduction by Jack Lindsay. Westport, Conn.: Greenwood Press, 1976.

CA   Matthew Arnold. "Culture and Anarchy." In *The Portable Matthew Arnold*, edited by Lionel Trilling. New York: Viking Press, 1949.

CSP   F. S. L. Lyons. *Charles Stewart Parnell*. New York: Oxford University Press, 1977.

CW   James Joyce. *The Critical Writings of James Joyce*. Edited by Ellsworth Mason and Richard Ellmann. New York: Viking Press, 1964.

E   Richard Ellmann. *James Joyce*. New York: Oxford University Press, 1982.

FW   James Joyce. *Finnegans Wake*. New York: Viking Press, 1939.

G   Don Gifford with Robert J. Seidman. *Ulysses Annotated: Notes for Joyce's Ulysses*. Berkeley: University of California Press, 1988.

L   James Joyce. *Letters of James Joyce*. Edited by Richard Ellmann. New York: Viking Press, 1966. *L* 1 refers to Volume 1, *L* 2 to Volume 2.

LCD   Dante Alighieri. *The Literary Criticism of Dante Alighieri*. Translated and edited by Robert S. Haller. Lincoln: University of Nebraska Press, 1973.

Inf   Dante Alighieri. *Inferno*. Vol. 1 of *The Divine Comedy*. Translated by Charles S. Singleton. Bollingen Series 80. Princeton: Princeton University Press, 1973.

Abbreviations

Pur   Dante Alighieri. *Purgatorio*. Vol. 2 of *The Divine Comedy*. Translated by Charles S. Singleton. Bollingen Series 80. Princeton: Princeton University Press, 1973.

Par   Dante Alighieri. *Paradiso*. Vol. 3 of *The Divine Comedy*. Translated by Charles S. Singleton. Bollingen Series 80. Princeton: Princeton University Press, 1975.

P   James Joyce. *A Portrait of the Artist as a Young Man*. Edited by Chester G. Anderson. New York: Viking Press, 1968.

U   James Joyce. *Ulysses*. The Corrected Text, edited by Hans Walter Gabler with Wolfhard Steppe and Claus Melchior. New York: Random House, 1986.

Unless otherwise indicated, throughout this book I cite *Ulysses* by reference to episode and line numbers (rather than page numbers) in the corrected text established by Hans Walter Gabler, with Wolfhard Steppe and Claus Melchior. Gifford's *Ulysses Annotated: Notes for Joyce's Ulysses* keys annotations to episode and line numbers as well, hence my references to that work are not to pages in it, but to notes identified by episode and line numbers.

Joyce's *Ulysses*

JOYCE *&* ARISTOTLE

That Aristotle was a major figure in Joyce's intellectual development, and in his earliest theoretical formulations of which subjects and forms authors needed to work with, has long been clear. During his second flight to Paris, in 1903, Joyce read Aristotle and kept a notebook of salient ideas that he collected in order to make the aesthetic theory that eventually, with the aid of "applied Aquinas," appeared in *Stephen Hero* and *A Portrait of the Artist as a Young Man*. Joyce's letters indicate that by the time he had begun *Ulysses* he had read Aristotle's *De Anima* (in a translation entitled *Psychology*), *Poetics*, *Metaphysics*, and *Rhetoric*.[1] While all four make appearances in the novel, Joyce made more of *De Anima* than any of the other three. Aristotle's definitions, from *Poetics*, of art and the artist, the subjects of the Paris notebook, are important topics in *Ulysses*, but subsidiary ones. Creation of an epic focused Joyce's intellectual attention on Aristotle's explanation of topics more encompassing than aesthetics. The dynamic structures of human mentality presented as instantiations of the dynamic structures of life itself—that epic purpose in *Ulysses* sent Joyce to Aristotle's systematic account of consciousness in *De Anima*, just as the autobiographical presentation of the artist had sent him to *Poetics* when he wrote the story of Stephen Dedalus's youth.

In 1917, at work on *Ulysses*, Joyce discussed Aristotle with Georges Borach, who recalls the conversation this way: "In the last two hundred years we haven't had a great thinker. My judgment is bold, since Kant is included. All the great thinkers of recent centuries from Kant to Benedetto Croce have only cultivated the garden. The greatest thinker of all times, in my opinion, is Aristotle. Everything, in his work, is defined with wonderful clarity and simplicity. Later, volumes were written to define the same things."[2] If to Alfred North Whitehead all philosophy was a footnote to Plato, this remark suggests that for Joyce, all philosophy proceeded from the original clarity and simplicity of Plato's pupil. The remark also makes Aristotle timeless, and so a contemporary for Joyce. Committed to portraying in *Ulysses* all things past, passing, or to come, Joyce required well-structured logical models for universality. The conversation with Borach suggests strongly that Joyce's favorite truth-teller was directly at hand to supply them.

Aristotle's *De Anima* is an account of the nature and activity of life in the here and now. Vitality's functions, not the personality's, are the subjects of Aristotle's *Psychology*. Joyce the novelist found there not a philosophy of character that could be drawn on for the creation of fictional people, but a general account of life itself, a description of the fundamental laws governing organic existence, and of the process by which human beings experience and understand those laws. *De Anima* must have appealed to Joyce the infidel largely because its analysis of the soul is general and impersonal, scientific rather than religious.[3] I think he absorbed the treatise's general principles, used them as primary structural devices in his novel, and, according to habit, insinuated in *Ulysses* that he had done so. What follows is a precis of *De Anima*, an examination of those places in *Ulysses* where Joyce tips his hat to Aristotle by alluding to or quoting the philosopher's works, and an account of concepts in *De Anima* that became principle elements in the novel's epic intellectual and aesthetic design.[4]

De Anima

Aristotle begins *De Anima* with the statement that inquiry concerning the soul is of the first importance in humanity's effort to acquire knowledge. All knowledge is beautiful and valuable, he says, and knowledge of the soul is so preeminently. The distinguishing qualities of knowledge are the degree of accuracy it achieves and the dignity bestowed on it by its object. On both counts knowledge of the soul is of the highest order. In addition, because the soul is the principle of life, knowledge concerning it contributes greatly to the study of nature, and thus substantially to the whole body of truth.

The first book of *De Anima* reviews previous theoretical accounts of the soul, including Plato's. Although Aristotle finds much to quarrel with in the other thinkers he surveys, the main disagreement is, as usual in Aristotle's work, with his former teacher. Plato had argued that the soul is immaterial, has three parts, is separable from the body, and is eternal. Aristotle rejects the tripartite division of the soul, substituting various functions of one substance for Plato's three souls. Most significantly he rejects the idea that the soul is separable from the body, or eternal, with the exception of its function as active intellect—an exception analyzed more throroughly later in this chapter.

After accounting for previous inquiries into the subject, Aristotle, in Book 2, presents his idea of the soul. He starts by discriminating three kinds of substance in existing things: matter, unrealized potential to become a certain individual thing; form, the shaping force that realizes any thing's potential individuality; and the combination of both. Bodies are substances, either living or not. The characteristics of life are self-sustenance, growth, and decay. A living body is a compound substance—natural matter in which the organic capacity for self-sustenance, growth, and decay is actualized by the formal presence of the soul. Aristotle puts it this way: "So the soul must be substance in the sense of being the form of a natural body, which potentially has life. And substance in this sense is actuality."[5]

Life, insofar as it is a definitive characteristic of a natural body, derives from the soul that informs the body. The soul thus defined is no more separable from the body than sharpness is from the blade of an ax, or sight from the eye. Any inquiry into life therefore involves an inquiry into the nature and function of the soul. Aristotle's method of inquiry in this treatise is empirical, as it almost always is throughout his works. Life is understood through observation of the activity of plants, animals, and human beings, natural bodies that all nourish themselves, grow, and decay. Such observation reveals six faculties of the soul: nutrition and reproduction under the heading self-sustenance, sensation (physical awareness of other bodies), desire, locomotion, imagination, and reason. These six faculties are the constitutive elements of the hierarchy Aristotle observed in living creatures. At the apex of natural life are human beings, who possess all six faculties. In descending order follow animals, who cannot reason, and finally plants, capable only of self-sustenance. According to Aristotle, the soul causes these six faculties to exist in a body in three senses: as the substantial essence of the body, as the source of all its actions, and as its final end. The entire realm of nature is at the soul's disposal, "for all natural bodies are instruments of the soul" (*A*, p. 89).

Aristotle's analysis of the soul's sensory and rational actions bears most significantly on Joyce's formal and conceptual innovation in *Ulysses*, especially on the protean analogies that universalize and unify the book's action. Although Joyce presents, at great length and very often, the other processes of the soul that Aristotle mentions—nutrition, reproduction, imagination, locomotion, and desire—he creates his representative man in *Ulysses* primarily by showing Bloom's senses and intellect at work. In those activities Joyce could continually show forms interchanging, the dynamic that he, following Aristotle, considered actuality's essence.

Sensation, as Aristotle defines it, is an activity in which the sensing body is acted upon by a motion that alters it. The sense organs have the potential to receive impressions, but that potential can only be actualized by an object outside the soul. The organs receive impressions and are thus altered—they do not alter themselves. Until sensation is in motion, it has no actual existence. Whatever is sensed impinges on the soul from objects outside it. Thus, sensation can never be produced by the soul in isolation.

Actual individual things are apprehended in sensation. As much of a thing as is capable of moving the sense organ is perceived by the subject. Aristotle begins his analysis of sensation with analysis of sight. Color, because it is visible, is the object of sight. By its nature color acts upon any transparent medium (air or water), actualizing the potential of that medium to be colored. The medium can only be made transparent by light. Light therefore is the prerequisite for sight, activating the potentially transparent and thus rendering it susceptible to the natural activity of color, the specific object of sight. Color sets a transparent medium (let it be air) in motion. The air in turn, because it is an extended continuum between the color and the eye, transfers the motion of the color to the eye. The potential to receive that motion, the perceptible form of a thing, is activated in the sense organ by the motion itself. In perception the sensible form and the sense organ coalesce, the sensible

impulse reproducing itself in the sensing faculty as a seal is repro-
duced in wax. Before sensation the sense organ and its object are
unlike each other. During sensation they have an identical form.
Sensation occurs in the other organs in the same way, although the
medium and objects are different for each different sense. The general action is this: A sensible object stimulates a medium which
extends as a continuum to a sense organ. The impulse, or perceptible form, without its matter, travels through the medium to the
sense organ, where sense and the sensible, the soul and an object
external to it, unite in an act of sensation.

Sensation, then, is the soul's faculty for identifying itself with
external objects through organic reception of their immaterial
forms. Like wax, the soul may receive the impress of a gold ring,
but not the gold, a quality of the object, not the matter of the object. Although a sense and its organ are in one way identical, since
both are potential recipients of sensible forms, they are in another
way fundamentally different. The sense organ is an extended magnitude to which the sense stands as a potential ratio. A range of
sensible objects exists for each sense organ. The sensible power in
each organ adjusts the organ's material reaction to stimulation received from the sensible objects in this range, maintaining throughout sensation equivalence between the motion on the organ and the
subsequent motion in the organ. If the ratio cannot be maintained,
because of excessive stimulation, perception will fail, and eventually the organ may be destroyed. Sensation is a mean then, between
the extreme motions possible in a sense organ. The mean, because
it is the midpoint between extremes, can be acted upon by both
extremes in all their various degrees. Tepid water is cooler than all
degrees of hot water and warmer than all degrees of cold water, and
therefore it can be changed into any degree of cold or hot water. So
it is with the soul in sensation, the activity by which a sense organ
adjusts itself to various motions received from sensible objects outside it. Because it is a mean, the soul, in its sensitive faculty, may
become identical to any sensible object existing within a given
range of extremes, and any sensible object in that range may become identical to the soul.

After briefly describing common sense as a faculty that responds
to all the activities of the five separate senses and their specific
objects and combines them to create a unified sensation of objects,

Aristotle defines imagination. Identifying itself with a sense object by receiving that object's perceptible form from the activity of the senses, the imagination stores that form for presentation to the rational soul, where the process of a living creature's identification with other existing things is perfected in the soul's highest function—thought.

The objects of thought are universals, the definitive essences of things and concepts. Thought works analogously to sensation. Just as senses are potentially receptive of sensible forms, so the intellect is potentially receptive of intelligible forms. When sensation occurs, the object sensed and the sensing subject are one being; so it is with the intellect, with two differences. Sensation requires the action of an external object to occur. Thought, deriving its actualizing form from the images of sensible objects already present in the soul as a result of sensation, does not. Sensation occurs in organs: thought, an immaterial motion, requires no organs and is independent, in its essential action, of the body. Because it is unmixed with matter, intellect is potentially receptive of and identical to all things. Aristotle compares the potential intellect to a blank tablet on which any letters can appear, because none are there intrinsically. This is not to say that the intellectual soul has no inherent essence, only that its essence is to receive and become all things. Before it acts, the intellectual soul has no knowledge and no real existence. This fact is emphasized to refute Plato's theory that the soul by its nature possesses universal knowledge that its existence in the body has obscured. Because thinking has no organ, it cannot, like sensation that occurs in organs, be destroyed or impaired by excessive stimulation. There is, consequently, nothing rational that the soul cannot think about, no intelligible object too enormous or complex for its intellectually assimilative power.

Although its function is independent of the body, the intellectual soul can only work on the material supplied by the senses. When the intellect receives the sensible form of an object from the imagination, it abstracts from the sensible form the object's intelligible form, its definitive, universal essence. Sensation is knowledge of a particular thing, thought is knowledge of the substantial nature, the universal essence of a particular thing. Through sensation the soul knows that something is red, through thought the soul knows the red thing as the substance "barn," and as a particular instance of that substance, "this barn." The actualization of sensation comes from forms outside the soul, the actualization of thought from forms within. Universal forms enter the soul when sensible forms do, and are abstracted from sensible forms by the intellect. Thus, incidentally, thinking is caused by objects external to the soul, but not immediately or essentially.

In addition to thinking about the essential definitive forms of particular things, the intellect can think about itself. Since any activated function of the soul is identical to what activates it, when the intellect is its own object, the soul identifies itself with itself. Sensations because they can only occur in organs with a limited potential for transformation, and because they can only be realized by the action of external things on the soul, can never realize themselves with such reciprocity. Thus there is no sensation of the power to sense, only of what is sensed. But thinking actualizes its own potential without organs, and without external objects. Receptive therefore to all things, thought may also think itself, and the soul may regard the soul, in perfect solipsism.

Having described the intellect as potentially all things, Aristotle explains how such potential is actualized. His explanation introduces the making mind, commonly called the active intellect. This topic, more than any other in *De Anima*, has fired unending argument among Aristotle's commentators, from Avicenna, Albertus Magnus, Averroes, and Aquinas down to Werner Jaeger, W. D. Ross, and G. E. R. Lloyd in this century. The following analysis is an attempt at simple exposition of Aristotle's concept, not an interpretation slanted toward Ross's position, or any other argumentative one. The active intellect is a positive state of the soul that makes potentially intelligible forms actually intelligible and the potentially receptive intellect actually receptive. Aristotle compares the activity of the active intellect in reasoning to the activity of light in sight. Without light, colors are only potentially visible—in the presence of light, which causes certain media to be transparent, and therefore receptive of colors, they are made actually visible. The active intellect is such a precondition for the soul's intellectual identification with all things. The active intellect makes what is potentially intelligible, in the sensible form presented to the mind by the imagination, actually intelligible, by abstracting the definitive essence of an object from the sensible impression of it and thus distinguishing the universal from the particular form. By virtue of this function the active intellect is the cause and agent of the passive intellect. The passive intellect is defined as the mind's capacity to receive and become all intelligible things. But this capacity can only function in the presence of intelligible forms. As information exists in the imagination it is unintelligible. Only after the active intellect has abstracted the intelligible information from images, their essential, definitive forms, can the passive intellect actually be passive, that is, receive the forms that it then identifies with itself.

As active intellect the soul is separable from the body, impassive (that is, not itself receptive of forms, not affected or moved by them, rather acting on them) and unmixed with any element. When isolated from the body, presumably after the death of the person in whom it functions, this aspect of the soul is eternal. There is no personal memory in the active intellect because it receives no forms, making things thinkable rather than thinking them. Thus, the immortality Aristotle claims for the soul here is not the personal immortality of Christianity. He says explicitly that of all the soul's functions only the active intellect is eternal, citing the death of the passive intellect as an explanation for the absence in the eternal soul of any memory of natural life.

In the eighth chapter of the third book of *De Anima* Aristotle gathers the implications and conclusions of his understanding of the soul's actions into a summary statement of life's capacity to unify dispersed and different objects.

> Now summing up what we have said about the soul, let us assert once more that in a sense the soul is all existing things. What exists is either sensible or intelligible; and in a sense knowledge is the knowable and sensation the sensible. We must consider in what sense this is so. Both knowledge and sensation are divided to correspond to their objects, the potential to the potential, and the actual to the actual. The sensitive and cognitive faculties of the soul are potentially these objects, *viz.*, the sensible and the knowable. These faculties, then, must be identical either with the objects themselves or with their forms. Now they are not identical with the objects; for the stone does not exist in the soul, but only the form of the stone.

The soul, then, acts like a hand; for the hand is an instrument which employs instruments, and in the same way the mind is a form which employs forms, and sense is a form which employs the forms of sensible objects. But since apparently nothing has a separate existence, except sensible magnitudes, the objects of thought—both the so-called abstractions of mathematics and all states and affections of sensible things—reside in the sensible forms. And for this reason as no one could ever learn or understand anything without the exercise of perception, so even when we think speculatively, we must have some mental picture of which to think; for mental images are similar to objects perceived except that they are without matter.

[A, pp. 179–81]

Life, whose essence is the soul, occurs in natural bodies, and, with the exception of the active intellect, is inseparable from natural bodies. The end of life is to participate, as much as possible, in the immortality of divinity, its first cause and originator. To this end living things reproduce themselves, creating new life to replace that which natural decay destroys. In human beings life assumes the highest form, reason. In reason, as in self-sustenance and sensation, the function of life is identification of all things with itself, reception and transformation of any existence into its own. Coalescence is the primary quality of life, shared by all the soul's functions. To live is to become all things, by virtue of the soul's capacity (limited in nourishment, sensation, desire, and imagination, unlimited in reason) to receive the forms of all things.

The soul, as Aristotle discusses it, is a biological substance, a natural fact. *Psychology* is an accurate enough transliteration of the Greek title (*On the Psyche*) but it has potentially misleading connotations. Aristotle's "soul" is not a permanent religious identity bestowed on human beings by God, nor is it the temporal sum of a person's experiences. The notions of salvation and free will, fundamental to so many religious accounts of the soul, especially Christian ones, have no place in *De Anima*. The investigation and analysis of personal history, the attention paid to emotions, dispositions, reminiscences, and all the other elements comprising the "mind" studied by scientists since Freud, are conspicuously absent in Aristotle's analysis. For him the soul is the organizing form of organic nature. That form's highest achievement, thought in human beings, is not nature transcending itself, as was true for Plato, but nature fully realizing itself.

De Anima and the Narrative of *Ulysses*

Joyce refers to Aristotle over thirty times in *Ulysses*. Six of those references are to *De Anima*. The first emerges in "Nestor" while Stephen is not teaching the pupils in his history class. During one boy's imperfect recitation of Milton's *Lycidas*, Stephen resumes speculation on Aristotle's ideas of historical change, which have been occupying him throughout the lesson that morning. He thinks:

> It must be a movement then, an actuality of the possible as possible. Aristotle's phrase formed itself within the gabbled verses and floated out into the studious silence of the library of Saint Geneviève where he had read, sheltered from the sin of Paris, night by night. By his elbow a delicate Siamese conned a handbook of strategy. Fed and feeding brains about me: under glowlamps, impaled, with faintly beating feelers: and in my mind's darkness a sloth of the underworld, reluctant, shy of brightness, shifting her dragon scaly folds. Thought is the thought of thought. Tranquil brightness. The soul is in a manner all that is: the soul is the form of forms. Tranquility sudden, vast, candescent: form of forms.[6]

This passage from "Nestor" initiates two associated concepts from *De Anima* that gradually and somewhat obscurely develop, through repetition, augmentation, and embellishment, across the novel into primary elements of its narrative and conceptual design: first, that everything existing is either sensible or knowable by the soul, and second, that the soul is identical, in a manner, to everything it senses and knows. These ideas, which Stephen variously cherishes, depends on, and chafes against in the narrative, also bear significantly on the intellectual order meticulously dispersed throughout the book's allusive symbolism, and provide means for integrating the novel's narrative and symbolic techniques.

To begin with the narrative here: Stephen is disgusted with his

students because they are rich and spoiled and do not know what
he knows. This last point is his excuse for berating them privately
and confounding them publicly with impenetrably obscure riddles
and flippant, inaccessible puns. Stephen shows more kindness to
Sargeant than to the other boys because this struggling, dim-witted
creature bears a physical resemblance to him as he was as a child
and seems an icon to him of his own futility. Stephen is a bad
teacher not because of ignorance (Joyce took extravagant and flattering pains to make his fictional shadow an intellectual wunder-
kind, a Young Turk familiar with the obscure systems of Joachim of
Floris and Jacob Boehme as well as the time-honored philosophy of
Aristotle and his scholastic devotees), but because of unanchored
bitterness and self-loathing that have alienated him from even the
simplest human discourse. How could this young man, who cannot
have breakfast until he has lacerated his host with accusations of
betrayal, and himself with guilty resurrections of his mother's
ruined corpse, teach schoolboys anything? His reminiscence of Aristotle during Talbot's faulty recitation of *Lycidas* is symptomatic
of Stephen's isolation, but it also reveals what he was like before
his disastrous return from Paris, and how he views the change.

While Talbot recites, Stephen thinks of Aristotle's idea that possibility must be actualized as possibility before any change from possible to actual can occur. This is a continuation of his earlier speculation about Aristotle's notions of history, and an answer to the last
questions Stephen asked himself before he set Talbot the task of
recitation, "But can those have been possible seeing that they never
were? Or was that only possible which came to pass? Weave,
weaver of the wind" (*U*, 2.52–53). Whether this weaver is Aristotle
or Stephen is impossible to determine, but the equivocal application of the term suggests very strongly that Stephen uses it to characterize both himself and Aristotle as futile intellectual seekers,
constructing absurd systems out of their own ignorance. By the
time Talbot has started reciting, Stephen has recovered from this
chronic bile and takes Aristotle seriously again, reconstructing the
argument he earlier sundered with grandiloquent obscurantism.
But instead of following Aristotle's argument, Stephen, influenced
despite his disgust for it by the classroom he is in, and the function
he is supposed to be carrying out, remembers his own time as a
student of Aristotle. The students in this Dalkey classroom are bab-

bling and indifferent to learning. He pursued Aristotle's difficult works in silence, in Paris, with a chaste devotion. To escape boredom and anguish, Stephen's mind drifts from the classroom to the library where he once pursued knowledge heroically. But the nostalgia does not relieve.

He remembers the readers around him in the library with eerie disgust. "Fed and feeding brains about me: under glowlamps, impaled, with faintly beating feelers." Like Armstrong, the rich Dalkey student who fondles figrolls before eating them during class, the students in the library have made thinking an occasion for feeding. Those inmates of Saint Genevieve were not finding the splendor of truth there: learning was an alimentary process for them, where it should have been radiant insight, as Stephen indicates it was for him. The metaphor of feeding is one more detail in Stephen's recollection that shows the influence of his present conditions on the escapist reverie. In front of Stephen, Armstrong feeds instead of learning on June 16, 1904, and Stephen, seeking to blot out Armstrong by remembering his own studies, remembers foreign students feeding. This disgust, aroused with the thought of food (a chronic problem for Stephen all day), catapults his reminiscence from realistic reconstruction to grisly surrealistic comedy, as Stephen transforms the feeding brains into insects, picturing the Parisian students not as investigators but specimens, "under glowlamps, impaled, with faintly beating feelers." Stephen's impulse to escape Dublin's squalor by remembering Paris has so far made the preferred past as disgusting and more gruesome than the present. By linking Saint Genevieve to the Dalkey schoolroom, Joyce indicates both the power of immediate physical details over Stephen's memory and imagination and the determining influence of his present disposition in the degraded scholar's retrieval of his past. Try as he may, Stephen cannot escape the world outside himself, or the world within.

Stephen read Aristotle in Paris as preparation for the achievement of the literary goal he had set himself at the end of *A Portrait of the Artist as a Young Man*: the creation of the conscience of his race. Back in Dublin for *Ulysses*, having created nothing but his own agony, Stephen throughout the novel regards Paris and his failed mission with longing indistinguishable from contempt. Whereas he once saw himself the fiery, holy rebel struggling to publish knowledge to a hypocritical and ignorant race whose vulgarity and cowardice had given license to the church's usurpation of knowledge and truth, he now remembers the incapacity that plagued the struggle (which he sees as feminine—the lady dragon "sloth" in his memory)—his timidity and hesitance, his weakness. But the passage does not end with discouragement. Instead it soars in Stephen's final thoughts to those moments when his eagerness and idealism for Aristotle's wisdom were consummated.

In the last four sentences of the paragraph Stephen remembers the exhilaration he felt in the library on understanding three crucial concepts in *De Anima*. The first is Aristotle's trinitarian account of the intellectual soul's capacity, in speculation, to be its own agent, subject, and object. "Thought is the thought of thought," Stephen remembers, continuing, "Tranquil brightness." The brightness and tranquility belong both to thought itself and to Stephen, who remembers escaping the sloth's restless darkness by understanding Aristotle's conception of thought. The metaphor of illumination is common to many descriptions of ecstasy, and more specifically, it is one conventional Christian term for the consummation of mystical insight. Augustine writes, "With the flash of one glance, my mind arrived at that which is"; St. Bernard of Clairvaux describes the experience with the same term, "When the Lord comes there is a consuming fire and his presence is understood in the power by which the soul is changed, and by the love by which it is inflamed; there ensues a certain sudden and unwonted enlargement of mind, an inpouring of light."[7] And, of course, there is Dante, whose progress through Paradise is an increasingly splendid ascent through ever more brilliant circles of light. It is worth noting that Stephen refers to the work of these Christian mystics more than once in the course of the day and that Joyce made Dante's epic a presence almost equal to Homer's in *Ulysses*. The ecstatic gleam the mystics describe is exactly what he recalls here, an intellectual rapture. As Dedalus continues he condenses two propositions from Aristotle's summary description of the soul: "The soul is in a manner all that is: the soul is the form of forms." Another memory of the rapture follows, this time climactic: "Tranquility sudden, vast, candescent." Consummation comes with repetition of the concept that gave him access to the long-sought splendor of truth: "form of forms." At last Stephen's effort to escape the painful present through reminiscence works: he does recall an unambiguous good in the Parisian debacle.

But of course he is in Dublin's neighboring Dalkey, remote from that tranquil brightness, and Joyce, true to his habit of constructing literary effects by contradiction, drops Stephen immediately back into the ignominy of the present moment. Talbot, throughout Stephen's revery, has been failing to recite *Lycidas* from memory, sneaking looks at the text that he's "propped . . . nimbly under the breastwork of his satchel" (*U*, 2.61–62). The metaphor "breastwork"—a hastily constructed wall for defense—indicates that Talbot believes he is fooling Stephen with this ruse, or at least that he is trying to by defending his crutch from teacher's glance. Teacher of course knows he has no authority in this classroom, and desires none. Talbot, like a broken record, sticks mechanically at the line "Through the dear might of Him that walked the waves,/ Through the dear might. . . . . ," breaking in, through stupidity, on Stephen's memory of intellectual rapture (*U*, 2.78–79).

Lycidas has many symbolic functions that bear on the conceptual design of the novel. I will mention only two ways here that the poem bears on the narrative: Talbot is struggling to keep his ruse afloat and sinks because he cannot remember the whole line describing the Savior who bore up the drowned Lycidas. Stephen has been struggling to fix his mind on better times, and hits on a memory of ecstatic deliverance, but he loses it because Talbot has not learned Milton's account of Christ, the Savior. "The dear might of Him that walked the waves" does nothing to help Talbot, who literally does not know it, and who forces Stephen down, through this ignorance, from a memory of deliverance, to the destructive floor of this wretched Dalkey classroom. So much for religious poetry, one thinks. But the judgment is premature.

Lycidas bears on Stephen's situation in two contradictory ways. The flight to Paris was made so that Stephen could save his race by creating for it a conscience. In this dual role as savior and creator Stephen is comparable to Christ, the dramatic hero of *Lycidas*, who created man and woman, according to Catholic theology, and who saved them. But the flight failed, and the failure made Stephen a different metaphoric son, Icarus, who drowned, like Lycidas, and who, unlike Milton's titular hero, was not saved. Stephen the would-be redemptive creator and Stephen the drowned youth are both present in Talbot's recitation, unbeknownst to Talbot, and perhaps to Stephen as well. The final allegorical stitch—Stephen as resurrected Lycidas—is deferred until Bloom appears two chapters later. Poldy is made Stephen's Christ repeatedly in the symbolism of the book. Backed by that association, Bloom closes the Miltonic symbolic account hundreds of pages later in "Eumaeus" when, speaking about the globe's water to Stephen, he mentions having once seen "a superannuated old salt, evidently derelict, seated habitually near the not particularly redolent sea on the wall, staring quite obliviously at it and it at him, dreaming of fresh woods and pastures new as someone somewhere sings" (U, 16.630–33). In the same chapter, twenty-four pages later, a narrative voice modeled on Bloom's consciousness repeats the reference: "Anyhow they passed the sentrybox with stones, brazier etc. where the municipal supernumerary, ex Gumley, was still to all intents and purposes wrapped in the arms of Murphy, as the adage has it, dreaming of fresh fields and pastures new" (U, 16.1725–28).

Before Bloom's intervention, Stephen, in terms of Milton's *Lycidas*, is Christ turned drowned boy, Icarus more than Lycidas. After Bloom's comically sacrificial salvation of Stephen in "Circe" (during which Poldy suffers a sadomasochistic execution symbolically identified more than once with the horrors of Golgotha), Dedalus may finally become the resurrected Lycidas, and the artist ready to twitch his mantle with exuberance for an epic project awaiting in the fresh new future. These are some primary ways Milton's elegy figures in the paradoxical double comparison of Stephen and Bloom to Christ, the major religious symbolism dominating the novel's narrative account of fathers and sons. Joyce floats the symbolic progress of *Lycidas* in his novel for more than five hundred pages, implicating it all along the way in many other systematic parallels (Yeats's "Who Goes With Fergus" is one). It is not accidental that the whole polyvalent business gets started while Stephen is thinking of *De Anima* and Aristotle's idea of the soul as a form that incorporates all other forms.

Casually plucked from the memory of his ecstatic vision by Talbot's defective mnemotechnic (a fault, incidentally, Bloom complains of in himself and his wife), Stephen drops even the pretense of authority and advises Talbot to go on cheating and turn over the page he's hidden under his satchel. "Turn over, Stephen said quietly.

I don't see anything" (*U*, 2.80). The counterpoint here is a beautiful example of Joyce's narrative style. Talbot has turned Stephen away from his memory of knowledge and light by not turning the obscured page of the text with which he tries to conceal his ignorance. Converted from light back to failure, Stephen reports his own condition when he sarcastically exposes Talbot's ruse with the remark "I don't see anything" (i.e., I don't, and you won't, see the line you've forgotten on this page—turn over to the next one where the poem you've supposedly memorized continues). The cheater's hidden page lacks the knowledge he seeks, as does the indifferent schoolmaster's darkened mind. With "I don't see anything," Joyce adds yet another metaphor to his description of Stephen's teaching: it is a case of the blind leading the blind. Dedalus was shy of brightness in Saint Genevieve; he's bereft of it as the master of a classroom in Dalkey.

Unlikely as it may seem that anyone could have an ecstatic reaction to Aristotle's prose, the response is understandable in Stephen's case. As Joyce characterizes him in *Portrait* and *Ulysses*, Stephen is an aficionado of Scholastic theology—a body of thought that is to a great extent the application of Aristotelian principles, many of them from *De Anima*, to Roman Catholic dogma. The Catholics diverged from pagan Aristotle considerably, naming the entire soul (not just the active intellect) immortal, and assigning it permanent personal identity, with salvation or damnation after death. Nonetheless, the religious account of man's essential, eternal nature (which Joyce first confronted in the Maynooth catechism he memorized at the age of eight) remained Aristotelian in fundamental ways: the soul there is called the first principle of life, and it is said to exist in three forms, vegetative, sensitive, and intellectual. *De Anima* must have been ironically familiar to Joyce when he first read it in Paris in 1904.

For a spiritual firebrand like Stephen, who has rejected religious faith to pursue a free artistic devotion but still believes that the rightful inheritance of his artist's soul is the full radiance of truth, Aristotle was the perfect new authority, the mind that gave Catholicism much of its intellectual mettle without being itself touched by the church's religious falsehoods and absurdity. Stephen, recalling the intellectual labors he undertook for the creation of the conscience of his race, first suggests the great importance of

Aristotle to his goal by retracing in "Nestor" his mind's progress toward luminescent insight into *De Anima*. The other appearances of this work in *Ulysses* further reveal the great extent of Stephen's intellectual debt to Aristotle. Since Joyce's intellectual development was the model for Stephen's, there is some reason to think that Joyce himself owed a similar debt to the Greek philosopher.

De Anima's next appearance in *Ulysses* comes in the first paragraph of "Proteus," again as part of Stephen's interior monologue. Walking along Sandymount Strand, Stephen thinks:

> Ineluctable modality of the visible: at least that if no more, thought through my eyes. Signatures of all things I am here to read, seaspawn and seawrack, the nearing tide, that rusty boot. Snotgreen, bluesilver, rust: coloured signs. Limits of the diaphane. But he adds: in bodies. Then he was aware of them bodies before of them coloured. How? By knocking his sconce against them, sure. Go easy. Bald he was and a millionaire, *maestro di color che sanno.* Limit of the diaphane in. Why in? Diaphane, adiaphane. If you can put your five fingers through it it is a gate, if not a door. Shut your eyes and see.   [*U*, 3.1–9]

The opening sentence here refers obliquely to Aristotle's conviction, stated in the summary of *De Anima* previously cited, that all thoughts derive from material supplied by the senses, and that no thought occurs without a mental image. Paraphrased to display its Aristotelian foundation, the first sentence would read: "If thought derives only from sense perception, and the most dominant sense perceptions are sights, the indispensable medium of thinking must be visibility, and intellectual activity must be at least the involuntary association of concepts with images." All this Stephen condenses into "thought through my eyes." Free of Deasy now (who tormented him in the previous chapter), idle, Stephen thinks again of Aristotle's psychology. This time he remembers the treatise's analysis of sensation, not his former visionary apprehension of the soul's capacity for universal identification with all objects of sensation and thought.

That universal function is transferred here from Aristotle's science to Christian mysticism. With the phrase "Signatures of all things I am here to read" Stephen refers obliquely to *Signatura Rerum* (Signature of All Things), a theosophical work by the Renaissance German mystic Jacob Boehme. According to Boehme, any intelligible reality was perceived through its opposite. He also believed that every created thing was infused with some portion of God's divinity. This spiritual portion, which made all things universal particulars, was God's signature in the created universe. By looking with visionary eyes at the world, a person might see a perpetual epiphany of God in the spiritual signatures infusing all matter. Boehme's works are elaborate expositions of the occult grammar that would enable people to read the epiphanic alphabet of God's material signature. The German mystic's works are comparable in the over-determined subtleties in which they formulate religious mysteries to the works of the Scholastics Stephen admires so much. Both theologies, although radically opposed in their premises and conclusions, operate in comparable ways: each is a perpetual motion machine whose primary action is the self-ordering proliferation of systematic expositions of God and humanity's access to him. The appearance of Aristotle, the patron of Scholasticism, and Boehme in the first sentences of "Proteus" reveals how conflicting Stephen's philosophical impulses are: attached to the clarity and certainty of Aristotle's experimental materialism (and its transformation in the works of medieval theologians), he also has a keen yearning for the obscure, mysterious spirituality charted and recharted in the esoteric syllogisms of heretical mystics.

The words "coloured signs" lead Stephen back to Aristotle's analysis of vision in *De Anima*, specifically to his account of the importance of the transparent (the diaphanous) for the sensation of colors. Doubting Aristotle's idea that colors appear at the limits of the diaphane in bodies, Stephen starts cutting up, making false difficulties and false solutions for Aristotle's theory. He reasons that because Aristotle defined color as an activity of a transparent medium in a body, the philosopher must have been aware of bodies before he was aware of colors. "How?" he asks. "By knocking his sconce against them, sure." The comparison is to Samuel Johnson's famous bullheaded refutation of Berkeley's idealism. To disprove the bishop's claim that reality is immaterial, Johnson, in Boswell's account, kicked a stone, dramatizing with his own pain Berkeley's ridiculous falsity. Johnson of course was philosophically astute enough to realize his gesture was not a refutation of Berkeley at all. He made it instead as a contemptuous reduction of philosophical

woolgathering to the level of common sense. Theories, he was saying with the kick, are useless when they cannot be squared with
immediate experience. Taking his cue from Johnson's ridicule of
Berkeley, Stephen makes a buffoon out of Aristotle by picturing the
ancient thinker butting his skull on a stone, stopping to analyze the
results, and then constructing his theory of sense perception. Johnson's assault on the innocent stone was a deliberate burlesque of
empirical investigation. But the object of the Englishman's scorn
was one fatuous conclusion arrived at through empirical procedure,
not the procedure itself. Stephen goes Johnson one better, subvert-
ing empiricism itself in his slapstick fantasy of an Aristotelian ex-
periment. It is interesting to remember that Berkeley, an Irishman,
was the preeminent theoretician of vision in his century, the specific sense on which Stephen has been dwelling throughout the first
sentences of this chapter. So it is doubly appropriate that a previous
sarcastic sophistry made to disgrace Berkeley should be used now
by Stephen to dismiss Aristotle's theory of vision as the bumbling
nonsense of a literally addlepated logician.

The construction of the joke is overly subtle, almost obscure, but
the comedy is not. The instant analogy displays intellectual dexterity, but nothing funnier than nihilistic hooting. The joke also casts
a faint political stain on Stephen. Johnson's sarcasm at Berkeley's
expense is one of hundreds of examples in *Ulysses* of English bru-
tality vanquishing Ireland's sons. Participating in the joke himself,
Stephen joins ranks, tangentially, with the oppressors, taking up
their spikey empiricism as a weapon against Aristotle, the intellectual sovereign of Roman Catholicism, the religion of the Irish Irish.
As if he were aware of all this, Stephen reproves himself with a
mocking parody of the voice of restraint and kindly reverence. "Go
easy" he tells himself. "Bald he was and a millionaire." These of
course are not reasons for Stephen to let up the ridicule—they
merely further characterize Aristotle as old and rich in addition to
doddering. The two details are from traditional ancient and medieval biographies of Aristotle. Stephen includes them as part of flippant ridicule for the reverence of the philosopher he has enjoined
on himself. In the Middle Ages that reverence resulted in the axiom
that ancient writers, especially Plato and Aristotle, together with
the Bible and the church fathers, could be appealed to for intellectual authority. This axiom gets recalled satirically when Stephen

thinks of the phrase in which Aristotle's preeminent literary champion in the Middle Ages, Dante, proclaimed the philosopher's authority over the thought of Christendom—"*maestro di color che sanno*"—master of those who know. The phrase is from the *Inferno* and is the first indication of dozens in the *Commedia* that Dante supplied and fashioned much of the intellectual order of his epic from Aristotle's works.[8] Stephen cannot go farther in jeering than to take Dante's naming of Aristotle's majesty in vain.

At the limit of scorn, Stephen starts questioning Aristotle again. Thinking still of vision, he observes, "Limit of the diaphane in. Why in?" Like the previous questions, this inquiry comes as much from the spoiler in Stephen as from the philosophical speculator. His answer to the problem is sophistry again, but this time more anarchic sophistry. The first reference to Johnson was at least made as part of an answer, however sarcastic, to a question. Stephen's response to the second question is not an answer at all, but a parody of Aristotle's habit of defining terms in the middle of an argument that has been constructed with them for quite some time. Again, Stephen refers to Johnson, this time heckling the good doctor as well as Aristotle.

His answer to why Aristotle conceived of the diaphane in bodies is this. "Diaphane, adiaphane. If you can put your five fingers through it it is a gate, if not a door. Shut your eyes and see." Stephen's response begins as an abbreviated reference to the exasperatingly miscellaneous logic characteristic (with few exceptions) of Aristotle's works. An Aristotelian paraphrase of the kind of reasoning Stephen is playing with in his two-word sentence would read as follows: To understand why the diaphane is *in* bodies, we must inquire into the nature of bodies and of the diaphane. Taking up the second topic first, we say of a visible body that it is visible when its diaphane is activated by light, or that it is invisible if light strikes not the diaphane, but its privation, the adiaphane. Stephen's curt "Diaphane, adiaphane" is a facetious condensation of *De Anima*'s argument that the objects of sight are not bodies themselves, but colors located in the diaphanous part of bodies. Stephen seems to be thinking that Aristotle would answer the question "Why in bodies?" by stopping everything to describe diaphane, getting sidetracked in a definition of adiaphane, taking up a new tangent, and perhaps never recovering the original topic.

In the first round of his mock inquiry into perception Stephen uses Johnson's empiricism to ridicule Aristotle's. In the second, Stephen ridicules the arbitrariness of Aristotle's definitions, and then turns the same ridicule on Johnson's. After mimicking Aristotle's logic with "Diaphane, adiaphane," Stephen does a quick closing parody of Johnson's definitions of words in his famous dictionary. "If you can put your five fingers through it it is a gate," Stephen says (i.e., if it has a grating though which a hand can pass), "if not a door." The Johnson entry Stephen refers to is this one: "*Door* is used of house, and *gates* of cities and public buildings, except in the license of poetry."[9] Aristotle often clarifies points in his arguments through analogical reasoning. Stephen, trying to answer a question about *De Anima* comically, forms his solution as Aristotle often seriously forms his, analogically. According to the logic of Johnson's definition, the solution to the difficulty of understanding why the diaphane is in bodies would be this. As a gate, whose body is composed of grating, can be penetrated by a hand, and as a door, whose body is composed of solid mass, cannot be, so a body that contains in its composition the diaphane can be permeated by light, and thus made visible, while a body deprived of the diaphane, containing as it were the adiaphane, cannot be so permeated and, consequently, cannot be seen. Thus the diaphane is *in* bodies as grating is in a gate, and it permits light to penetrate a body, as a grate allows a hand to penetrate a gate. This is how a ruined Jesuit amuses himself.

The logical minutiae of the opening paragraph of "Proteus" justify Buck Mulligan's complaint against Stephen in "Telemachus": "you have the cursed jesuit strain in you, only it's injected the wrong way," and Professor MacHugh's comparison in "Aeolus" of the morose, inactive author to Antisthenes, of whom, MacHugh tells Stephen, it is said "none could tell if he were bitterer against others or against himself" (*U*, 1.209, 7.1036–37). In "Nestor," the first time Stephen thinks of *De Anima* in *Ulysses*, he remembers its central concepts and his previous pursuit and ecstatic apprehension of them without ridicule. Here in "Proteus," Aristotle's theories and the "maestro" himself fall victim to the vitriolic scorn Stephen reserved for himself in earlier chapters. The ancient words of *De Anima* are not mystical conduits of spiritual light and vision here, but ciphers insufficiently explaining physical light and sensory perception. This ambivalence toward Aristotle in the narrative dimension stems from the conflicting forces of ambition, remorse, obscurantism, and rationality in Stephen. The narrative ambivalence has its counterpart in the symbolic role *De Anima* plays in *Ulysses*, where it is pitted against Bruno's theories of the soul, constructed in large part to refute Aristotle. But that is a topic for the second chapter. For now there are other, less complicated uses of *De Anima* in the novel's plot to consider.

The next entrance of *De Anima* is in "Scylla and Charybdis." There Stephen invokes Aristotelian philosophy to refute A.E.'s argument that Platonic mystical insight is art's purpose, and the great source and accomplishment of Shakespeare's plays. Using Aristotle's empiricism as an intellectual credential, Stephen argues that artists depict not the timeless spiritual essences Plato called Forms, but the events of their own lives. Exploiting the implications of Aristotle's comment in *De Anima* that "the soul is in a manner all that is: the soul is the form of forms," Stephen argues that all the narrative and symbolic forms of Shakespeare's plays (and by implication of any artist's work) are representations of the consequences in the artist's soul of his sexual submission to domination and betrayal by a woman. (Only men are artists in Stephen's theory.) The artist's submission is his initiation into the eternal battle of the sexes, which men always lose. That battle is the fundamental human reality, Stephen argues, and until a man enters it, he cannot recreate experience in art because he as yet knows nothing about it. The forms of any work of art are only the forms of life emerging in the soul of the artist: all other poetics are fraudulent evasions of art's great purpose, which is the reconciliation of the artist, and through him of mankind, to the lifelong suffering caused by sexual warfare. For a man of genius, an artist, Aristotle's remark that "the soul is in a manner all that is" has a special meaning. Stephen argues that to a genius who is an artist his own image is the standard of all experience. Consequently, when he regards the world he finds there images of his own life, discovering within the world only the actualization of some potential in himself. All the forms and subjects of an artist's works will always proceed from his contemplation of his own experience of life's inevitable sexual conflict; whatever he makes will bear the scars of a soul sundered by passion from the happy bonds of natural life.

Aristotle's works are the general source for Stephen's imperfectly empirical aesthetics, but they are not deployed systematically or entirely explicitly in his argument. When they do come up, they are quickly inserted either as refutations of a point someone has made against Stephen or as part of the witty panic of those secret thoughts that accompany his whirligig public debate. The first reference comes after A.E. has pronounced the symbolist credo: "Art has to reveal to us ideas, formless spiritual essences. The supreme question about a work of art is out of how deep a life does it spring. The painting of Gustave Moreau is the painting of ideas. The deepest poetry of Shelley, the words of Hamlet bring our minds into contact with the eternal wisdom, Plato's world of ideas. All the rest is the speculation of schoolboys for schoolboys" (U, 9.48–53). Stephen is about to use A.E.'s biographical explanation for literary merit against the mandarin mystic, and he begins by responding: "The schoolmen were schoolboys first,. . . . Aristotle was once Plato's schoolboy. . . . That model schoolboy . . . would find Hamlet's musings about the afterlife of his princely soul, the improbable, insignificant and undramatic monologue, as shallow as Plato's" (U, 9.56–57, 76–78).

The musings would be improbable and insignificant to Aristotle because he had written that personal immortality for the soul did not exist. Hamlet's belief in it would seem to Aristotle shallow for the same reason Plato's did: both imagine the soul can be separated from the body, neither distinguishes the soul's only eternal function—impersonal active intellect—from its other functions, such as memory, sensation, character, and so forth. The musing would be undramatic because it contributes nothing to the action of *Hamlet*, a violation of the criteria for plots as set down in Aristotle's *Poetics*. (Improbability and insignificance also violate that work's standards for drama.) Finally, it is worth noting that A.E.'s original deprecation of Stephen's literary theory as the work of a schoolboy becomes in Stephen's hands a compliment and a weapon.

Dedalus observes that A.E.'s schoolboys grew to be schoolmen. With this remark, he signals a change in his relationship to Russell. Stephen, once a member at the outer limits of A.E.'s school, has left it for good. Aristotle, once Plato's schoolboy, grew and founded his own school in which revision of Plato was a main objective. That school achieved its highest level of influence in medieval Europe, in the extensively Aristotelian theology of the Roman Catholic Scholastics. Stephen has cast off Dublin's Plato, Russell, and is obliquely casting himself as a modern Scholastic here, an alumnus (like his hero Aquinas) of the school of Aristotle.

The next reference to *De Anima* in "Scylla and Charybdis" is comic. Stephen, during a lull in the literary debate, remembers with chagrin that Russell, whom he's now arguing against, once lent him money that he has not repaid. Trying to justify his intellectual aggression against a creditor and annul the embarrassing debt, Stephen indulges in the following half-serious sophistry.

> Wait. Five months. Molecules all change. I am other I now. Other I got pound.
>
> Buzz. Buzz.
>
> But I, entelechy, form of forms, am I by memory because under everchanging forms.   [*U*, 9.205–9]

Philosophy gets the better of biology in this little game, as Stephen admits that his soul, the form of all forms that his everchanging physical and mental existence might take, remains constant throughout all such changes. The evidence of this constant identity is memory, the soul's power to recognize and retain permanent actuality, the entelechy by which an individual life acquires and assimilates constantly various new physical and mental existence. The phrases "entelechy" and "form of forms" are both from *De Anima*, where both are used as definitions of the soul. "Form of forms" is repeated from Stephen's classroom memory of St. Genevieve in "Nestor," showing up as part of a comic subterfuge here, instead of an object of mystic contemplation. *De Anima's* complex account of identity, once a source of religious experience for Dedalus, is equally at hand for trivial, snickering dishonesty. The joke here reveals both how habitual Stephen's recourse to Aristotle is and how thoroughgoing: *De Anima* serves him as text for literary debate, literary heroism, and the evasion of literary creditors. The same treatise, in the symbolic design of the novel, allowed Joyce to make his story of Leopold Bloom a literary image of life's informing principles.

Ulysses: Body and Soul

The repeated citations of *De Anima* in Stephen's critical personal
and intellectual moments do more than characterize Dedalus. They
also disclose a large part of the submerged logic of this book's unusual structure. The two concepts from *De Anima* that figure in
the formal design of *Ulysses* more than any others are, first, the
proposition "the soul is the form of forms" and, second, its corollary, "the soul is in a manner all that is." Applying these statements
to analysis of Joyce's realism and symbolism, and their integration
in *Ulysses*, casts new light on the matter and manner of Joyce's art,
and the knowledge it displays. In the early essay "Drama and Life,"
Joyce required of literary art that it shine with "the splendour of
truth." Lest readers remain in utter darkness confronted with the
unprecedented artifice of *Ulysses*, Joyce, at crucial moments in the
novel, flashes Aristotelian spotlights, thereby suggesting, with the
cunning he trusted more than frankness, a way that leads attention
successfully to the truth hidden in the new Dedalian labyrinth.

There is a close correspondence between Aristotle's account of
the relationship of the soul to the body and Joyce's construction of
Ulysses. He made Bloom's story an epic of the body, by sustaining
an allegorical schema throughout the novel in which chapters and
details of chapters are symbolically associated with various organs
and organic systems (respiratory, nervous, and the like). The point
of this analogical identification of character and culture with bodily
functions is Aristotelian: the soul is not separable from the body;
the reality of human experience, individual or social, always has an
inalienable material basis; consciousness in any mode is, somehow,
always of the flesh.

If *Ulysses* is an epic of the body's life in this Aristotelian way, it
must also be an epic of the soul. The soul of *Ulysses*, as the title
indicates, is Homer's story of Odysseus's wandering and eventual
return to Ithaca after the Trojan war. This story Joyce presents as
the universal story, the form by which his book contains the soul of
nature, the source and principle of life itself. As a vital natural body
is formed, caused, and actualized by a soul, so the literary body of
Ulysses is formed, caused, and actualized by a soul, a principle giving precise artistic vitality to all the details in the book's multiple
structures and establishing for all those details and structures the

same integrity and coherence that order human life. The Homeric parallel, and the other systematic and isolated parodies, symbols, and analogies suspended in it, are not derived from the narrative or stitched onto it in *Ulysses*: they stand to its plot and characters as Aristotle says the soul does to the body, as formal cause.

By claiming that Joyce portrayed the soul as the first principle of reality, I am not arguing that he was a Byzantine allegorist who transformed the *Odyssey* into a hieroglyph of transcendent immaterial existence.[10] The universality Joyce saw in Homer's epic was not this occult one. Gnostic itineraries of the soul's journey before birth and after death are at the lunatic fringe of *Ulysses'* encyclopedic realism and symbolism. They were central in the intellectual life of Dublin's artists in 1904 and so could not be left out of Stephen's fictional encounter with the literary life of his nation, or Joyce's historical summary of what he perceived as Ireland's mental ruin. In the book's conceptual order metempsychosis, Buddhism, and theosophy are part of Joyce's encyclopedic plan to include in *Ulysses* all those metaphysical accounts of the soul's universality that rivaled his own, and then either make them compatible with his, or laugh them out of existence. The soul Joyce portrays with Homer's *Odyssey* and subsidiary symbolic narratives in his epic is, in large measure, the soul as Aristotle conceived it: organic nature's essence, the substantial reality of life on this earth as it appears in inescapably physical bodies.

This Aristotelian account of the soul supplies much of the logic for the encyclopedic, polysemous design of Bloomsday. By absorbing a foreign body's sensible or intelligible form, the soul identifies itself with that body. In this manner the soul is all that is: the mediating factor between individual consciousness and external objects, the substance continually transformed by other substances, but under all transformations changeless, undivided, permanently individual. This quality of the soul, its integrity and its multiple transfigurations, is the most important Aristotelian idea in *Ulysses*. The idea has conceptual and technical applications in the novel. Taking up the technical applications first, I want to suggest what the idea does for the realistic surface and for symbolism, analogy, metaphor, and parody in the figurative structure of the book.

Joyce's style in *Ulysses* displays two opposite techniques. One is imagistic precision, governed by the scrupulous meanness of *le mot juste* that creates definite, singular impressions. Joyce uses this technique in descriptions and in dialogue, for conversations and interior monologue. The following passages show this precise, realistic technique at work. The first comes at the end of Stephen's walk with Mulligan and Haines in the opening chapter. "Buck Mulligan sat down to unlace his boots. An elderly man shot up near the spur of rock a blowing red face. He scrambled up by the stones, water glistening on his pate and on its garland of grey hair, water rilling over his chest and paunch and spilling jets out of his black sagging loincloth" (*U*, 1.687–91). The next excerpt is from a barroom conversation in "Lestrygonians."

—Well, what'll it be? Paddy Leonard asked.

—I'll take a stone ginger, Bantam Lyons said.

—How much? Paddy Leonard cried. Since when, for God' sake? What's yours, Tom?

—How is the main drainage? Nosey Flynn asked, sipping.

For answer Tom Rochford pressed his hand to his breastbone and hiccupped.

—Would I trouble you for a glass of fresh water, Mr. Byrne? he said.

—Certainly, sir.

Paddy Leonard eyed his alemates.

—Lord love a duck, he said. Look at what I'm standing drinks to! Cold water and gingerpop! Two fellows that would suck whisky off a sore leg.   [*U*, 8.996–1007]

The last citation is from Bloom's rumination in "Sirens." "I too. Last of my race. Milly young student. Well, my fault perhaps. No son. Rudy. Too late now. Or if not? If not? If still?/ He bore no hate./ Hate. Love. Those are names. Rudy. Soon I am old" (*U*, 11.1066–69). The mimetic accuracy this kind of writing displays has caused critics to identify Joyce as the one novelist working in English who perfected the realistic prose invented and developed by the French novelists of the nineteenth century, especially by Flaubert, Zola, and the Goncourt brothers.

The second, opposite technique is prodigal allusiveness. In this mode Joyce clusters any number of singular impressions and definite meanings around one subject and sets them all competing for primary control over that subject. The first technique fixes a topic in one context; this one surrounds a topic with numerous, variously interdependent contexts. These multiple contexts do not always converge on their topic all at once. Often they are distributed in spiralling groups whose elements touch down in the story line at many different places in changing sets. By incremental repetition and variation of multiple contexts above, below, and in between lines, Joyce exceeds the unilinear limits of the realistic style in *Ulysses*.

Here is an accreted symbolic passage from "Oxen of the Sun." Stephen is elaborating on Dixon's comment that Beaumont and Fletcher shared one mistress.

Greater love than this, he said, no man hath that a man lay down his wife for his friend. Go thou and do likewise. Thus, or words to that effect, saith Zarathustra, sometime regius professor of French letters to the university of Oxtail nor breathed there ever that man to whom mankind was more beholden. Bring a stranger within thy tower it will go hard but thou wilt have the secondbest bed. *Orate, fratres, pro memetipso.* And all the people shall say, Amen. Remember, Erin, thy generations and thy days of old, how thou settedst little by me and by my word and broughtedst in a stranger to my gates to commit fornication in my sight and to wax fat and kick like Jeshurum. Therefore hast thou sinned against my light and hast made me, thy lord, to be the slave of servants. Return, return, Clan Milly: forget me not, O Milesian. Why hast thou done this abomination before me that thou didst spurn me for a merchant of jalaps and didst deny me to the Roman and to the Indian of dark speech with whom thy daughters did lie luxuriously? Look forth now, my people, upon the land of behest, even from Horeb and from Nebo and from Pisgah and from the Horns of Hatten unto a land flowing with milk and money. But thou hast suckled me with a bitter milk: my moon and my sun thou has quenched for ever. And thou hast left me alone for ever in the dark ways of my bitterness: and with a kiss of ashes hast thou kissed my mouth. This tenebrosity of the interior, he proceeded to say, hath not been illumined by the wit of the septuagint nor so much as mentioned for the Orient from on high Which brake hell's gates visited a darkness that was foraneous. Assuefaction minorates atrocities (as Tully saith of his darling Stoics) and Hamlet his father showeth the prince no blister of combustion. The adiaphane in the noon of life is an Egypt's plague which in the nights of prenativity and postmortemity is their most proper *ubi* and *quomodo*.

[*U*, 14.360–86]

The language here comes from: the psalms of desolation, Ecclesiastes, Christ's moral injunctions in the New Testament, the Mass and Tenebrae services of the Catholic Church, the Jewish prayer service, the climax of the Exodus story, Thomas Moore's song "Let Erin Remember the Days of Old," Moses' song in Deuteronomy, the Song of Solomon, the Apocryphal Gospel of Nicodemus, Thomas Browne's *Christian Morals*, Cicero's *Tusculan Disputations*, *Hamlet*, *De Anima*, Nietzsche's *Thus Spake Zarathustra*, Stephen's theory of *Hamlet*, his vampire poem, and the nightmare vision of his dead mother. Each reference is implicated through analogy with all the others: together they all portray Stephen's conviction that Ireland is bent on destroying his artist's soul. And they all occur before this passage and again after it, in different configurations, aligned with different subjects and characters. The dominant analogy in this passage is composed of Stephen's comparisons of himself to the crucified Christ, made in the typological language of the Tenebrae service. In this service, held on Good Friday, passages from Jeremiah's Lamentations, Psalms, Exodus, Deuteronomy, and Isaiah are combined to form Christ's Reproaches, a litany in which the Old Testament passages are all identified as forecasts of Christ's passion. The typological comparison of the Old Testament and the New Testament that characterizes so much of Christian thinking, especially Catholic thinking in the Middle Ages, is part of Joyce's symbolic construction of Bloom's position in Dublin, as well as Stephen's, and when it sounds here in Stephen's passage, it identifies the young martyr with the old one, the Irish victim with the Jewish one, the Son with the Father, Telemachus with Odysseus, Prince Hamlet with King Hamlet.

This symbolic mode in Joyce's style is a development of the mimetic one, as algebra is a development of arithmetic, or polyphony of plainsong. In the mimetic style Joyce works with one effect at a time, uniting them in sequence, one after another. In the symbolic one, he combines discrete effects into scrambled, overlapping sets whose members and relationships are always changing. The language in *Ulysses* fluctuates between realism and symbolism; most of it combines both.

The prominence and extent of realism's control varies according to Joyce's symbolic purpose in any given passage, but its essential quality does not. Its scrupulous meanness, its mimetic accuracy, are immutable constants variously exploited throughout the novel but nowhere substantially diminished or increased. Irreducible facts appear in this imagistic style: Bloom making a nosegay of his big toenail, Stephen's mother's vomit in a bowl, flowers on Howth Hill or in Gibralter, Miss Kennedy's breasts cresting in the satin of her blouse. These images, and hundreds more like them in *Ulysses*, are implicated in very complex, symbolic patterns, but they do not lose their material fixity, no matter how extravagant the formal permutations may be. Objectivity, the soul of the realistic mode in *Ulysses*, like virginity, does not admit of degrees.

But the allusive style does. Throughout the novel it varies in density and complexity. At times elements from five or six systematic parallels converge on a narrative detail or sequence. At times no more than one is present. *Don Giovanni*, the *Odyssey*, Christmas pantomimes, *The Arabian Nights*, *Robinson Crusoe* and "The Legend of Sleepy Hollow" at different points appear separately and in various combinations as analogues for some part of Bloom's story. These and dozens of other sustained parallels never appear the same way twice in *Ulysses*: they rotate through the novel shifting alliances among themselves and constantly changing their points of contact with the narrative.

For example: *Hamlet* in various aspects is part of the portrayal of Stephen and Bloom at different times for different reasons. In one aspect though, as the extravagant mourner, the prince is a constant element of Stephen and Bloom, who both wear mourning all day. Stephen wears it for himself as well as for his mother, much as Hamlet does in mourning for his father. Bloom, who has lost a father and will soon be commemorating that death, wears black for Paddy Dignam, a very casual acquaintance. Stephen's extravagant obsequies express alienation, resentment, and wounded pride. Bloom's display formal responsibility to social conventions and kindliness. Ironically, Bloom's mourning suit signals that he, like Stephen, is an alien in Dublin. Bloom is a pariah shunned by acquaintances; Stephen chooses his status as outsider to guarantee what he mistakenly perceives as spiritual and artistic integrity. These opposite extremities of solitude are both indicated by one narrative detail, clothing, which implicates the characters in opposed ways in the same systematic analogy, *Hamlet*. A subtitle for *Ulysses* might have been "The Black and the Black" (*pace* Stendhal). Bloom's color poignantly, whimsically represents his innocent pretense that he too is part of Dublin society, and his half-farcical sense of connection to all life ("hed go into mourning for the cat," Molly complains in "Penelope") (*U*, 18.1310). Stephen's color bitterly signals the stillbirth of his artistic plans. This unity of the two is an especially clear example of what comparison (whether allusion, parody, or symbol) is in *Ulysses*: identification of two separate elements, established by a fact common to both, one that simultaneously displays the elements' uniformity and difference.

The sartorial unity of Stephen and Bloom derived from the *Hamlet* parallel dovetails with their unity as Father and Son in the trinitarian symbolism. That symbolism is transposed throughout the novel in the unity of Hamlet senior and junior, as Stephen describes it in his aesthetic theory; the unity of Odysseus and Telemachus in the Homeric parallel; of Dante and Virgil in the analogy to Dante's *Commedia*, and so forth, and so on. The point is that Joyce's comparisons in *Ulysses* are not so many isolated arithmetic equivalences, but parts of an organic system in which the elements that are distributed and integrated are always changing.

Here is a simple instance in which a symbol changes narrative partners in one scene. In "Telemachus" (*U*, 1.569–602), Buck Mulligan and Haines play Rosencrantz and Guildenstern to Stephen's Hamlet, trying, for reasons Stephen considers treacherous, to make him reveal his theory of *Hamlet*. Mulligan wants Stephen to get money from Haines, who could publish the theory, but Stephen insults the Englishman and ruins the plan. When Dedalus appears ready to discuss his theory, Mulligan interrupts him and makes the imminent recitation an excuse to drink. The parallel to *Hamlet* 2.2 emerges distinctly in this sentence where Stephen stops to observe his interlocuters: "In the bright silent instant Stephen saw his own image in cheap dusty mourning between their gay attires" (*U*,

1.570–71). He is Hamlet, dressed in black, they are Rosencrantz and Guildenstern, the treacherous friends in gay attire plotting against him. A strange thing happens next. Mulligan, provoked by Haines's mention of a theological interpretation of *Hamlet* (one similar to Stephen's theological ideas about *Hamlet* and to major ideas in the book's conceptual order), interrupts the discussion. "Buck Mulligan at once put on a blithe broadly smiling face. He looked at them, his wellshaped mouth open happily, his eyes, from which he had suddenly withdrawn all shrewd sense, blinking with mad gaiety. He moved a doll's head to and fro, the brims of his Panama hat quivering, and began to chant in a quiet happy foolish voice" (*U*, 1.579–83). He proceeds to chant blasphemous songs, mocking himself, insanity, and Christianity.

Buck behaves this way all day. The unusual factor in this exhibition is the link Joyce makes between it and *Hamlet*. Hamlet has been Stephen's role so far, especially its brooding resentment. Why now does Buck upstage Stephen, doing Hamlet's feigned insanity himself, as he "puts on" an antic disposition here, reenacting Hamlet's strategy for protecting his secret and evading Claudius's henchmen, Rosencrantz and Guildenstern? He does so to prevent Stephen from reciting the theory, partly because he doesn't want to hear it, partly because he thinks that in another situation Haines might still be willing to pay for it. Mulligan is sure to plunder that payment if it ever comes Stephen's way, and Joyce displays that greed here by having him usurp Stephen's identification with England's primary dramatic victim of usurpation.

He repeats the same usurpation in "Scylla and Charybdis," this time while Stephen does explicate his *Hamlet* theory. Again the topic is paternity. Stephen has just finished a theological interpretation of paternity in *Hamlet* (recall Haines in *U*, 1.577–78), when Mulligan says: "—Himself his own father, Sonmulligan told himself. Wait. I am big with child. I have an unborn child in my brain. Pallas Athena! A play! The play's the thing! Let me parturiate!" (*U*, 9.875–78). Here, combining classical Greek literature with *Hamlet* 2.2.633–634, Buck mocks not only Dedalus's theory but the very symbolic structure through which Joyce has created Stephen—the analogy of Hamlet to Homer's prince. Telemachus, like his father, is befriended by Athena, who, disguised, visits him in the opening of the *Odyssey*; Dedalus (who thinks of himself as Hamlet more than once in the novel) is also befriended by Athena, who comes to him in the guise of a milkmaid in the opening of Joyce's book (*U*, 1.389). When Buck, playing Zeus, calls on that virgin goddess to end his anguish and be born, he steals not only Stephen's thunder, but Joyce's as well. That theft comes clear in Buck's parodic characterization of the artist as an Olympian creator-god, a characterization Dedalus and Joyce make repeatedly in their parallel careers, often adding Jehovah and the trinitarian Father to Zeus.

Stephen's final word for Mulligan in "Telemachus" is "usurper." The accusation expresses Stephen's resentment that Ireland prefers doctors, those who deal with the body, over artists, who deal with the soul. Early in the chapter, while Mulligan banters condescendingly with an ignorant milkmaid (whom Stephen views as Ireland personified, and whom Joyce portrays as Homer's Athena, disguised even from herself in Dublin), the alienated artist thinks, "She bows her old head to a voice that speaks to her loudly, her bonesetter, her medicineman: me she slights" (*U*, 1.418–19). This resentment over Mulligan's worldly success and his own penury is part of a more intimate fear on Stephen's part that Mulligan's proffered friendship is exploitative and dangerous, a conviction that Mulligan's actions throughout the day, especially at Westland Row Station that night, justify. Finally, affecting aestheticism and decadence years after the fashion has died out in England, Mulligan has made flippant homosexual overtures earlier that morning to Stephen, who responds to them with icy contempt. Sex of any kind is out of the question for this bilious young man, and even if it were not, he has no inclination to participate in Mulligan's lewd, hypocritically Bohemian carousing. Buck has usurped Stephen's professional place in Ireland; offering false friendship and scabrous love, he would also rob Stephen of his emotional and spiritual integrity, and so kill the artist in him. For all these reasons, Stephen names him "usurper," and Joyce casts him as Antinous in the Homeric parallel—the bestial parasite who befriends Telemachus only to plot his murder. Mulligan is one of the funniest people in *Ulysses*. In any other comedy his sense of humor would make him very attractive. It does not in this book, at least not after the first few pages. As the novel progresses it becomes clear that Joyce has not made him a Dublin Falstaff whose geniality and absurdity go far in commending even his vices, but a fatuous timeserver, a stage Irishman bent on destroying the soul of an artist, a sin for which there is no forgiveness in *Ulysses.*

When Buck takes over Stephen's symbol, Hamlet, he is doing in the symbolic order of the book what he does in the narrative— usurping. These are deft, unobtrusive instances of Joyce using symbolism to denote character. Mulligan's temporary usurpation of Stephen's symbolic identity occurs in the background of these primarily realistic chapters. In later chapters, especially in "Circe," such usurpation will become a prominent device, whereby characters think other people's thoughts, details from parodies show up as part of the narrative, and symbols shift from one narrative detail to another. What at first had a narrative function as characterization takes on much broader conceptual value as the book continues. In "Telemachus" Joyce is warming up, gradually acquainting his audience with a style that eventually dominates the closing chapters of the book. The distribution of one symbol to two opposite characters in one scene from that chapter is partly a device of characterization and partly an instance of Joyce's habit of changing anything, by virtue of some symbolic realignment, into anything else in his novel. A conceptual purpose animates this shape-shifting in *Ulysses*. Embedded in the comedy and technical dexterity is an image of the operation of the soul as Aristotle conceived it in *De Anima;* an image Joyce presents as a fundamental principle of experience, namely, that living things take their being, according to a fixed yet perpetually changing pattern, from identifying interchange with other living, and inert, things.

The two interdependent styles of *Ulysses*, realism and symbolism, allowed Joyce to make the novel both drama and literature, as he defined those terms in his early essay "Drama and Life." In the realistic style he portrays the accidental humors, the circumstances and whimsicalities of particular people in a particular place. This much is literature. In the symbolism, that sustained influx into one narrative form of as many other forms as he could muster (literary, philosophical, theological, musical, biological, historical, geographical, political, et al.), from as much of the past and present as he had time to ransack, Joyce shows the changeless laws, the universal principles (or fixed pattern), as becoming "involved and over-wrapped" (adjusted) in local mundane circumstances. The factor any symbol has in common with a narrative detail (separation between spouses in the case of Rip Van Winkle, Odysseus, and Dublin's Bloom) provides the formal unity of the "dramatic" and "literary" dimensions of the novel. The differences between those symbolic and narrative elements (Odysseus's mortal grandeur and Rip Van Winkle's drugged sleep are not part of Bloom's story, for instance) make up a large part of the novel's comedy. It is interesting to note, as an aside here, that Irving's "The Legend of Sleepy Hollow" is itself a parody of Homer's two epics, in which the American revolutionary war substitutes for the Trojan one and Rip Van Winkle avoids the conflict (as Odysseus unsuccessfully tried to) not with a ruse, but by sleeping through it. Like the Ithacan king, Van Winkle returns after a twenty-year absence to the place that knows him no more. Here is one more instance of Joyce's inweaving symbolism: another comic parody of the *Odyssey* existed, and it had to be in Joyce's to satisfy the Irishman's universalizing aspirations. Metaphors, analogies, systematic parallels, and random parodies, while they almost always have a precise narrative function, either as devices of characterization or projection of the action, are all part of the system by which *Ulysses* becomes an encyclopedic, joyous image of the great dramatic subject as Joyce conceived it—life's changeless passion, the changing realization of human verity.

In Joyce's early conception, the underlying passions were the primary subject of "drama"—the motley agents and the circumstances that carried them out were only incidentally part of the work. That thesis ruined Joyce's only play, *Exiles*, an ethical sexologist's closet drama in which Love and Freedom struggle far above the heads (and other relevant organs) of their motley agents Richard and Bertha Rowan and Robert Hand. Even today when Dublin playwrights are asked about their latest project, a standard reply is, "I'm working on a dramatization of *Exiles*." The great achievement of *Ulysses* is the fully imagined integration of changeless principles and changing circumstances. The human verities do not appear "in all their nakedness and divine severity" in Joyce's first epic, but they do appear, wrapped up in the multicolored fabrics of comic symbolism.

Aristotle's *De Anima* furnished an intellectual foundation for Joyce's symbolic method and its integration with the narrative one in *Ulysses*. Just as the changing laws of being endure through all historical permutations, governing their development, so the soul endures through all experiences of any life, assimilating and unifying its constitutive elements through all their countless transformations. As changeless laws and changing circumstances are inseparably bound in human history, so the soul and body are inseparably bound in nature, two components of a compound entity. So also the narrative and symbolism of *Ulysses* interpenetrate one another, indivisibly, thoroughly.

The soul and life are equivalent terms in *De Anima*, much as Ulysses and life were equivalent terms to Joyce. In different ways both were synonyms for universal experience—Ulysses because he had done everything, and the soul because, through sensation and intellection, it might become anything. "The soul is in a manner all that is," Stephen remarks in "Nestor," "the form of forms." Odysseus's life is such a form, reincarnated through literary metempsychosis, in Bloom's. Two ancient Greek images of universality are bestowed on *Ulysses* by its symbolism: Homer's narrative one and Aristotle's philosophical one. Because Bloom's story is a symbolic equivalent of Odysseus's, it contains, like the Greek's, all stories; because the *Odyssey* is the soul of *Ulysses*, the novel can absorb any other form. As the soul is equally present in all parts of the body in Aristotle's account, so the capacity for symbolic association is present in any narrative element of *Ulysses*. The realistic body of this novel, by virtue of its Odyssean soul, contains in all its parts (characters, events, places, even objects) the capacity for identification with any other form.

Since Bloom is the image of Odysseus, the soul causing *Ulysses* to be what it is, his symbolic potential is actualized more conspicuously and extensively than any other in the novel. Odysseus, "the man of many ways," reveals himself in the multiple symbols clustered around Bloom as much as he does in Bloom's actions and thoughts. But Stephen, Molly, soap, a horse, Parnell, *Don Giovanni*, and most other elements of the realistic narrative Bloom moves in also receive the same symbolic treatment he does, in lesser degrees. By virtue of his presence, they are forms that employ other forms; by virtue of his identity with the universal Odysseus, Bloom, in all the particulars of his story, is "in a manner all that is." The point is made very eloquently by Fritz Senn in his essay "Book of Many Turns." "*Polytropia* in *Ulysses* then is not limited to any one feature, or level, or any one person—not even to persons. It is poly-tropically distributed and incarnated throughout. Animals too, like Stephen's Protean dog on the beach or the dog following Bloom into the byways of Circe, perform feats of amazing versatility. Even in-animate objects, such as Bloom's newspaper, his wandering soap, or Stephen's ashplant, are capable of transformation."[11]

In Aristotle's conception the souls of human beings put nature and all experience at their disposal, identifying them with anything they encounter. By constructing the symbolism of *Ulysses* in part according to Aristotle's conception of the soul in *De Anima*, Joyce achieved something comparable—he put an encyclopedic range of forms and topics at his artistic disposal and successfully composed with them an image of one man's life as universally identical to all human life. And he finally gave coherent philosophical value to the vague terms "human verity" and "changeless passion" that dis-played intellectual ambition, and little more, in his early critical work.

As *Ulysses* proceeds from chapter to chapter, the book becomes more and more elaborate symbolically. The narrative and allusive elements that appear in the first chapter are constantly restructured to fit the new forms entering the book in each chapter. The progres-sive complexity of the novel's narrative and conceptual design is in part an imitation of the complexity in any day's development, and the complexity of any individual life's development, carried on in the soul's constant integration of newly absorbed forms with those already present. As an image of the soul's activity *Ulysses* is an image of the process of life itself—constant proliferation and order-ing of new forms. Such dependence on a theory of the soul for an aesthetic design is not a unique event in literary history. Dante worked the same way in his *Commedia* (a fact that Joyce made part of his novel, as the third chapter of this book argues). Joyce's con-temporary Yeats also wrote to indicate the progress of the soul. But what Joyce originally perceived as Yeats's spiritualistic evasion of reality separated the novelist from the poet. Joyce announced the dispute in his most explicit description of *Ulysses'* stance vis-à-vis the material world, written years before the novel was conceived. "Life we must accept as we see it before our eyes, men and women as we meet them in the real world, not as we apprehend them in the world of faery." This was Joyce in 1900 in "Drama and Life." Yeats of course went on to do more than dream of "the world of faery," and Joyce accordingly stopped this kind of carping. He even included one of Yeats's faery poems, "Who Goes with Fergus," in *Ulysses* as a significant part of his own literary confrontation with men and women in the real world. Still, there is justice in the young critic's daring scorn for Yeats's notion of literary art, and an arresting determination to be worldly about the soul, to defy religious or literary devaluations of mundane circumstances, to make words live as Aristotle said the soul and all human beings do—in things.

c h a p t e r   t w o

JOYCE & BRUNO

J oyce began reading Giordano Bruno's Italian dialogues in his first years at University College, Dublin, 1898–1900. He was eighteen years old at the end of that time, and in full-scale rebellion against the church. Bruno's heretical doctrines of the world-soul and the coincidence of contraries, together with his furious and unrelenting outcry against intellectual or spiritual domination of men by institutions, must have helped inspire the young Joyce to pursue his own genius, to choose the perilous freedom of exile from Ireland. By 1914, when he started *Ulysses,* Joyce must have thought more about Bruno's hardship and ultimate fate than he did about Nolan's glorious zeal. After ten years of exile in which he lived the way Bruno did—traveling from city to city in Europe, usually poor, dependent on patrons for survival, harassed or cut off from the literary establishment—Joyce had even more cause to identify himself with the martyred Italian than he had at University College when he was a heroically ambitious teenager. At sixteen and eighteen Bruno the Nolan was an example for Joyce; at thirty-three, a fellow victim.

The personal devotion Joyce felt for Bruno has been documented in Stanislaus Joyce's *My Brother's Keeper* and described in Richard Ellmann's biography, *James Joyce;* William York Tindall's *James Joyce: His Way of Interpreting the Modern World;* and some of the personal recollections of Joyce that appear in Willard Potts's *Portraits of the Artist in Exile.*[1] These sources, and others, all provide essentially the same picture: Joyce's discovering in Bruno a model of the values and circumstances that made up his life as an artist— faultless courage in the face of hostility and persecution, contemptuous defiance of established authorities, vaulting ambition, disappointment at ignorant abuse, rapture at life's mystery, and most significantly, solitude.

The evidence of how Joyce thought about Bruno, or even which of the Italian's dialogues he read, is not as abundant or clear as the evidence for his knowledge of Aristotle. Nevertheless, Joyce did speak out about Bruno, and not only to lionize him or take on his mantle. In 1903 Joyce reviewed J. Lewis McIntyre's *Giordano Bruno*, the best book in English at the time on the Italian martyr's life and thought. Joyce was qualified to judge McIntyre's book by his study of the Italian dialogues of Bruno with Father Ghezzi in college, the same Ghezzi scornfully included in Stephen's diary entry on Bruno in *A Portrait of the Artist as a Young Man*. His remarks about Bruno in this review (McIntyre's name is never mentioned) are very puffy, but they have enough intellectual focus to show what Joyce thought Bruno's contribution to modern intellectual life was.

> As an independent observer, Bruno, however, deserves high honour. More than Bacon or Descartes must he be considered the father of what is called modern philosophy. His system by turns rationalist and mystic, theistic and pantheistic is everywhere impressed with his noble mind and critical intellect, and is full of that ardent sympathy with nature as it is—*natura naturata*—which is the breath of the Renaissance. In his attempt to reconcile the matter and form of the Scholastics—formidable names, which in his system as spirit and body retain little of their metaphysical character—Bruno has hardily put forward an hypothesis, which is a curious anticipation of Spinoza. [*CW*, p. 133]

Two ideas from these paragraphs dominate Joyce's conception of Bruno: that the Nolan was sympathetic to nature as it is, the world of mundane experience, and that he found in that world opportunity for spiritual activity. Bruno's attempt to join the scholastic terms "form" and "matter" resulted from his mystical apprehension of nature's divine unity. In *Ulysses*, Joyce elaborated this mystical conception of reality, preserving Bruno's rapture and abandoning the militancy that he found so compelling in 1903. One very powerful idea unifying the interpenetrating schemas of *Ulysses* in which Joyce presents nature and its secret life is Bruno's conception of the coincidence of contraries. Scholars have noticed this conception in Joyce's work so often and so casually that it has become one of the clichés in Joyce criticism (especially criticism of *Finnegans Wake*).² Like all clichés this one is true, but rarely understood or spoken with penetrating or precise intentions. In this chapter I want to show, with more detailed analysis than is normally given to the subject, exactly how Joyce understood Bruno's concept of the unity of opposites. First I will examine one of the Nolan's Italian dialogues that Joyce knew from his college study with Ghezzi and from its detailed presentation in McIntyre's book, and then I will make a preliminary investigation of how some ideas from that dialogue appear in *Ulysses*.

Renaissance Abstrusiosities

Cause, Principle, and Unity (the English translation of the Italian work *De La Causa, Principio et Uno*) is divided into five dialogues, each of which has a speaker, Teofilo, who delivers Bruno's anti-Aristotelian conception of reality in response to friendly and hostile interlocutors, especially Dicson and Gervase. After an extended apologia in the first dialogue (a gesture Bruno's cantankerous bearing toward the intellectual establishment made necessary over and over throughout his career), the Nolan begins his argument about the interdependent relationship of the concepts of cause and principle in the second dialogue.

For Bruno, the first cause and principle of all things is God. This absolute origin of being is inaccessible, but its vestiges, the proximate cause and principle of all things, are available to human understanding through observation of nature, where they abide. No other avenue of knowledge is available; no mystical bypass of things as they appear to the senses is conceived or allowed by Bruno. Understanding reality is not, however, simply a matter of observing nature, but the reward of reasoned observation, reason in this case denoting a new method for discovering the secret cause and principle of nature, truths that have been obscured by Aristotle's doctrines, especially his ideas of causality and the mutual exclusiveness of opposites. Bruno's new method involves redefinition of the concepts of cause and principle, and the assertion that opposites, despite Aristotle's rules, coincide in nature.

Cause and principle, according to Bruno, both bring about the existence of all things but differ in the manner of their activity. Principle he defines as "what intrinsically contributes to the constitution of a thing and remains in the effect."[3] To clarify this definition he says, "For the point is the principle of the line, but not its cause; the instant is the principle of activity; the position-whence is the principle of motion, but not its cause; the premises are the principle of an argument, but not its cause" (*C*, p. 80). Cause, on the other hand, "contributes to the production of things from outside and has its being outside the composition, as is the case with the efficient cause and with the end for which the thing produced is destined" (*C*, p. 80).

Having distinguished his main terms, Bruno goes on to describe their functions. He takes up cause first, specifically the universal efficient, formal, and final causes of nature. To define the universal efficient cause he brings in the Neoplatonic idea of the world-soul, which he calls the "universal form" (*C*, p. 81). This world-soul is the "formal cause" of nature considered in its entirety, as a single organism composed of all that has been, is, and will be. This formal cause gives each item its essential reality, its structure. "As for the efficient cause," he declares, "the universal physical efficient cause is the universal intellect, which is the first and principal faculty of the world-soul" (*C*, p. 81). This efficient cause (universal intellect) actualizes the structures implanted in nature by the formal cause (world-soul).

The efficient cause is the genetic code, as it were, of the organic universe, the systematic organizer of predetermined form. After comparing the universal intellect to Plato's demiurge, the Pythagoreans' universal agitator, and the Magi's sower, Bruno gives his own metaphor to the term.

As for us, we call it the inner craftsman, since it forms matter and shapes it from within, as from within the seed or root is sent forth and unfolded the trunk, from within the trunk are thrust out the branches, and from within the branches the formed twigs, and from within these the buds are unfurled, and there within are formed, shaped, and interwoven, like nerves, the leaves, flowers, and fruits. As from within, at certain times, the sap is recalled from the leaves and fruits to the twigs, from the twigs to the branches, from the branches to the trunk, and from the trunk to the root.   [C, p. 82]

It is important to notice that this "inner craftsman" has two opposite skills, unfolding forms from matter and retracting them. The final cause guiding this complex activity of the universal intellect is the perfection of the universe, the realization of all forms contained in the world-soul. Since the universal intellect works from within matter, unfolding forms rather than imposing them extrinsically, it follows that all forms have an actual existence in matter, and are unfolded now in one kind of material composition, now in another.

Having discussed "cause," Bruno is ready to explain what he means by "principle." Here he introduces the first unification of opposites in the work, arguing that principle, the intrinsic organization of being, is identical to cause, the extrinsic organizer. He returns now to the similarity already observed between the universal intellect as efficient cause, and its original definition as cause's opposite, principle.

Dics. But how can the same subject be at once principle and cause of natural things? how can it have the nature of an intrinsic part and not of an extrinsic one?

Teo. I deny that there's any impropriety in that, if we consider that the soul is in the body like the pilot in the ship, and the pilot, insofar as he shares the ship's motion, is part of it; yet, insofar as he is understood as the ship's guide and mover, he is seen, not as a part, but as a distinct efficient cause. Likewise the soul of the universe, insofar as it animates and informs, comes to be an intrinsic and formal part of the universe; yet insofar as it directs and governs, it is not a part, it does not rank as a principle, but as a cause.   [C, pp. 83–84]

Bruno presents here a radically ambiguous nature, governed by an immanent principle that also operates as an extrinsic, transcendental cause. Natural things all participate in material and immaterial being; they operate on two systems, the limiting defining action of principle, which works from within matter to make it now a tree and now a star; and the limitless, infinite action of the universal intellect, an efficient cause that works from without matter, changing trees into stars into knives, actualizing all forms enclosed in matter. These two systems are aspects of one system, reciprocal oppositions in the limitless process by which spirit and matter interchange states to create nature. It follows that all particular things in nature are universal particulars, since, actualized from within by the universal intellect acting as principle, their fixed form presents all forms to the shaping force of the universal intellect acting from without as efficient cause. This vexing ping-pong metaphysics finishes up in the mantric observation of Anaxagoras: all in all.

That idea leads Bruno to conclude the second dialogue of *Cause, Principle, and Unity* by arguing not only that the form of the universe is a living soul, but that all forms of all natural objects are souls, and that everything in nature, therefore, lives. Recalling Aristotle's *De Anima*, Bruno argues that just as the soul of an individual is entirely present in all his or her parts, so the world-soul is entirely present in every part of the world. Faced with the obvious distinction between organisms and other objects, Bruno clarifies his assertion that everything that is, is alive, in the following passage: "Let a thing be as small and diminutive as you like, it still possesses in itself a part of spiritual substance which, if it finds a suitable subject, becomes plant, becomes animal, and receives the members of one or other of the bodies that are commonly called animate; for spirit is found in all things and there is not the least corpuscle that doesn't contain internally some portion that may become alive" (*C*, p. 87).

All things are alive because they all contain forms that, in the right material setting, can develop into organisms. The form of a lotus lies curled in the lid of a jar, and can unfold when the kaleidoscopic shiftings of matter, governed by the universal intellect of the world-soul, have replaced the wood and metal of the lid with veins, roots, pigments, and odor. As Bruno puts it:

Teo. If then spirit, soul, life, is found in all things and in various degrees fills all matter, the certain deduction is that it is the true act and the true form of all things. The world-soul, it follows, is the formal constitutive principle of the universe and all contained in it. I say that if life is found in all things, the soul must be the form of all things: that which presides throughout over matter, holds sway over composite things, and determines the composition and consistency of their parts. And hence such form is no less enduring than matter is.

I understand it to be one in all things. But, according to the diversity of matter's dispositions and the power of the material principles, active and passive, it comes to produce diverse configurations. . . . [C, p. 89]

Having analyzed the unified opposition of cause and principle in the world-soul, Bruno, in the third dialogue, turns to the activity of this ambiguous force in nature and sets out the unified opposition of the world-soul with matter, which is itself a unified opposition of cause and principle. He concludes the third dialogue with the argument that matter not only displays the same unified opposition as the world-soul, but is indistinguishable from that soul, identical to it. The created universe—nature, the simulacrum of God—displays one principle that is also one cause; nature's integrity and perfection are discovered only through intellectual apprehension of that paradoxical unity. Grasping nature's coherence, a mind grasps as much of life, or reality, as it will ever know.

All considerations of matter as a substance separate from form, Bruno argues, begin with the analogy between nature and art. Just as artists require subjects for the embodiment of the forms in their imaginations, so nature requires a substance for the embodiment of the forms present in the world-soul and universal intellect, nature's first cause and principle. Just as the artists' subjects have no artificial form until the artists work on them, so matter, the substance nature's forming intelligence works on, has no natural form until the universal intellect, the active intelligence of the world-soul, operates on it. Finally, just as wood in the case of a carpenter has no artificial form until the carpenter shapes it, and just as wood can have as many forms as the minds of carpenters can create, remaining substantially unchanged—wooden—throughout all artificial transformations, so matter, the subject of nature's artist, the universal intellect, has no form in itself, but can be shaped in as many forms as the universal intellect contains (in this case an infinite number), maintaining throughout all the embodiments its original substantiality.

One crucial difference distinguishes natural creation from human artifice. Artists can only operate on subjects already formed by nature (craftspeople on wood, or iron, etc., imaginative artists on human experience), but nature works with an absolutely formless subject, matter, which is not corporeal or dimensional in Bruno's argument, but the infinite capacity to be formed. Following Aristotle here again, Teofilo argues that artists work by applying an extrinsic form to their subject. The idea of Helen exists in the mind of a sculptor—not as Michelangelo, Bruno's contemporary, held, in the stone—and is attached to the stone through skilled technique. Nature, in Bruno's argument, works as Michelangelo said he did—not from without, but from within matter. The result of this distinction is that the substratum of nature—matter—cannot be observed (being formless) as the substratum of art, formed matter, can be. Wood, colors, and characters and events can be observed by the senses in the products of artists; the matter of nature is known only through intellection. It is not felt or seen but apprehended, Bruno says, "with the eye of reason" (*C*, p. 102).

In the following paragraphs, Bruno sketches out what unity the eye of reason would see observing matter.

Teo. Don't you see that what was seed becomes stalk, and what was stalk becomes corn, and what was corn becomes bread—that out of bread comes chyle, out of chyle blood, out of blood the seed, out of the seed the embryo, and then man, corpse, earth, stone or something else in succession—on and on, involving all natural forms?

Gerv. I see that easily.

Teo. There must then exist an unchanging thing which in itself is not stone nor earth nor corpse nor man nor embryo nor blood nor anything else in particular, but which, after it was blood, became embryo, receiving the embryonic being; and after it was embryo, received the human being and became man. In the same way, in that which is formed by nature and constitutes the subject of art, what was tree becomes table and receives the being of table; that which was table, receiving the being of door, becomes door.

Gerv. Yes, that I understand quite well. But this substratum of nature, it seems to me, cannot be body, nor of a certain quality. For, escaping as it does into one form and natural being, and then into another, it does not manifest itself corporeally, like wood or stone, which always appear what they materially are, or serve as a subject, no matter what the form.

Teo. You put it well. [C, pp. 102–3]

Nothing in nature produces itself, Bruno argues: in all things there is a distinction maintained between the agent of an action and the result or object of an action. The soul (form) is the agent of nature, Bruno maintains, and matter (the soul) is the object. In this next passage he clarifies his bald distinction between agent and object in nature: "Hence we declare that there are three things in nature's body: first the universal intellect inherent in things, secondly the soul which vivifies all, and thirdly the substratum" (C, p. 108). The world-soul vivifies nature; its essential characteristic, the universal intellect, acting from within matter as principle, bestows on matter its power to be formed, and acting from without matter as efficient cause draws out all particular and shifting formal compositions from matter. These two together (the world-soul and universal intellect) are the form of nature; their field of action, the object of their agency, is the substratum Bruno has defined in the third dialogue: matter, the infinite capacity of nature to be formed. When Dicson, Bruno's reliable, friendly interlocuter, asks for an explanation of how forms are unfolded from a natural principle, Bruno develops his earlier argument concerning the identity of cause and principle.

Principle, "what intrinsically contributes to the constitution of a thing and remains in the effect," is identified with matter, nature's substratum. But this same principle is also cause, "what contributes to the production of things from outside and has its being outside the composition," a potency identified with the world-soul.

Matter is the principle from which all forms are unfolded, and matter is the cause (the world-soul) by which they are unfolded. Bruno extends this identity of principle and cause to an analogous set of oppositions unified in matter: possibility and actuality.

> Therefore, there is nothing which can be said to exist, if it cannot also be said to own the capacity of existing. And this aspect corresponds so precisely with active potency that passive and active cannot exist in any way without one another— so that, if there has always been the potency to make, produce, create, [cause, form] there has also always been the potency to be made, produced, created [principle, matter]. One potency implies the other. I mean that in positing one we necessarily posit the other. [*C*, p. 111]

The conclusion: matter is all that is and all that can be, the substratum of all forms (the first principle) and the forming agent operating on the substratum (the first cause). In this way it resembles God, in whom cause and principle, form and matter, act and power, are one.

But God's unity, although present in the natural cooperation of form and matter, differs in one crucial way from the mundane unity of matter and soul. God is all that is and all that can be without differentiation of time and place; all being is perfectly and absolutely present at once in Him, whereas nature is all it is and can be through the successive transformation of matter from one form to another. In God, the supreme principle, every potentiality and actuality are enfolded and unitary: in nature potentiality and act are disjointed, and unified only through the infinite succession of forms dispersed and multiplied through kaleidoscopic composition with matter. God's unity is implicated, nature's explicated—God is the great chord, nature the infinite melismatic dispersion of it.

Nature, as a whole and in all its parts, is the universal particular. A tree is in fact only one thing, but it contains the potential, which nature realizes through time, to become all things. As active potency (considered relatively), as a succession of compositions that decay, "the universe is all that it can be—in an unfolded, dispersed, and distinct way" (*C*, p. 112). As passive potency (considered absolutely), as the infinite capacity to produce natural compositions, as a principle in which matter and form are identical, the universe "is all that it can be, in a unified and undifferentiated way, since all is there all and identical in the utmost simplicity, without difference or distinction" (C, p. 112).

Matter and form are identical, as principle and cause are, by virtue of matter's double status as active and passive potency. In the world of nature that they create, act (form's being) and power (matter's) are unified. The universe participates in God's essence, it contains and depends on that essence for its being. Taking its being from unified God, displaying His unity in its own way, the universe is called by Bruno a "rational organism," a living, integrated creature. The whole substance of nature is one thing, Bruno concludes, integrated by a first principle that is indistinguishably material and formal. As his pupil Dicson puts it, "though in the descent of nature's ladder we encounter a duality of substance; one spiritual, one bodily—yet in sum they are both reducible to one being and one root" (C, p. 116).

In the fourth dialogue Bruno repeats his argument that contraries coincide in the soul, extending the coincidence to the identity of bodiless forms that transcend nature and all the embodied forms nature contains. In the fifth and last dialogue, Bruno finally explains the unity of individual souls and the world-soul, arguing for the final time that all things have souls, and that the soul of anything makes it identical to all other things, makes it all in all. "The universe then is one, infinite, immobile. One, I say, is absolute possibility, one is act, one is form or soul, one is matter or body, one is being, one is the maximum and the best. It is not capable of comprehension and therefore is endless and limitless, and to that extent infinite and indeterminable, and consequently immobile" (C, p. 135).

So begins the fifth dialogue. The world-soul, a derivative of God's unity, is the animating principle of this infinite universe. Bruno takes up the nature of infinity at the beginning of this last section.

And if in the infinite is found no differentiation, as of part from whole and as of one thing from another, certainly the infinite is one. In the comprehension of the infinite, no part is greater and no part is lesser, since any part however large conforms no more to the infinite's proportion than does any part however small. . . .

... You do not come any nearer to proportion, likeness, union, and identity with the infinite by being a man than by being an ant, by being a star than by being a man; for you do not draw any closer to that being by yourself being a sun or a moon than by being a man or an ant. And so in the infinite these things are indifferent. And what I say of them I mean of all things of particular substance. [C, p. 136]

Since all being is unified and infinite, no part of that being, no particular soul or thing (they are equivalent terms in Bruno, all things being animated, as he argued in the second dialogue) has more being than any other. Each contains the capacity to become all things, and in this way contains all things, since capacity is equal to activity in Bruno's argument. But this equality is simultaneous and perfectly achieved only in God. In the universe, the simulacrum of God, the identity of capacity and activity, or possibility and actuality, comes to be only through ceaseless transformation of matter from one form to another. This breach in nature of possibility and actuality is healed through the agency of the world-soul, which perpetually draws forth and recombines forms from plenipotentiary matter, creating the multiplicity of nature in order to realize nature's latent unity.

So although each soul contains all other souls, all the world-soul, and all being, it does not contain them all totally, but only in a specific mode limited by the accidents of quality, quantity, relation, and the other Aristotelian categories of matter that govern natural compositions. Every soul encloses a unity only part of which it can unfold. Every soul is infinite and unified, as well as limited and incomplete. Every soul is a universal particular. As Bruno puts it, "Everything we take in the universe has in itself that which is entire everywhere; and so it comprehends in its mode the whole world-soul (though not totally, as we've already pointed out). That soul is entire in any part whatever of the universe. Therefore, as act is one and constitutes a single being, wherever it is, we are not to believe there is in the world a plurality of substance and of that which is truly being" (C, p. 139).

The multiplicity of forms in nature results from the many different modes through which substance (the world-soul) must dispense itself when limited by the corporeal qualities matter displays in the physical universe. "The substance in the part" is a good motto for Bruno's cosmology, expressing succinctly the ambiguity on which his argument rests (C, p. 141). Each natural soul is a part of substance (the world-soul) and thus identical to all that is, and each natural soul is a formed part of matter (the same substance as the world-soul). As a material composition, each soul is unique, since matter's active potency can only produce one natural composition at a time. In the first case the unity of being is disclosed by the identity of all souls in nature, in the second the unity is disclosed by the unique status of each soul. In both cases a perfect infinite One appears; as the maximum absolute unity of substance when the world-soul is viewed as the substratum of nature, its principle (substance in the part); and as the minimum, relative unity of substance when the world-soul is viewed as the unrepeatable form of a unique particular, its cause (again, substance in the part).

The last proof of nature's unity, of the world-soul's status as all in all, comes when Bruno analyzes "the signs and verifications through which we wish to conclude that contraries coincide in unity" (C, p. 145). The signs of the world-soul's capacity to unite contraries Bruno draws from mathematics.

Hence, as regards signs, tell me: What thing is more unlike the straight line than the circle? what thing is more contrary to the straight line than the curve? Yet in the principle and in the minimum they coincide; since, as the Cusan, discoverer of geometry's most beautiful secrets, has divinely observed, what difference will you find between the minimum arc and the minimum chord? Further, in the maximum, what difference will you find between the infinite circle and the straight line? Don't you see that the circle, the larger it grows, approximates with its arc more and more to straightness? [C, p. 145]

These mathematical proofs suggest a truth verifiable through observation of nature. To Bruno's eye of reason all natural phenomena variously indicate one truth: coincidence of contraries. He observes:

Where does the physician seek the antidote more profitably than in the poison? who offers a better theriac than the viper? In the worst venoms are the best medicines. Is not one potency

common to two contrary objects? Now, where do you believe this comes from if not from the fact that, as the principle of being is one, so is the principle of conceiving the two contrary objects—and that, as the contraries are relative to a single substratum, so are they apprehended by one and the same sense?
. . .

In conclusion, he who wants to know the greatest secrets of nature should regard and contemplate the minima and maxima of contraries and opposites.   [*C,* p. 149]

The capacity of contraries to coexist in one subject comes to nature from the world-soul which animates it, and in which the fundamental contraries, principle and cause, power and act, form and matter, possibility and actuality, derive their unified existence from the perfection of God. This world-soul, present entirely in each particular of the universe, although not in all its possible modes and forms, animates the created world and makes each natural or celestial composition a soul from which all of reality can be explicated, that is, discovered and drawn forth. The universe is infinite, and every part of it is infinite: nothing in the natural or celestial world (unified contraries of matter) has more or less being than anything else. Hence, the world can be seen, as Blake put it, "in a Grain of Sand."[4] To quote him again in the same vein, "If the doors of perception were cleansed everything would appear to man as it is: infinite."[5]

In the natural world particular things, unstable compositions, will go through ceaseless transformations, receive and cast off an infinite number of forms, as the world-soul operates to heal the natural breach between power and act in the created universe. That perpetually closing, never closed breach displays the dependent identity of nature to God; it teaches those with eyes to see that the world of time is the moving image of God's world, eternity. Every form in time's world is a discrete ensouled unity that contains the capacity to produce and display all other forms time has contained and will contain. Under time's law, every natural form will give rise to all others by giving place to all others in corporeal matter's infinitely patterned and restless round. The crucial fact to observe here is the pattern, the unity giving out and holding in all differences in nature. Because God's unity is inaccessible to human beings, they must strive for knowledge of God's vestiges in nature, the world-soul. Understanding the world-soul's unity in nature, present entirely in all that is, human beings come as close as they can to understanding reality. When they understand their own souls, or the soul of any existing thing, they grasp all in all.

I have tried, in this analysis of Bruno's alternately exhilarating and frustrating dialogue, to present accurately the main thrust of his argument: that reality is a dynamic interchange of identical oppositions, and that the world-soul, through metempsychosis, organizes this interchange and composes its fluctuating partners. This world-soul, implicit and explicit in every existence, reveals itself to the diligent meditator on the unity of contraries manifested everywhere in nature. Here Bruno reverses a primary concept governing Aristotle's thinking about the soul and everything else. In *Metaphysics* Aristotle argues that opposites cannot exist simultaneously in the same subject. Bruno argues that existence is nothing but the coincidence of opposites in the world-soul.

For Aristotle, the soul is "in a manner all that is," as it is for Bruno, but the crucial difference comes in Aristotle's characteristic qualifier, "in a manner." Unlike Bruno, Aristotle has no concept of a world-soul unifying particular souls. Each soul is a discrete item in Aristotle's thinking, logically equivalent to all other souls, but not substantially identical to them. The soul, as he understood it, is a register, both camera and film, by which human beings experience material and immaterial substances outside themselves. The soul identifies human beings with all that is by reproducing in them the forms they encounter and so making these forms available to thought, sensation, and the other activities of the human animal. In the awareness the soul provides (which does not amount to absolute identification with the objects perceived) human beings and nature coalesce; in the simulacrum of nature presented to individuals in and by their souls, and only in that simulacrum, can they become, in Aristotle's guarded sense, all that is. The soul does not dissolve the opposition of human beings and everything else that is, but mediates it. Nowhere in Aristotle's *De Anima*, or any other work, does he conceive the power for unity that Bruno gives the soul.

Bruno hated Aristotle for that omission. Where Aristotle saw only a power for mediation and representative identity between human beings and nature, Bruno saw perfect unity; interchange of forms in matter, not mediation; and absolute, not representative, identity among all material and immaterial compositions. A human being and a stone would always be different, opposite things to Aristotle; such absolute difference doesn't exist for Bruno, who holds that all beings share one substratum in which they are identical—matter, which is also the world-soul. Only organic beings have souls in Aristotle's view: everything lives in Bruno's, through the omnipresence of the world-soul as unity of cause and principle, form and matter, and the like. In Bruno's thought, through the power of the world-soul resident in all beings, all is in all everywhere. Contradictions demonstrate being to Bruno; they do not prove its absence, as his detested Aristotle argued. Aristotle's failure to observe the unity of opposites in the soul led Bruno to the following kind of outburst, taken from *Cause, Principle, and Unity*:

> Aristotle, among others, did not grasp the one, did not grasp being, did not grasp the true, because he never realised how being is one; and though he was free to adopt a significance for being common to both substance and accident, and further to distinguish his categories according to so many genera and species, so many differentiations, he has not avoided being any the less ignorant of the truth, through a failure to deepen his cognition of this unity and lack of differentiation in constant nature and being. And, as a thoroughly arid sophist, by his malignant explanations and his frivolous persuasions, he perverts the statements of the ancients and sets himself against the truth—not so much perhaps through weakness of intellect as through force of jealousy and ambition.   [*C*, p. 139]

Bruno and Aristotle share one intellectual objective that makes them useful for Joyce's artistic and intellectual purpose in *Ulysses*: they both want to explain what the highest object of knowledge is, what unity human intelligence can discover in experience; and they both offer the operations of the soul as a model of that unity.[6] In significantly opposed ways both thinkers argue that analysis of the soul will yield principles of universality by which all experience may be understood. Joyce, who wanted to represent all experience in his first epic, found in both thinkers useful and interdependent strategies for making one existence, Bloom's, contain all existence. He also used the very different identification of soul and matter in Bruno and Aristotle as sources for his unusual identification of symbolic and realistic representation in *Ulysses*. The religious, symbolic achievement of Blake's prophecies and the dense, detailed worldly report of Defoe's works, the idea and the fact, the two extreme modes bounding literary enterprise in Joyce's view, coalesce in *Ulysses* thanks to the theories of the soul provided by Aristotle and Bruno (*CW*, p. 214). Aristotle offered an explanation for why opposites had to occur together in nature, and how the soul mediates them; Bruno developed that explanation into a theory in which opposites not only had to occur together, but were dialectically identified. The words of the Greek scientist and the Italian heretical mystic on the subject of the soul appear both in Stephen's mind and in Bloom's, and in the symbolic clusters that spin around these two men throughout the novel. Like these theories of the soul, Bloom and Stephen are contraries that coincide at dozens of places in the narrative and symbolic order of *Ulysses*, most explicitly in "Ithaca" when Stephen is named "Stoom" and Bloom "Blephen" (*U*, 17.549, 551). Relying on both theories, Joyce recapitulates in his art Bruno's antithetical development of Aristotle's conception of the soul and so dramatizes his own conviction that all being is unified, and that its unity is preeminently displayed and understood in the human soul.

Joyce displays Aristotle's *De Anima* prominently in the narrative of *Ulysses* in ways that suggest its conceptual and formal value in the novel. Bruno's work, although equally central to the book's structure, is never explicitly named. Some slanted quotations and indirect allusions do surface in the narrative, but Bruno, like Homer, works underground for the most part, or to put it another way, works, as the world-soul in his theory does, everywhere unseen. In the next section of this chapter I want to bring to light some of the many buried moments where Bruno's thought is at work in *Ulysses*, before making conclusions, in the third and final section, about how Bruno's thought shapes the effort of *Ulysses* to be universal, and why what I think is a major presence in the novel remains virtually anonymous throughout the book.

Bruno and the Moth:
Ulysses under the Rule of *Vice Versa*

In *A Portrait of the Artist as a Young Man*, Stephen Dedalus records in his diary in Chapter 5 a conversation in which he mentioned Bruno: "Then went to college. Other wrangle with little round-head rogue's eye Ghezzi. This time about Bruno the Nolan. Began in Italian and ended in pidgin English. He said Bruno was a terrible heretic. I said he was terribly burned. He agreed to this with some sorrow."[7] One part of this conversation appears in *Ulysses*, greatly transformed. There the reference to Bruno does not appear in Stephen's thoughts or speech, but as one part of Bloom's fantasy life dramatized in the "Circe" episode. While Bloom talks with three whores, Florry, Zoe, and Kitty, in Bella Cohen's whorehouse (where he has come to rescue Stephen), his grandfather Lipoti Virag appears to him and alternately upbraids, derides, and exhorts Bloom about his sexual proclivities, his knowledge of occult medical formulas and cures, his defective mnemotechnic, and his studies as a naturalist.

While Virag interrogates Bloom, a moth flies around the mauve shade covering one of Bella's lamps (the same shade that Stephen fractures later in the chapter during the hallucination in which the ghost of his mother appears).

VIRAG

(*head askew, arches his back and hunched wingshoulders, peers at the moth out of blear bulged eyes, points a horning claw and cries*) Who's moth moth? Who's dear Gerald? Dear Ger, that you? O dear, he is Gerald. O, I much fear he shall be most badly burned. Will some pleashe pershon not now impediment so catastrophics mit agitation of firstclass tablenumpkin? (*he mews*) Puss puss puss puss! (*he sighs, draws back and stares sideways down with dropping underjaw*) Well, well. He doth rest anon. (*he snaps his jaws suddenly on the air*)

THE MOTH
I'm a tiny tiny thing
Ever flying in the spring
Round and round a ringaring.
Long ago I was a king,

Now I do this kind of thing
On the wing, on the wing!
Bing!

(he rushes against the mauve shade, flapping noisily) Pretty
pretty pretty pretty pretty pretty petticoats.   [*U*, 15.2460–77]

Some further clarification of Virag's stuttering interest in
Gerald's metamorphosis, and an explanation for the stutter, come a
few pages later. Bella Cohen has by this time entered the room, and
Bloom's unconscious response to her is being dramatized. He is
now the female servant of Bello, the whore-mistress made male.

BELLO

(guffaws) Christ Almighty it's too tickling, this! You were a
nicelooking Miriam when you clipped off your backgate hairs
and lay swooning in the things across the bed as Mrs. Dandrade
about to be violated by Lieutenant Smythe-Smythe, Mr. Philip
Augustus Blockwell M.P., signor Laci Daremo, the robust
tenor, blueeyed Bert, the liftboy, Henri Fleury of Gordon Bennet
fame, Sheridan, the quadroon Croesus, the varsity wetbob eight
from Old Trinity, Ponto, her splendid Newfoundland and Bobs,
dowager duchess of Manorhamilton. *(he guffaws again)* Christ,
wouldn't it make a Siamese cat laugh?

BLOOM

(her hands and features working) It was Gerald converted me
to be a true corsetlover when I was a female impersonator in
the High School play *Vice Versa*. It was dear Gerald. He got that
kink, fascinated by sister's stays. Now dearest Gerald uses
pinky greasepaint and gilds his eyelids. Cult of the beautiful.   [*U*, 15.2998–3013]

Once this second passage identifies Gerald as Bloom's high-
school transvestite, homosexual friend, Virag's mysterious naming
of the moth comes clear. Knowing Gerald's homosexuality makes
understanding Virag's second sentence much easier, "Will some
pleashe pershon not now impediment so catastrophics mit agitation of firstclass tablenumpkin?" The inverted word order, together
with "pleashe," "pershon," "mit," and "tablenumpkin," in addition
to embodying Gerald's sexual inversion, identifies Virag as Aus-

trian. In the sentence Virag impersonates the endangered, fay moth's fright (the dramatic cause of Virag's stutter) by taking on Gerald's lisping ("pleashe," "pershon"), oh so *genteel* ("agitation of firstclass tablenumpkin"), theatrical style ("catastrophics"). If Gerald in his guise as moth could talk, Virag is saying, this is how he would say help!—"Save me from myself, help me from the light by waving one of those *divine* firstclass table napkins at me!" Overwrought Gerald may be, but tinkling elegance remains his style. The mix of German syntax, vocabulary, and accent with theatrical perversion not only characterizes Virag and Gerald but identifies them in the sentence. Gerald moth's song brings the themes of metempsychosis and the circular transfer of form and matter through nature into the scene. The meaning of that insertion will be dealt with in a later paragraph. Here it is enough to observe that those ideas are cast in the tawdry glamor of Gerald's theatrical sexuality, in the opposite voices of deliberate naiveté and rueful cynicism that begin and end his music-hall song.

As the moth flaps up against the mauve shade he cries out "Pretty pretty pretty pretty pretty pretty petticoats." "Mauve shade" is a nice ambiguity. "Shade" of course refers to lamp shade, but it also means darkness, ghost, Hades, and color, in this case the color of the lamp's covering. The mauve shade is a shade of purple; purple, like lavender, is a conventional badge of homosexuality, as well as royalty and mourning. "Shade" seems appropriate to Gerald in at least four ways: as the tone of a color denoting his sexual orientation, his former royalty (vide the song), his status as a doomed creature of darkness, and his bodiless, ghostly presence in the moth. When he is badly burned Gerald moth will go to Hades, the land of shades; Virag, pointing to Gerald's peril, mourns the death before the fact. It is no accident then that the petticoats Gerald flies to are purple.

Finally there is the word "pretty" repeated six times. The word means artful; clever; delicately, gracefully pleasing; conventionally beautiful; apparently pleasant but lacking strength, purpose, and, to Joyce's mind, manliness (i.e., insipid). "Pretty" in Gerald's case denotes artful; clever; deceptively pleasant but unmanly; weak. In the moth's it also denotes deceptively pleasant. In Bloom's case the word denotes both deceptively pleasant and unmanly. The petticoats he has dressed in, and watched Gerty dressed in while mas-

turbating in "Nausicaa," insofar as they provide the thrills of voyeurism and transvestite sexuality, are deceptively pleasant but unmanly. For the moth the petticoats are a lamp shade covering destructive light; for Bloom and Gerald they are lingerie on male
bodies, his own in Bloom's case (in addition to a female model,
Gerty), presumably other men's as well in Gerald's.

Bloom stands with Gerald in danger of being burned. His confession, as a female, of participating in Gerald's theatrical schoolboy
crossing of sexual barriers brings more unified contraries into the
long list already circling the deadly light with the moth. Bello's
exposé of Bloom's fantasies enacted after the purchase of Mrs. Dandrade's underwear ["You were a nicelooking Miriam" etc. (*U*, 15.
2999–3007)] forces Bloom to identify Gerald, and so answer Virag's
earlier question, "Who's dear Gerald?" The forced explanation also
presents a wildly improbable list of Lady Bloom's adulterous lovers.
This burlesque epic catalogue, in which Bloom, dressed in a prosti-
tute's clothes, imagines his services extended to a sports team from
Oxford, a member of Parliament, a lieutenant, a dog, a duchess, an
alias of himself when male (Henri Fleury), and the imaginary Laci
Daremo, the robust tenor, balances Bloom's own burlesque epic
catalogue in "Ithaca" of adulterers serviced by his female counterpart, Molly. Joyce plays tit for tat with this list, making Bloom's
adulterous adventures even more preposterous than Bloom makes
Molly's.

Her violators, although hypothetical, are all real people of the
opposite sex. His, also hypothetical, include men, women, a dog,
and two phantasms, the second of which, signor Laci Daremo,
unites this catalogue again to Molly. Along with anal depilation
(clipped "backgate" hairs) and the perverse couplings opposed in
Bloom's list (a man dressed as a woman imagines heterosexual intercourse that is in fact homosexual—with male violators—and homosexual intercourse that is in fact heterosexual—with the duchess), there is masturbation, signified by Bloom's coupling with
Henri Fleury (himself) and explicitly presented in the name of the
robust tenor, Laci Daremo. His name comes from the duet in Mo-
zart's *Don Giovanni* in which Giovanni almost seduces the bride-
to-be Zerlina on the day of her marriage. "*La ci darem la mano*":
"Let us give each other's hands," Giovanni sings; "*Vorrei e non
vorrei*": "I do and don't want to," Zerlina answers. The duet, sung

by Molly and various basses in the past (and on the program sched-
uled by her Giovanni, Boylan), has been on Bloom's mind, in a mistaken version at times, all day; appropriately enough, since his Zerlina has no doubts about her betrayal of him and in fact takes no
pains to hide it. Molly's giving of hands leads to long-needed heterosexual satisfaction; Bloom's giving of hands (masturbation while
fantasizing, in women's clothes, three perverse couplings) is doubly
contrary to hers. It involves no real adultery, and it involves only
one person whose lust may be natural, but is certainly not normal,
as Molly's is.

The play that prefigured Bloom's phantasmagorical status as a
costumed night-bird in Bella's house was *Vice Versa*, a farce by
Francis Anstey (the pseudonym of the Englishman Thomas Anstey
Guthrie), which depicts the conflict of father against son (*G*, p.
413). The title, like the moth, contains numerous oppositions. It
incidentally pits the author's real name against an alias, as well as
referring to the sexual transference involved in homosexuality and
transvestism, the normal union of contraries in heterosexual love,
and the ongoing coincidence of opposed wills in persons of one sex
and one flesh that occupies both Stephen and Bloom throughout
the novel—the problem of fathers and sons. In the play Dick Bultitude, the son, exchanges bodies, through the law of metempsychosis, with his father, Mr. Bultitude. The farcical happenings teach
the father what suffering his tyrannical treatment of the son entails. Stephen's *Hamlet* theory and the trinitarian symbolism of the
novel both display the same paradoxical unity in more elegant
terms: whether the son is Dick Bultitude, Jesus, or Hamlet, he is in
the father, and the father is in him. The play's title condenses in a
commonplace phrase one major effort of Joyce's art in this epic: the
struggle to portray an interdependent unity among experiences that
seem irreconcilable; the heroic attempt to say with magnanimous
comedy and philosophical precision what Stephen in "Scylla and
Charybdis" says to scorn A.E.'s mystical presumptuousness: "This
verily is that" (*U*, 9.63).

One final topic falls into Gerald moth's endangered orbit: the
literature of Ireland which Joyce repudiated. Bloom tells Bello,
"Now dearest Gerald uses pinky greasepaint and gilds his eyelids.
Cult of the beautiful" (*U*, 15.3012–13). Overwrought, theatrical homosexuality and overwrought, cultish art, especially literature, had

met in Joyce's Dublin in the person of another Dubliner, Oscar Wilde. Wilde tried to jettison moral approaches to art's subjects that characterized late Victorian aesthetics and replace them with worship of "the beautiful" in art. By that term Wilde meant the necessarily amoral delight in pure form (usually form that shaped impure subjects) that alone made an imaginative work "artistic." Wilde's homosexuality was not a necessary component of this aesthetic, but Joyce here presents it as a symbol for the new theory's insistence on art's unnatural, amoral, exquisite barrenness, and in a more polemical vein, on art's connection to spiritual purity. At the end of the century some men took up Wilde's conviction that art was exquisitely rarified form that freed men from moral and intellectual responsibility in the world, but they did not take up his flamboyant sexual politics. Yeats, Pater, Dowson, Johnson, and other "decadent aesthetes," as they were called in the nineties, could espouse Wilde's ideas without being practicing homosexuals (or, in the ambiguous cases of Pater and Johnson, without proclaiming how "artistic" their deviation from the sexual norm was).

The insistence on art's uselessness and freedom from realistic reporting cleared space for two related developments in literature: what Joyce in an early essay called "the world of faery," and theosophical mysticism (CW, p. 45). Yeats took part in both faiths, as did George Russell. Lady Gregory and Douglas Hyde eschewed the metaphysics of the theosophists led by Russell. Although these antiquarian mythologists had political motives for adding Irish legends and superstitions to the storehouse of Irish literary invention (the creation of an Irish imagination being the necessary precondition, in their minds, to the creation of an Irish state), they concentrated on literature's power to be fanciful and mysterious instead of mundanely informative, and so implicated themselves in the first purpose of A.E.'s cabal and in Wilde's cult of the beautiful. A.E., Yeats, and Lady Gregory are singled out as members of that cult in the following places in *Ulysses*. Stephen, mocking Russel's thought, makes a silent parody of it in "Scylla and Charybdis" in which the following sentence appears: "Hiesos Christos, magician of the beautiful, the Logos who suffers in us at every moment" (*U*, 9.62–63). Later in the same chapter Mulligan castigates Stephen for insulting Lady Gregory in print and says:

O you inquisitional drunken jewjesuit! She gets you a job on
the paper and then you go and slate her drivel to Jaysus.
Couldn't you do the Yeats touch?

He went on and down, mopping, chanting with waving grace-
ful arms:

—The most beautiful book that has come out of our country
in my time. One thinks of Homer.   [*U*, 9.1159–65]

In addition to its emphasis on homosexuality, the "cult of the
beautiful" concentrated on representation of the femme fatale,
among other things. Wilde's play *Salome*, and Pater's description of
the Mona Lisa in his chapter on Leonardo Da Vinci in *The Renaissance* (a description Yeats included as the first poem in his edition
of *The Oxford Book of Modern Verse* as late as 1936) are the most
famous examples of the figure, who also appears in Stephen's villanelle in *A Portrait of the Artist as a Young Man* and, usually
comically, all over *Ulysses*.[8] In a context where painted whores are
presented as sirens luring men (moths) to their destructive flame
(Bella's purple-shaded lamp), Wilde's cult of the beautiful (which
worshipped form enameled to the point that moral value in art was
suffocated, or more accurately, vaporized) fits perfectly, in fact begs
to be included.

Joyce settled a personal score and did some aesthetic theorizing
of his own by grouping so many of his Irish literary contemporaries into this cult and sending them with Gerald and the moth
into immolation in a whorehouse. A.E., Yeats, Lady Gregory, and
Douglas Hyde all made up the literary establishment young Joyce
tried unsuccessfully to storm, and for years afterward resentfully
scorned. Stephen's exclusion from the literary soiree to be held on
the night of June 16, 1904, dramatized in "Scylla and Charybdis,"
documents what Joyce took to be the establishment's snub of him
(*U*, 9.301–13). In "Circe" Joyce avenges the snub by grouping the
aesthetes and the fairy revivalists into one aerial circle of destruction—Gerald moth's—imitating in this his beloved Dante, whose
enemies were confined to underground circles of torment in an earlier autobiographical encyclopedic epic of the soul's progress. The
inclusion of the cult of faery is not accidentally or only maliciously
connected through a pun to homosexuality. This whole corps of his
contemporaries, Joyce thought, had turned their back on art's func-

tion—the impersonal affirmative revelation of the truth about life in the body—and so given up their "virtue" in the Latin sense, their manliness. They fall, for that failure, on the damned side of contraries united in the moth. Their counterpart, who has been rejected from their cult, and managed thereby to escape the destruction it entails, has no name in Bloom's biographical sketch of Gerald, but it seems safe enough to assume Joyce saw himself in that part—the mature Dedalus who soared safely past the dangers that assailed and singed him as a young man. The most beautiful book to come out of Ireland, Joyce implies by damning the cult of the beautiful, the book to make one think of Homer, was not to be Lady Gregory's retelling of Cuchulain legends, to which Yeats affixed a version of the fawning viciously preserved in Mulligan's remarks, but Joyce's own *Ulysses.*

But if opposites coincide in the moth, Joyce must somehow identify his own effort with the cult of the beautiful. If this is that, that must also be this. Joyce's symbolic literary avatar, Icarus (Stephen's prototype), died after all of the danger Gerald moth courts: flying into a burning light. In the case of Joyce's literary effort, the identity with the cult of faery and the theosophists appears in three dimensions. Joyce put in his time as a theosophist and a writer of evanescent, dainty verse: in these ways his own career matches the work of the other Irish writers scorned in Bloom's history of Gerald. Joyce, like Yeats, Russell, Lady Gregory, and Hyde, wanted to put Dublin on the cultural map, and to put it there grandly, in a place of preeminence befitting its station as "the seventh city of Christendom." This goal identified him with the other writers of his time, however much he detested their methods. Moreover, if the members of the cult of the beautiful were doomed to mental and spiritual destruction by practicing their well-received art, Joyce had reason to fear that physical hardship might bring him martyrdom while he was writing his unpopular books. During much of the time he wrote *Ulysses* Joyce's professional life was what it had been since he left Ireland in 1904: penury, struggle, and a protracted series of battles with publishers who only gave fledgling life to his work. Joyce had every reason when he wrote the lines about Gerald the moth and the cult of the beautiful to fear that his work faced a fire of material devastation as dangerous as the spiritual fire the cult of the beautiful flirted with. Implicit in Joyce's attack on

Wilde, Yeats, and crew is the exile's fear that despite his superior genius, he too might be ruined, not through the wrong faith, as they were, but through personal misery, the destructive force of censors, and the malice of publishers and printers.

One more answer to Virag's question, "Who's dear Gerald?" remains. In the narrative dimension of *Ulysses* Gerald has one historical identity to which many symbolic identities accrue. The chief of these, the symbolic figure that makes the rest possible, Joyce has obscured. Readers of *Ulysses* who know *A Portrait of the Artist as a Young Man* in precise and intimate detail may hear that novel's identification of Giordano Bruno as a heretic "terribly burned" echoing in Virag's sarcastic "O, I fear he shall be most badly burned." The echo of "Giordano Bruno" in "Gerald" and "burned" is one more indication of the moth's secret identity. Readers who know Bruno's work will know why his symbolic presence draws together so many pairs of contraries and how it unites them all in one subject, the moth imperiled by deadly burning. Those readers will also recognize that Bloom, Virag, and Stephen all acquire some qualities of Bruno in the scene where Gerald appears. Virag with his insistence on occult cures presents Bruno, the Renaissance Magus, who delved into the secrets of nature searching out coincidence of contraries. He also presents Bruno's other exotic intellectual preoccupation, the development of a system of memory, with his repeated injunctions that Bloom exercise "mnemotechnic." Bloom and Stephen both are in danger of the martyrdom Bruno suffered: Bloom, because like Bruno he rejected the cultural and civic authority of the Church in favor of secular humanism ["Free money, free rent, free love and a free lay church in a free lay state" (*U*, 15.1693)]; Stephen, because like Bruno he has rejected the church's intellectual and spiritual authority, and seeks Truth in the operations of his own soul as it imbibes wisdom from mystical philosophers. Bloom, in fact, like Bruno, is burned at the stake for his heretical pains in "Circe" (*U*, 15.1926–56).

Four ideas from *Cause, Principle, and Unity* clarify the functions of Bruno's ignominious, comic transformation into a whorehouse moth whose doomed flight depicts, among other things, a very minor character from Bloom's past. Gerald's motto *vice versa* encodes in a semaphoric flash Bruno's conviction that the universe exists in the world-soul, which exists in God; that the world-soul is entirely present, though not entirely explicated, in every particular of the universe (that all is in all); and consequently, that every particular is a universal particular in which opposites coalesce.

The world-soul's serial and creative progress through nature appears in Virag's musical impersonation of Gerald the moth. It is diminished and risible there (a sure sign in this crafty, comic book that something crucial to its conceptual design has emerged).

> I'm a tiny tiny thing
> Ever flying in the spring
> Round and round a ringaring.
> Long ago I was a king,
> Now I do this kind of thing
> On the wing, on the wing!
> Bing!   [*U*, 15.2469–75]

The song recapitulates Bruno's idea that the world-soul, moving through time, unfolds its perfected being now in one natural form, now in another, perpetually transforming itself and nature to realize the only variety of unity the world of time allows—succession, the moving image of the simultaneous presence all things have in God. Each particular form contains all that can be, but only unfolds one variation of that plenitude; every particular is entirely what it is, but not all it can be. Through cyclical fluctuation of natural compositions the world-soul reconciles the opposition of universal and particular being in the world of time, unfolding from each composition all the other possible compositions it can yield, thus dynamically locating all in all. So, through cyclical fluctuation of motifs, symbols, styles, voices, and narrative details, the structure of *Ulysses* locates all in all in the portrayal of Bloom.

The process of the world-soul in nature at large also operates individually in each particular life, where it is called metempsychosis, the transmigration of souls. Bloom explains the idea with little success to Molly in "Calypso," from which point it recurs in crucial moments at least sixteen times explicitly, and many more times implicitly throughout the novel. Gerald's song presents every item in Bruno's description of the world-soul's natural oscillation through particulars to the universal: the cycle is here—"Round and round a ringaring"; the perpetual generation of new forms from old ones—"Ever flying in the spring"; the entire presence of the world-soul in the smallest particular—"I'm a tiny tiny thing"; and its constantly varied composition—"Long ago I was a king, / Now I do this kind of thing." According to Bruno's conception of all in all, Virag, Bloom, Stephen, and all the other characters associated with the moth are included in Gerald's transformations. Insofar as they participate in the world-soul they were all present in Gerald when he was a king, as they are when he is a moth, and will be when death from the gas jet (Bing!) transforms him, under the rule of metempsychosis, into some other tiny thing. They are all transformed in the design of *Ulysses*, each in unique ways, but each new incarnation, each tiny thing in the springing round of nature (and Joyce's literary imitation of it) always contains, via its presence in the world-soul, all the forms discarded and not yet taken up by each other tiny thing.

Virag, a phantasm of Bloom's memory, conjures up someone else from Bloom's memory who appears as a moth who sings a song. This is the narrative situation, one in which all the figures are distinct from Bloom, and yet identical to him since they are his projected memories, not, apparently, present to others in Bella's house. In this realistic dimension, Bloom unfolds characters distinct from and identical to him, gives them shape for a while, and then retracts them all, emerging from his hallucination, forgetting Virag and the others, only to unfold them again later, in new configurations. The psychology of hallucination in the narrative recapitulates the dynamic unity of opposites that organizes the world-soul's natural transformation, a unity represented in the symbolic dimensions of the hallucination through slanted conjuration of the martyred Bruno—"terribly burned"—and parodic quotation of his ideas: the moth's song and the title of a transvestite farce, *Vice Versa*. The structure of *Ulysses* in these scenes from "Circe," and in many others there is no space or time to analyze here, is like the structure of Bruno's reality: a dynamic interchange of opposite states in one substance. Fritz Senn puts the point nicely in his essay "The Rhythm of *Ulysses*":

> There is "infinite variety everywhere," but the poles of sameness and difference, and the process of transformation bringing them about, underlie everything, including such concepts and themes as metempsychosis, incarnation, trinity, identity, Ho-

meric parallels, analogies, Viconian schemes, "history repeating itself with a difference," and the representativeness of Joyce's Dublin. It is the "same old dingdong always" (167) but—*mutatis mutandis*. And part of the vitality lies in the transmutations.[9]

Nothing in *Ulysses* is single, or only what it seems to be—either an item solidly contained in the narrative, or part of a symbolic nimbus in which wild abstrusiosities glow. Opposites in the narrative coalesce, opposites in the symbolism coalesce, and the opposed narrative and symbolic dimensions coalesce. At the moments under consideration for so many pages by now, this ringing round takes place in an imperiled moth, whose circling recapitulates the obscure cyclical cosmology of an occult heretic.

Joyce has symbolically elaborated the narrative surface of the moth more than the narrative surface of most other details in the book, less than that of some (keys, or the handbill announcing the coming of Elijah, for instance). But not even the most thoroughly elaborated symbols of the book—Bloom's status as Christ, Moses, and Odysseus—are explicitly present in all the narrative details of the novel. Most of the identities in *Ulysses* are implicated one with another by associative logic. Gerald as moth explicitly portrays only one opposition, father and son in the farce *Vice Versa*, just as a moth only explicates one natural form the world-soul can take, but that one highlighted title stands as an emblem for the artistic strategy of *Ulysses* at large—Bloom is and is not Odysseus. The same logic appears throughout the book in hundreds of trivial moments: Stephen is and is not Lycidas in his schoolroom, Molly's lamp is and is not the rose of Paradise Beatrice led Dante to, and so forth, ad infinitum (or to be more precise, until all the coalescing opposites in the novel have been put through all the permutations established for them by Joyce's scatter-shot symbolism; which is virtually, if not in fact, ad infinitum). Some details will yield more explicit and precise connections than others, but even the scantiest symbolic functions of the tiniest details lead to consideration of topics that organize the novel as a whole.[10]

Epic representation of universals requires some model. Joyce could not tell every person's story to depict all of human experience, so he told Everyman's; depicted a universal particular. Everyman by nature is any man or woman; what is said of him must be true of all people. So it is with a theory including the concept of a universal particular: any and all particulars must manifest all other particulars and all particulars must also be particular universals. It is this principle, drawn from Bruno, that permeates *Ulysses*, allowing Joyce to establish so many hidden interconnections and identities between narrative and symbolic particulars. Those identities, in which Joyce depicted his sense of the universal conditions of life, would have been infinite, as life is, if Joyce could have managed to keep adding details to *Ulysses* forever. Phillip Herring's and A. Walton Litz's books *Joyce's Ulysses Notesheets in the British Museum* and *The Art of James Joyce*, which show that Joyce's novels were composed by accretion even after their submission to printers, suggest that only publishing deadlines prevented this.[11] Joyce's lifetime preoccupation with Dublin's lower middle-class, and his habit of somehow including all his previous fiction in *Ulysses* and *Finnegans Wake*, as if each epic were an amplification of the previous achievements, also suggest devotion to the idea that all could be seen and said at once, that life was ceaseless variation of one eternal substance.

In *Ulysses* Joyce wanted to write all of life into and out of one life, hence he gave the book an unprecedented wealth of narrative facts, locating in Bloom's story some variety of everything that can happen to one man in one place and time. From that narrative matter he extrapolated, through parody, analogy, and encyclopedic allusions, a symbolic representation of everything that happens to all people at all times, unfolding the history of the body from Bloom's thirty-eight-year-old form, the history of consciousness from Bloom's experience, and the history of human culture from Bloom's city, Dublin. In accordance with this double structure that implicates and explicates everything through one subject—Bloom—Joyce wrote a book in which all narrative and symbolic details are dynamically interchangeable (and in which a great many are elaborately interchanged); a book that at any point can be read into and out of any and every one of its details. Of course writers before Joyce had written books in which all the details interlock in mutual suggestiveness. In fact, it would be perfectly sound to argue that literary art is nothing but that kind of organization of words. But no one before Joyce, or since, makes the principle of all in all so thoroughly functional. And no one connects it to Bruno's thought in the way Joyce does.

The philosophical precedents for this literary device that Joyce could have drawn on besides Bruno, or in addition to him, are multiple. Pre-Socratic philosophers, especially Anaxagoras, and many Eastern and Western mystics, especially Plotinus, all have some variation of the formula "all in all." I have elaborated Joyce's reliance on Bruno's conception of this ancient idea because he felt biographical affinity for the harassed, martyred Italian (like Stephen's man of genius, he saw his own image in Bruno's work), and because Bruno expressed the idea in terms of the coincidence of contraries, a formula obviously useful for the creation of an epic in which a Greek military ruler is recast as a cuckolded Jewish adman, the subject, not the ruler, of a kingdom; worse, an empire. Nicholas of Cusa provided many of Bruno's ideas about the unity of contraries, although the friar and the cardinal disagree at many places. Joyce included Bruno's debt repeatedly in *Finnegans Wake*, linking him and Cusanus over and over again as the sages of coinciding contraries. Whatever the cause, Joyce did not cite Cusanus in *Ulysses* but left the idea squarely in Bruno's camp.

Bruno's thought and presence enter *Ulysses* at many other points besides Bloom's memory of Gerald and vision of Virag. The previous analysis of Gerald is offered as a touchstone of the Nolan's importance to the novel. The following paragraphs point out just a few of Bruno's multiple appearances elsewhere in Joyce's epic of *vice versa*.

In "Lestrygonians," Bloom, thinking of the differences between eating on Olympus and in Dublin while he wonders whether statues of goddesses include the beloved anatomical detail that empties the human alimentary canal, makes the following observation: "Quaffing nectar at mess with gods golden dishes, all ambrosial. Not like a tanner lunch we have, boiled mutton, carrots and turnips, bottle of Allsop, Nectar imagine it drinking electricity: gods' food. Lovely forms of women sculped Junonian. Immortal lovely. And we stuffing food in one hole and out behind: food, chyle, blood, dung, earth, food: have to feed it like stoking an engine. They have no. Never looked. I'll look today" (*U*, 8.925–31). The opposition Bloom makes between the eternal and mundane realms contains an allusion to Bruno's explanation of how divinity's static perfection is reduced to a series of fluctuating forms in the world of matter. *Cause, Principle, and Unity*, in a passage already cited in this chapter, makes the point this way: "Don't you see that what was seed becomes stalk, and what was stalk becomes corn, and what was corn becomes bread—that out of *bread comes chyle, out of chyle blood*, out of blood the seed, out of the seed the embryo, and then man, corpse, earth, stone, or something else in succession—on and on involving all natural forms?" (emphasis mine; *C*, p. 102). Bloom has changed the order of Bruno's catalogue, and left reproduction out of his musings, but the subjects and observations in both lists are otherwise identical: life in nature undergoes physical permutations to perfect itself, whereas life in the celestial sphere does not. Bloom does not think of how the two spheres are connected; that observation is left for a reader familiar with the argument from Bruno quoted in the excerpt to make for himself.

The natural cycle that Bloom describes takes place slowly through long periods of time. The same cyclical transformation, used to describe a quick series of actions performed by one creature, shows up in the following excerpt from "Proteus," a chapter of shape-shifting.

The dog yelped running to them, reared up and pawed them, dropping on all fours, again reared up at them with mute bearish fawning. Unheeded he kept by them as they came towards the drier sand, a rag of wolf's tongue redpanting from his jaws. His speckled body ambled ahead of them and then loped off at a calf's gallop. The carcass lay on his path. He stopped, sniffed, stalked around it, brother, nosing closer, went round it, sniffling rapidly like a dog all over the dead dog's bedraggled fell. Dogskull, dogsniff, eyes on the ground, moves to one great goal. Ah, poor dogsbody. . . .

. . . His hindpaws then scattered the sand: then his forepaws dabbled and delved. Something he buried there, his grandmother. He rooted in the sand, dabbling, delving and stopped to listen to the air, scraped up the sand again with a fury of his claws, soon ceasing, a pard, a panther, got in spousebreach, vulturing the dead. [*U*, 3.343–45, 359–64]

Stephen, who watches this scene, is "dogsbody," as he names himself in the first episode, "Who chose this face for me? This dogsbody to rid of vermin?" (*U*, 1.136–37). The dog's circling round another dog's corpse presents to Dedalus an analogical image of God's cyclical self-realization through history. The phrase describing the circling dog—"moves to one great goal"—first appears in "Nestor," the episode preceding "Proteus," when Deasy says to Stephen, "All human history moves towards one great goal, the manifestation of God" (*U*, 2.380–81).

In this passage three of Bruno's ideas converge: God's perfection is manifested through the transformation of forms in time in the created universe; every particular form (a dog or Stephen) is an explication of the world-soul, and so contains implicitly all other forms it will, but has not yet, become; and in the union of particular and universal that all forms display, opposites are united. Read against these ideas, the passage may be interpreted as follows: The living God is a living dog who circles round a dead one (the world, God's simulacrum, his "brother"), and the dog, living and dead, is also a man, Stephen Dedalus, made, like the world, in God's image, who has turned, like the world, away from Him. Stephen, in heretical bitterness, thinks of God as operating like a carrion and scavenger in the two dogs, in himself, and in the world at large. In the passage, God, Stephen, the world, and the dog (God's orthographical contrary) become bear, wolf, calf, horse, fox, leopard, panther, vulture, and corpse; a series of transformations organized exactly according to ideas from Bruno cited in Bloom's thoughts about food on Olympus versus food on earth, and present again in this subsequent passage in "Proteus": "God becomes man becomes fish becomes barnacle goose becomes featherbed mountain" (*U*, 3.477–79). Stephen follows this second list with a gloomy meditation on the cyclic interflux of dead forms in nature. Readers familiar with Joyce's biography know that the series beginning with "God" celebrates life, not death, by ending in a metaphor for Joyce's *summum bonum*. "Barnacle" goose brings Joyce's Nora into the picture: "featherbed mountain" refers not only to a real mountain in Ireland, or to pillows made of goose down and feathers, but to that venereal pillow, the elevation in Nora and all other women where life begins, a promontory never far from Joyce's mind. Once more opposites coincide in a passage built on Bruno's thought.

Describing the world-soul's hidden and revealed presence in God, Bruno, in a passage already quoted, cites Ps. 139:12. The English version of the Latin reads, "Yea the darkness hides not from you, but the night shines as the day: the darkness and the light are both alike to you" (*C*, pp. 114–15). This same association of the world-soul with dark light occurs in *Ulysses* in Stephen's thinking about Arab and Jewish medieval thinkers who made Neoplatonic commentaries on Aristotle's works, especially *De Anima*, that extended the Greek's thought in the same direction Bruno did later. "Gone too from the world," Stephen laments, "Averroes and Moses Maimonides, dark men in mien and movement, flashing in their mocking mirrors the obscure soul of the world, a darkness shining in brightness which brightness could not comprehend" (*U*, 2.157–60).

Another Mideastern man of dark mien, the Jew Bloom, is associated with a dark reflecting mirror in "Nausicaa." Wandering on the strand [where in "Proteus" Stephen thought of Aristotle's analysis of the soul, and where he composed mentally the lines "Darkness is in our souls do you not think? Flutier. Our souls, shamewounded by our sins, cling to us yet more, a woman to her lover clinging, the more the more" (*U*, 3.421–23)], Bloom, exhausted by his own experience with a shame-wounded soul, Gerty, unwittingly imitates Stephen by composing his own commemoration of a sexual misdemeanor in the sands where it occurred. "Some flatfoot tramp on it in the morning. Useless. Washed away. Tide comes here. Saw a pool near her foot. Bend, see my face there, dark mirror, breathe on it, stirs. All these rocks with lines and scars and letters. O, those transparent!" (*U*, 13.1259–62). Before he gives up on the whole business, Bloom does write one message that he quickly effaces, "I. . . . Am. A" (*U*, 13.1258, 1264).

Stephen's passage recurs, in fragments, in Bloom's. In Stephen's, the obscure soul of the world is flashed by dark men with mirrors; in Bloom's, Poldy sees his own dark face in the dark mirror of the tidal pool. Joyce's mosaic interlocking of the passages identifies Bloom with the soul of the world from Stephen's thoughts, the dark (see Stephen's "obscure") light flashed in a mocking mirror; the mockery in Bloom's case stemming from his knowledge that the motion of this watery mirror over the message he has written will render the act of composition, as he puts it, "Useless." Bruno's idea that the world-soul is the created image of God occurs twice in the "Nausicaa" excerpt. The account of creation in Genesis, in which God breathes on the waters, and the Roman Catholic theological exposition of it, which held that God created the world for solipsistic magnification of his own glory, both bear on Bloom's simple act of looking into the tidal pool. God created in darkness by breathing on water to make a moving image of his own glory: Bloom looks into the tidal pool to see himself, and then remarks how the image "stirs," that is, multiplies itself in ripples when he breathes on it. Bruno's idea that nature is the moving image of God, because the world-soul that creates it is, commands attention in a passage where a figure identified by implied symbolism with the world-soul imitates God's manner of creation.

Joyce filled his novel with paraphrases of Bruno's ideas about the world-soul in which that term never appears. The following are some of the most conspicuous. From Seymour Bushe's speech on the law of evidence in the Childs murder case, a description of Michelangelo's Moses:

> that stony effigy in frozen music, horned and terrible, of the human form divine, that eternal symbol of wisdom and prophecy which, if aught that the imagination or the hand of sculptor has wrought in marble of soultransfigured and soul-transfiguring deserves to live, deserves to live;   [U, 7.768–71]

from Stephen's Hamlet theory:

> —As we, or mother Dana, weave and unweave our bodies, Stephen said, from day to day, their molecules shuttled to and fro, so does the artist weave and unweave his image. . . . In the intense instant of imagination, when the mind, Shelley says, is a fading coal, that which I was is that which I am and that which in possibility I may come to be;   [U, 9.376–78, 381–83]

and later in the argument,

> He [Shakespeare] found in the world without as actual what was in his world within as possible. Maeterlink says: If Socrates leave his house today he will find the sage seated on his doorstep. If Judas go forth tonight it is to Judas his steps will tend. Every life is many days, day after day. We walk through ourselves, meeting robbers, ghosts, giants, old men, young men, wives, widows, brothers-in-love, but always meeting ourselves;   [U, 9.1041–46]

from "Oxen of the Sun":

> What is the age of the soul of man? As she hath the virtue of
> the chameleon to change her hue at every new approach, to be
> gay with the merry and mournful with the downcast, so too is
> her age changeable as her mood;   [*U*, 14.1038–41]

from Stephen's "Pornosophical philotheology" in "Circe":

> As a matter of fact it is of no importance whether Benedetto
> Marcello found it or made it. The rite is the poet's rest. It may
> be an old hymn to Demeter or also illustrate *Coela enarrant
> gloriam Domini*. It is susceptible of nodes or modes as far apart
> as hyperphrygian and mixolydian and of texts so divergent as
> priests haihooping round David's that is Circe's or what am I
> saying Ceres' altar and David's tip from the stable to his chief
> bassoonist about the alrightness of his almightiness;
>   [*U*, 15.109, 2087–93]

from J. Alexander Dowie, American evangelist appearing as Elijah
in "Circe":

> Have we cold feet about the cosmos? No. Be on the side of the
> angels. Be a prism. You have that something within, the higher
> self. You can rub shoulders with a Jesus, a Gautama, an Inger-
> soll. Are you all in this vibration? I say you are. You once
> nobble that, congregation, and a buck joyride to heaven be-
> comes a back number. You got me? It's a lifebrightener, sure.
> The hottest stuff ever was. It's the whole pie with jam in;
>   [*U*, 15.2197–2202]

and finally, from "Ithaca":

> He reflected that the progressive extension of the field of indi-
> vidual development and experience was regressively accompa-
> nied by a restriction of the converse domain of interindividual
> relations.
> As in what ways?
> From inexistence to existence he came to many and was as one
> received: existence with existence he was with any as any with
> any: from existence to nonexistence gone he would be by all as
> none perceived.   [*U*, 17.63–69]

Each one of these passages offers a model for reading *Ulysses*, for following the logic in its permutations of styles, and narrative and symbolic facts, and each one also condenses the primary ideas of Bruno's *Cause, Principle, and Unity*; that opposites converge, and that all is in all in the world-soul. I list the excerpts here to give some sense of how extensive Bruno's intellectual presence is in *Ulysses* and to indicate that his thought appears as *thought* in the novel, and not only in trivial symbolic snippets like the whorehouse moth.

Before making conclusions about Joyce's use of Bruno in Bloom's epic, I want to mention one last trivial snippet in which Poldy and the Nolan are identified. John Wyse Nolan, in "Cyclops," lists the names of Irish soldiers who have fought for the British in the past only to be betrayed. One of them is "Ulysses Browne of Camus that was fieldmarshal to Maria Theresa" (*U*, 12.1383–84). As is normally the case when the Irish discuss their history in *Ulysses*, Nolan gets his facts wrong. As Don Gifford points out :

Nolan is confusing two field marshals: Ulysses Maximillian, Count von Browne (1705–57), the Austrian-born son of one of the wild geese; he was one of the most distinguished field marshals in the army of Maria Theresa (1717–80), queen of Hungary and Bohemia and Archduchess of Austria. He was killed while leading a bayonet charge at the battle of Prague. And George, Count de Browne (1698–1792), born at Camus (thus "of Camus") in Limerick. He became a soldier of fortune and a field marshal in the Russian army. He was regarded as a favorite of Maria Theresa and Catherine the Great.

[*G*, 12.1383–84n]

The elision, besides depicting how the Irish compromise their just grievances against England's abuses through indifference to historical accuracy, also identifies Bloom and Odysseus with Bruno.

Collapsing two Brownes by accident, Nolan presents another instance of Bruno's idea that opposites coincide. In this case an exiled Irishman and honorable soldier in the Austrian army coincides with a native Irishman who left the island, joined the Russian army, and, as a military philanderer, became the sexual pet of two empresses. Both men display Bruno's name in their own, and both are conjoined by an Irish double of the Renaissance Italian; John

Wyse *Nolan* (emphasis mine). "Wise" here adds the evaluation of Bruno's philosophical effort as a sage accomplishment. The two soldiers also repeat qualities of Homer's Odysseus; the first in his name and military honor, the second in his wily self-advancement, military prowess, and sexual connection to two women rulers (recall Odysseus's time with Calypso and Circe). Both men figure in Bloom's situation, first by their identity with Odysseus, and in more particular ways: Ulysses Browne by birth in Austria, the country once part of an empire with Hungary, Bloom's ancestral homeland, and George Browne by amorous connection to the queen of Bloom's ancestral homeland. George Browne, servant to the sexual pleasure of two women rulers, recapitulates Bloom's sexual subservience to two ruling women, Molly and Bella Cohen, who are identified in Joyce's novel with Odysseus's illustrious paramours, Calypso and Circe. George Browne also ironically reflects one more Odyssean trait in Bloom—his imperfect success as an adventurer, a wily self-advancer; as Molly calls him, an unceasing plotter and planner (*U*, 18.1008–9). This tiny item in which four men are identified with Bruno, introduced by an Irish "Wise" Nolan, indicates not only how thoroughgoing, but also how precise and sly Joyce's use of Bruno can be in *Ulysses*.

Soultransfigured and Soultransfiguring

At the end of the last chapter two styles in *Ulysses* were distinguished; imagistic precision, associated with the narrative, documentary report of mundane experience, and prodigal allusiveness, associated with the novel's symbolic depiction of the universal laws governing that experience. With reference to *De Anima*, the styles were shown to be mutually dependent—as the body and soul were to Aristotle—with Bloom's narrative operating as the body and Homer's *Odyssey* operating as the soul of Joyce's creation. Read against Aristotle's thought, the book appears a living embodiment of universal principles of being, a literary body animated by the reincarnation of two Greek souls, Homer and Aristotle. Bruno's concepts recapitulate the alignment of matter and form, body and soul, narrative and symbolism, imagistic precision and prodigal allusiveness, with one major change. Whereas Aristotle enabled Joyce to depict the interdependence of perpetually transformed experience and its unchanged universal laws, Bruno enabled him to show the identity of these two subjects.

The alignment of *Ulysses'* realism and symbolism with Bruno's ideas of the soul, superimposed on the book's Aristotelian design, suggests that Joyce was not entirely satisfied with Aristotle's thinking and needed to modify the Greek's materialism. Dublin and Ithaca, Bloom and Odysseus, matter and form, narrative and symbolism—all the oppositions holding *Ulysses* together—are only associated in mutual dependence under the auspices of Aristotle: Bruno's dialogue makes the contraries concretely identical, not only opposite substances similar in some aspects, but thoroughly the same—one thing. Read against Aristotle, the symbolism of *Ulysses* is substantial form for the material reality concretely present in the narrative. Bruno's thought identifies the two contrary organizations, making all items in the book symbolic and narrative.

The universal law Bruno supplies to *Ulysses* holds that any particular in experience coincides with its opposite, and with all other particulars, and with all these others is always in the process of being rendered universal by the activity of the world-soul, the power identifying all with all. This universal law accounts, among other things, for the artistic logic governing prolix symbolic elaboration of so many details in *Ulysses*, for the dense parodies of "Oxen of the Sun" for instance, or the obscure musical figures in "Sirens," in which the narrative seems to have vanished completely under the pressure of apparently irrelevant (and on Joyce's part self-indulgent) analogy. In such instances, Joyce displays the universalizing function of the world-soul, its capacity as "principle" or "universal intellect" to bring all forms out of one form. In the imagistic, narrative writing—the description of men eating in "Lestrygonians," for instance—Joyce displays the particularizing function of the world-soul, its capacity as "cause" to bring one form out of plenipotentiary matter (narrative matter in the case of a novel) and fix its borders, temporarily; to make something, as Bruno says "all that it is," before making it, through transformation, "all that it can be."

Aristotle's presence in the novel implies, among other things, that the unity of *Ulysses* derives from Joyce's symbolic association of Bloom with Odysseus, and of both these with the soul, the form of forms. Bloom's association with the soul, in the logic Bruno's presence bestows on the novel, extends the Aristotelian unity of narrative and symbolism into identity. Symbolic abstraction and narrative representation, according to the Aristotelian logic of *Ulysses*, coincide as form and matter do in organisms, as opposites that remain opposites throughout their cooperative actualization of any life. In the order Bruno's thinking gives *Ulysses*, representational narration and abstracting symbolism are not only two opposite modes of one act, but two identical acts. They are the minimum and maximum explication of Bloom's power, as one soul in the world-soul, to become all things; the particular and universal expressions of the power *Ulysses* has, as the book of books, to present all things, and in that way to be all things.

The following excerpt from "Ithaca," in which Bloom and Stephen gaze at constellations symbolically identified with Dante's starry images of universal order ("The heaventree of stars hung with humid nightblue fruit") is one of many model explanations Joyce offers in *Ulysses* for the contrary styles of the novel (*U*, 17.1039). Its minimizing narrative and maximizing symbolism are both identically capable of infinite extension, and for that reason both identical representations of the dynamic actualizing universal being.

With what meditations did Bloom accompany his demonstration to his companion of various constellations?
Meditations of evolution increasingly vaster: of the moon invisible in incipient lunation, approaching perigee: of the infinite lattiginous scintillating uncondensed milky way, discernible by daylight by an observer placed at the lower end of a cylindrical vertical shaft 5000 ft deep sunk from the surface towards the centre of the earth: of Sirius (alpha in Canis Maior) 10 lightyears (57,000,000,000,000 miles) distant and in volume 900 times the dimension of our planet: of Arcturus: of the precession of equinoxes: of Orion with belt and sextuple sun theta and nebula in which 100 of our solar systems could be contained: of moribund and of nascent new stars such as Nova in 1901: of our system plunging towards the constellation of Hercules: of the parallax or parallactic drift of socalled fixed stars, in reality evermoving wanderers from immeasurably re-

mote eons to infinitely remote futures in comparison with which the years, threescore and ten, of allotted human life formed a parenthesis of infinitesimal brevity.
Were there obverse meditations of involution increasingly less vast?
Of the eons of geological periods recorded in the stratifications of the earth: of the myriad minute entomological organic existences concealed in cavities of the earth, beneath removable stones, in hives and mounds, of microbes, germs, bacteria, bacilli, spermatozoa: of the incalculable trillions of billions of millions of imperceptible molecules contained by cohesion of molecular affinity in a single pinhead: of the universe of human serum constellated with red and white bodies, themselves universes of void space constellated with other bodies, each, in continuity, its universe of divisible component bodies of which each was again divisible in divisions of redivisible component bodies, dividends and divisors ever diminishing without actual division till, if the progress were carried far enough, nought nowhere was never reached. [*U*, 17.1040–69]

Increasingly vaster evolution, where infinity appears uncondensed and evermoving, and increasingly smaller involution, where infinity appears perpetually condensed, where the universal is concealed in particulars, each of which is composed of increasingly smaller parts, all of them concealing more condensed universality: this opposition accounts perfectly, and in Joyce's typical way, comically, for the symbolism in *Ulysses*, which allusively extends Bloom's story until it includes all stories, and the narrative, which dwells consistently on one day of Bloom's life, breaking it down (often through internal monologues) into highly specified parts, each of which, in continuity, contains its own universe of perpetually divisible component parts. The analogy to Bruno's conception of explication that is implication, principle that is cause in the world-soul, is not hard to see.

Readers of *Ulysses* at all points in the novel practice the same meditations Bloom does watching the stars, as they observe the book ascend toward infinite symbolic magnification and collapse into infinite narrative specification of one man in one place and time. Bloom can not contemplate evolution and involution at once;

he must switch from one to the other. Readers of *Ulysses* are forced by Joyce to be fully aware of both modes of infinity simultaneously, to read all symbols as narrative details and vice versa. To absorb, to order all this complexity, Joyce needed a literary structure that was flexible and stable, one that simultaneously preserved unity and multiplicity. To a large degree he found the conceptual model for that structure in Bruno's revision of Aristotle's ideas of the soul. And like Bruno, Joyce was fond of expressing the universal particularity of the world-soul, in which opposites such as maximum and minimum coincide in every part, with mathematical figures. Immediately after Bloom meditates on the constellations, he thinks about mathematics in the following way.

> ... some years previously in 1886 when occupied with the problem of the quadrature of the circle he had learned of the existence of a number computed to a relative degree of accuracy to be of such magnitude and of so many places, e.g., the 9th power of the 9th power of 9, that, the result having been obtained, 33 closely printed volumes of 1000 pages each of innumerable quires and reams of India paper would have to be requisitioned in order to contain the complete tale of its printed integers of units, tens, hundreds, thousands, tens of thousands, hundreds of thousands, millions, tens of millions, hundreds of millions, billions, the nucleus of the nebula of every digit of every series containing succinctly the potentiality of being raised to the utmost kinetic elaboration of any power of any of its powers. [*U*, 17.1071–82]

If this kind of complexity can be unfolded from one number, what order of complexity suits the representation of a life, which, unlike a number, is always changing? The idea that every number in the series contains the potential to be explicated into the maximum of the series displays Bruno's idea that every part of the world soul, every minimum form actualized in matter, contains the whole universe in potential. Analogously, every detail in *Ulysses*, Joyce's image of the world-soul, is a condensation of two opposite and identical notions of infinite, universal being represented, in a literary mode, in the novel's narrative and symbolism.

Finally, the comedy of Bloom's imagination of an encyclopedia (a multivolume work printed, like the *Britannica*, on India paper) created to represent the "complete tale of its printed integers" applies to *Ulysses* itself, a massive book with aspirations and formal properties (cross references, lists, tables, etc.) identical to the *Britannica's*. If all the works alluded to in the novel were set back to back on a shelf, they would certainly outstrip any encyclopedia, and probably come close to the space occupied by the number raised to "the 9th power of the 9th power of 9." The comic comparison of *Ulysses* to reference works has one clear ethical function as well as these formal literary ones. Insofar as *Ulysses* takes on the epic function of educating, as Homer's work did for centuries, it educates people in the operation of their own souls, where "encyclopedic" (that is "universal" and "circular" in the original Greek) magnification and reduction of all being takes place.

Joyce begins the lesson in Stephen's classroom memory of Aristotle's *De Anima* in "Nestor," where Aristotle's idea that the souls of human beings make them the simulacra of all things first enters the book. He then extends Aristotle's account of the soul, through increasingly predominant analogy, parody, and allusiveness that begins in "Wandering Rocks" and climaxes in "Circe," into the radically mystical conclusions of Bruno, who held that people's souls identified them entirely with all being. By putting the two thinkers in one continuum (the increasingly symbolic narration of Bloom's day), Joyce implies that the divorce between them that Bruno insisted on is not final. Both theories locate universal principles of being in human consciousness, Aristotle's through scientific observation, and Bruno's through scientific observation governed by spiritual insight. This identity holds through all the differences isolating the two thinkers in intellectual history and in their appearance in Joyce's "chaffering allincluding most farraginous chronicle" (*U*, 14.1412).

Two short excerpts from *Finnegans Wake* tell perfectly what truth Joyce found in Bruno's thought. First: "But look what you have in your handself! The movibles are scrawling in motions, marching, all of them ago, in pitpat and zingzang for every busy eerie whig's a bit of a torytale to tell."[12] In addition to being perhaps the most ingenious description of masturbation in English (a fact which demonstrates, as so many others in that wild book do, that *Finnegans Wake* is probably also the dirtiest nonpornographic book in English), these sentences display Bruno's theory of the transformations of life in the world-soul. The same principle animating the created universe, Joyce suggests here, animates writing (an activity not uncommonly thought of as masturbatory). Each letter and each word, like every particular and all its parts, are "movibles" perpetually marching to universality, seeds (sperm) stirring to deliver their particular composition of the life of the world-soul. The symbolic narrative of *Ulysses* depicts life itself, as Joyce conceived it with Bruno; not only Bloom's life, or human life in general, but the secret life of everything that is. Aristotle's *De Anima* gives philosophical resonance to Joyce's insistence in *Ulysses* that experience is somehow always bodily; Bruno's dialogue goes past that concrete limitation, rendering the body itself a form, not a cause or absolute source of experience: a mode of life no more or less complete than the mode life takes in words, ideas, dust, sperm, or Molly's last word on the subject, "rocks."

The idea that life in the world-soul entirely fills every existence results in the logic of this second sentence from *Finnegans Wake*: "When a part so ptee does duty for the holos we soon grow to use of an allforabit" (*FW*, pp. 18–19). This presentation of Bruno's answer to the Platonic problem of the One and the Many glosses the kind of unity that particular universals give the aesthetic and conceptual design of *Ulysses*. Bloom's story and everything in it is an "allforabit": an alphabet and a universal particular, a representation and a presentation of life mediated by language and immediately, wholly present in it. These ideas, extensively developed in *Ulysses*, overran the structure of *Finnegans Wake*. In many ways *Ulysses* today looks like a toy model for that monstrously vital work, a prospective budget for Joyce's seventeen year expense of spirit.

Aristotle is the counterbalance that distinguishes *Ulysses* from the nighttime epic. Bloom's day is primarily a scientific one, a depiction of the rational soul analyzing what it encounters in life, whereas Earwicker's night is a religious mystery, among other things—a depiction of the living soul's experience of death in sleep. Opposed to Aristotle, Bruno, by his own logic, coincides with him in *Ulysses*. The vitality Bruno describes runs in tandem with Aristotle's idea of life in the first epic, forcing the novel past the Greek's materialism without outstripping it entirely. The two temperaments Joyce needed in order to write, the scientific and the artistic, owe as much to Aristotle as they do to Bruno. Joyce's contrary doubles, Bloom and Stephen, who both represent both temperaments in *Ulysses*, display Bruno's occult science in various ways, and pursue the Italian's mysterious art—"the divination of opposites"— usually without knowing it. But they also practice Aristotle's scientific method, and display, in their narrative and symbolic roles, the importance to Joyce of Aristotle's aesthetic, which requires that artists study the actual to make valid generalizations about the probable.[13] Bruno's conception of universal particularity is not so incompatible with Aristotle's aesthetic as one might first think. The Greek's insistence that art tells what should happen, instead of what has happened (the subject of historians), is based on his conviction that artists represent universal principles as they appear in particular lives, and are therefore like philosophers who examine what is necessarily so.[14] Bruno identifies the subjects Aristotle's aesthetic kept separate, but otherwise he repeats in his theory of the world-soul the two-fold reality Aristotle analyzes in *Poetics* and again in *De Anima*. These two works (especially the second one) authorized Joyce's experimental portrayal of universal laws of being in *Ulysses*. Bruno's thought takes much of its value in the novel from that authorization. The book is about fathers and sons, from the father's point of view, mostly. Hence Aristotle, like Bloom vis à vis Stephen, holds his own against the more exotic thinking of Bruno.

Stephen, however, not Bloom, grew up to write *Ulysses* (although Bloom helped make Stephen's maturity possible). In the same way Bruno's mysticism eventually outstripped Aristotle's common sense in Joyce's career, helping to create, together with the Italian Vico, Joyce's maturest work, *Finnegans Wake*. In *Ulysses* Joyce has shown the last moment in his own career when Aristotle still held sway; the moment in family life when sons imperfectly displace, for the first time, fathers; the moments of waking consciousness when reason distinguishes contraries that the mind's irrational power is busy uniting. The balance of contrary authorities in *Ulysses* tips in favor of Bruno as the book progresses, but not so much that Aristotle becomes negligible. Just as the *Odyssey* portrays Telemachus's helping Odysseus to assert his authority, so *Ulysses* portrays Stephen's helping Bloom in his struggle to repossess his house (and being helped in turn by Poldy in his adolescent struggle to possess himself). Bruno, the badly burned martyr, like Dedalus and like Telemachus, serves his father's purpose in Joyce's retelling of Greek mythology: he extends Aristotle's theory of the soul. Joyce's transformation of Homer's story involves an enlargement of the son's role as dispossessor, but stops short of the preoccupation with the subject displayed in *Finnegans Wake*. Bruno's ideas of the world-soul are powerfully at work in *Ulysses* together with Aristotle's *De Anima*, not at the expense of the Greek philosopher, but as magnification of the importance he placed on the soul.

One last meaning of Bruno's presence in Bloom's story remains: its secrecy. Why, if Bruno's ideas of the soul have as much to do in the novel as Aristotle's, is the martyr's name submerged, never once directly presented either in the narrative or symbolic structure of the book? The answer lies partly in Bruno's own theory, which persistently argues that the world-soul, although omnipotent and omnipresent, is not available to unaided observation, but only to "the eye of reason," and then only after long, arduous meditation has cleansed that inner eye's doors of perception. By implicitly referring to Bruno's martyrdom, partially quoting one of the Italian dialogues, and including inconspicuous translations and transliterations of Bruno's name, *Ulysses* dramatizes two of Bruno's conceptions about the unity bestowed on life by the world-soul: its obscurity to all but the initiated, and its presence in even the smallest particular. The rational coherence of the created universe, according to Bruno, could be found by a properly disposed mind in any detail of that universe. The rational coherence in *Ulysses'* portrayal of universal being derives, in large measure, from Bruno's thought, which can be found at work in any and all details of the novel. It is entirely appropriate for the thinker fixed on unified oppositions, who envisioned life's unity as secret and omnipresent, to appear disguised in a book where his occult idea of unity is ubiquitous.

Bloom's meditation on the "uncondensed milky way" accounts nicely for Bruno's faint identification in the novel. Watching the stars Poldy recalls a commonplace of folk science—that the milky way shines during the day as it does at night, a fact people are not normally aware of because sunlight overpowers starlight. If, Bloom imagines, a daytime observer were placed out of the sun's influence "at the lower end of a cylindrical vertical shaft 5000 ft deep sunk from the surface towards the centre of the earth," he would see the stars. This observer would be cleansing his perception and seeing what Stephen, thinking of Neoplatonic theories of the world-soul, calls "darkness shining in brightness which brightness could not comprehend" (U, 2.160). Bruno's ideas are always at work in *Ulysses*. Discovering their author's presence, though, requires shutting out the seemingly domineering logic of Aristotle, just as seeing the evershining stars during the day requires shutting out the sun's light. Like the milky way at noon, Bruno's thinking shines in Aristotle's in this novel. Readers eager to penetrate Joyce's new Dedalian maze have a better chance if they can see, with the inner eye of reason, this second light, if they can intuit the crucial implications of scant clues and innuendos where Bruno's form glows as faintly as the milky way would to that unfortunate, hypothetical creature in Bloom's mile-deep shaft.

There is one more reason for the secrecy: Joyce's attitude toward the spiritual insight Bruno's thought requires. Joyce abjured Catholicism utterly in his youth and never took it back, convinced that his soul could not live under the church's law of obedience. The problem in Joyce's case was not faith, but submission to the moral and intellectual authority of Christian theologians. When he left the Jesuits, he left Christ, the Virgin, the saints, the Trinity, and all other Catholic items of belief. He continued to use Christianity as an artistic source in his work, but he made his infidelity to its religious precepts unmistakably clear by pitching the imaginative substance of Christianity as far into blasphemy as his literary genius, at its most lurid, allowed. Blasphemy abounds in *Ulysses*, but there is not one pious Catholic feeling in the novel, a significant absence in a book claiming to portray everything that is; an absence that indicates Joyce saw no truth in the religion he had abandoned.

Speculation about the soul, however, does appear prominently in the book. The functions of Aristotle's *De Anima* and Bruno's *Cause, Principle, and Unity* in the symbolic realism of *Ulysses* suggest that Joyce never lost faith in the powers of the soul but turned to a pagan logician and to a heretical magus for accounts of spiritual reality. Aristotle supplied an intellectual authority that replaced the church's (readily, since the church's thought was so Aristotelian, thanks to Aquinas), and a philosophical vocabulary for analysis of the soul, but little scope for Joyce's powerfully mystical inclinations. Bruno's outlawed religious principles of the unity of being, and the life of all things, offered the alienated rebel a romantic precedent for his own solipsistic religious convictions. Throughout his career Joyce treated his literary genius with religious devotion; everything in his life was second to it, and many things in his life, including to a great extent his familial relationship with his parents and brother, and later with his wife and children, were sacrificed when they interfered with it. When he wrote, "I have found no man yet with a faith like mine," the object of that audaciously proclaimed faith was his artist's soul (*L*, 1:53). Stephen's remark to Bloom, "But I suspect . . . that Ireland must be important because it belongs to me" (*U*, 16.1164–65) could easily be extended in Joyce's case to this proposition: experience is important because it occurs to me, the genius who can provide its most permanently beautiful form. In Joyce's most extreme posture as an artistic creator-god, one that he strikes over and over in *Ulysses*, the proposition takes this form: experience is important because it emanates from me.[15]

Bruno's idea that all reality is present in any one soul, and can be discovered there by eyes trained in observation of unified contraries, must have seemed very attractive to an audacious, abused genius, trying to write an unprecedentedly documentary account of the victimizing country and people who were present to him only in memory. The creation of *Ulysses* was an extremely introspective business, both because its two characters are autobiographical projections and because, aside from letters sent by friendly Dubliners, or conversation with those who had also wandered into exile—or its shorter variety, vacation—Joyce had only his own impressions, his internal recreation of the city, to work with. Here is the Aristotelian bedrock (the psychological fact) for Joyce's posture as the creator-god, which Bruno's theory cast as spiritual heroics. What pride made desirable, geography made necessary: the universality of *Ulysses* had to proceed from Joyce, as any book has to proceed from its author's consciousness, but with a special result in the case of this isolated, ostentatiously Satanic Dubliner. He made, I think, of the writing of *Ulysses* an occasion to confirm for himself a heretical faith that located all being in the soul.

Recall again Joyce's letter to Lady Gregory in which he first declared that faith in 1902.

> I do not know what will happen to me in Paris but my case can hardly be worse than it is here. I am leaving Dublin by the

night boat on Monday 1st December and my train leaves Victoria Station for Newhaven the same night. I am not despondent however for I know that even if I fail to make my way such failure proves very little. I shall try myself against the powers of the world. All things are inconstant except the faith in the soul, which changes all things and fills their inconstancy with light. And though I seem to have been driven out of my country here as a misbeliever I have found no man yet with a faith like mine. [L, 1:53]

Saying the soul fills all the world's inconstant things with light, claiming the statement as an article of dangerous heretical faith that elevates him above the country it alienates him from, Joyce recapitulates Bruno's thinking and Bruno's isolated heroism. By 1922 he had managed to transfigure such thinking about his own soul into the creation of Bloom's. In the process he transformed romantic Satanism into domestic comedy, and adolescent longing into adult prudence, forebearance, and temperate expectation. The change shows clearly in his comic presentation of Bruno's metaphysics, and of the martyr himself. In "Circe," (U, 15.2512–27) the idea that unified contraries guide the artist's faith in his own soul comes up comically, when the Siamese twins Philip Drunk and Philip Sober confront Stephen on the subject of his ruined career, offering contradictory advice for its restitution. These two embody an apocryphal story about justice meted out by Alexander the Great's father, Philip of Macedon, and the contrary impulses in Matthew Arnold's idea of culture—"Hellenism" and "Hebraism"—both of which impulses they bring to bear on Stephen's dilemma. The twins can be such a wacky example of metempsychosis in action largely because of Bruno's intellectual contribution to *Ulysses*, a fact that one final piece of information hidden in their names, with Joyce's jovial cunning, obliquely confirms. Before he took the religious name "Giordano" on entering the priesthood, Bruno was "Filipo."

chapter three

JOYCE & DANTE

Dante was the first European to make his own life the subject of an epic poem, and thereby the pattern for a universal explanation of reality and humanity's place there. His choice of vernacular Italian over Latin for this undertaking is commensurate with the exaltation of individual experience to encyclopedic understanding. Long before Wordsworth, Dante elected to be a poet speaking to his audience in their own language, making his sensibility the standard for cultural regeneration. Unlike Wordsworth, Dante had a sensibility, and a poem to preserve it, dignified by a meticulous, copious understanding and original development of the philosophical and literary tradition inherited from classical antiquity and transformed in Christianity. This intellectual order and range in Dante's autobiographical epic, the genius that added right thinking to right feeling in order to depict right doing, made the *Commedia* an indispensable means for Joyce's universalizing end in *Ulysses*. Being the means to an end, Dante's poem is both fixed and transformed in Joyce's book. What results from that double action, how Dante's conception of the soul's universality informs a modern work that systematically and drastically reforms that conception, and all other constituent precedents, occupies this chapter.

Dante's Poetics

Dante conceived of poetry as an intellectual discipline, a mode of study that could provide knowledge subject to the same rules of validity and utility that governed philosophy, medicine, or mathematics. As those sciences all had methods, systematic procedures established and authorized by traditions derived from classical antiquity, so did poetry, which operated according to rules derived from various systematic interpretations of classical authors, especially Virgil. Writing poems as well as reading them was an intellectual accomplishment analogous to working out Euclid—all three activities could be taught and, when learned, ended in knowledge. The discipline of poetry was carried out, as all disciplines were in Dante's world, in Latin. Alongside, or beneath this authorized discourse, poets all over Europe were also writing poems in various vernaculars, establishing literary traditions on the basis of common speech and the exotic, nonclassical topic of "courtly" or "romantic" love. By Dante's time vernacular poetry in Italy had accumulated so much intellectual and artistic capital that poets could claim for it cultural authority equivalent to that of classical Latin. That is precisely what Dante did in his Latin prose treatise *De Vulgari Eloquentia* (*On Eloquence in the Vernacular*, 1304–9), a work which argues that all modes and forms of discourse, including the grandest, can be conceived and composed in the vernacular.

Cultural stability and continuity, the preservation of religious wisdom—these norms for civilization that Latin had safeguarded were endangered by the instability, idiosyncracy, and ignorance that afflicted human language after Babel. Starting with that Biblical catastrophe, Dante argues that Latin was invented by grammarians to replace the universal vernacular that men and women spoke from their first moments in Eden until the hubristic engineering feat of the tower. The pride which led to Babel persisted as punishment after its destruction in the isolation of individual will that separate, incommunicably various languages represented. The scholars feared, Dante argues, "that, because of the change in language which issues from the will of individuals, we would be able to understand either not at all or at least imperfectly the authoritative ideas and histories of the ancients or of peoples whom the difference of place makes different from us."[1]

The universal communicability of Latin is its great virtue. That virtue pertains because of Latin's systematic eloquence, the invention of academics. Dante asserts that stable eloquent speech can proceed from the vain wills of people separated by custom and geography when those people are poets of the first order who naturally observe the systematic excellence native to their own common tongue. The aesthetic insights of such poets are superior to the rational schemas of the grammarians for ameliorating the isolation and ignorance that afflicts polyglot humanity, because poetry's beauty commands closer attention than the alien elegance of the grammarians' dialect. Putting poets at the summit of wisdom in this fashion has endeared Dante to many writers, not the least among them Joyce, who shared with the Italian epic poet the conviction that literary art was the highest perception of value.

Having established the most eloquent vernacular as Tuscan, Dante goes on to argue that only the best poets writing about the best subjects should use it. The best poets provide their vernacular art the greatest learning and natural talent. To identify fit topics for demonstrating the excellence of these poets in the vernacular, Dante relies on ideas of the soul that originate in Aristotle's *De Anima*. Human beings, having tripartite souls, have three primary ends: to realize the demands of their vegetative souls they seek what is useful, for the demands of their animal souls what is delightful, and for the highest requirements of their rational souls, what is honest. The highest usefulness being self-preservation, the highest delight love, and the highest honesty virtue, vernacular poets should treat those activities that best actualize these ends: "prowess in arms, the flames of love, and the direction of the will" (*LCD*, p. 35). The treatise, unfinished, ends by analyzing the appropriate form for these topics, the canzone, its proper styles (tragic, elegiac, or comic), and appropriate meters and rhymes. In all these distinctions, the standard of propriety is both aesthetic and intellectual, the desirable practice being in all cases that which presents the soul's ends most beautifully and intelligibly. To sum up—Dante argues in this treatise that poetry's most illustrious subject is the operation of the human soul. This subject can be treated with all the dignity it receives in Latin by the best poets working in the vernacular, who by natural instinct work according to rational principles of eloquence equivalent in intellectual authority (and superior in rhetorical power) to the rules of Latin created artificially by grammarians.

According to Dante, not only the subjects of poetry, but the ordering of a poem's parts, its aesthetic and conceptual structure, derive from the operations of the soul and must conform to them. Some remarks from *La Vita Nuova* and *Epistle X* (the letter to Can

Grande) indicate how he conceived this formal identity of literary activity and the nature of the soul.

Committed to the idea that poetry informed people of truth, Dante felt compelled to justify its ostentatiously fictive devices, especially its figurative language. In *La Vita Nuova*, an autobiography and an anthology of love poems, Dante justifies the rationality of figurative language in poetry by preceding and following each poem with a systematic exegesis. The interpretation, or "division" (Dante's term for exegesis), preceding each poem accounts for its autobiographical occasion; the division following each poem declares its subject, analyzes the stages of the argument, and reveals whatever truth structures the arrangement of parts into unity in each lyric. The divisions frame the poems because Dante believed no poet should write fictively unless he was prepared to explain in prose the intelligible purpose of every comparison, apostrophe, or story in the poem. The same requirement applied to all conceptual, dramatic, metrical, stylistic, and formal elements of any work. In Chapter 25 of *La Vita Nuova* he writes: "But to prevent any crude persons from drawing any wrong inferences, I say that the poets did not write this way [figuratively] lacking a purpose, nor should those who use rhyme write in this manner without there being a purpose behind what they say. For it would be a disgrace to someone who dressed his rhymes in the figures or colors of rhetoric if later, on demand, he could not strip his discourse of this dress to show what he had really meant" (*LCD*, pp. 117–18).

The process of division could be extended to justify every explicit and implicit detail in all the poem's structures: the precision of each analysis being governed by Dante's sense of the difficulty of any given poem and his willingness to tell the laity his love. In Chapter 19 he writes of one lyric:

But because this last section is easy to understand, I will not bother with further divisions. But I will say that a deeper understanding of this *canzone* would require the use of even more minute divisions. However, anyone who does not have enough intelligence to be able to understand it through those divisions I have already made will not offend me if he lets the matter rest here, since I am in fact afraid that I have already communicated too much of its meaning in making only the divisions I have, if it should happen that many people were to hear them. [*LCD*, p. 87]

This excerpt shows how Dante matched his poetic practice to the operation of human intelligence (the rational soul). Following Aquinas and Aristotle, Dante held that the intellectual soul divided objects of knowledge into component parts and integrated them according to whatever inherent principle of unity they might display or suggest. He makes this point explicit when he writes to Can Grande to explain the third division of the *Commedia*, *Il Paradiso*, to him.

[5] As the Philosopher says in the second book of the *Metaphysics*, "As a thing is with respect to being, so it is with respect to truth" [Aristotle, *Metaphysics* 2.1]; . . . And so, of all things which have being, some are such that they have absolute being in themselves, others such that their being is dependent upon a relationship with something else. . . . Because such things depend for their being upon another thing, it follows that their truth would depend upon the truth of the other; . . . [6] Therefore, if one should wish to present an introduction to a part of a work, it is necessary to present some conception of the whole work of which it is a part. For this reason I, who wish to present something in the form of an introduction to the above-mentioned part of the whole *Comedy*, have decided to preface it with some discussion of the whole work, in order to make the approach to the part easier and more complete. [*LCD*, p. 98]

The citations from *De Vulgari Eloquentia*, *La Vita Nuova*, and this letter indicate that Dante thought poetry presented the soul to the soul as an object of knowledge, in structures that insured understanding by recapitulating the intellect's natural process—analytic division that ended in synthetic discovery of truth.

The *Commedia* displays a much more conceptually and imaginatively complex figural structure than the love poems of *La Vita Nuova*, and so it required more complex exegesis than Dante offered in the anthology. In the autobiographical collection poetic license results in personification and extended comparisons more than anything else. But the epic's meaning is allegorical on the grandest scale and involves not only symbolic depiction of one man's love for his lady, but the figural presentation of all experience, the narrative analysis of everything that can happen to a soul and to the bodily world it moves in. Before Dante says anything else to Can Grande about *Il Paradiso*, he makes this universalizing function of the poem's figural structure clear by describing how he has given the poem multiple meanings and subjects.

[7] For the clarification of what I am going to say, then, it should be understood that there is not just a single sense in this work: it might rather be called *polysemous*, that is, having several senses. For the first sense is that which is contained in the letter, while there is another which is contained in what is signified by the letter. The first is called literal, while the second is called allegorical, or moral or anagogical. And in order to make this manner of treatment clear, it can be applied to the following verses: "When Israel went out of Egypt, the house of Jacob from a barbarous people, Judea was made his sanctuary, Israel his dominion" [Ps. 113:1–2, Vulgate; Ps. 114:1–2, King James Version]. Now if we look at the letter alone, what is signified to us is the departure of the sons of Israel from Egypt during the time of Moses; if at the allegory, what is signified to us is our redemption through Christ; if at the moral sense, what is signified to us is the conversion of the soul from the sorrow and misery of sin to the state of grace; if at the anagogical, what is signified to us is the departure of the sanctified soul from bondage to the corruption of this world into the freedom of eternal glory. . . .

[8] This being established, it is clear that the subject about which these two senses play must also be twofold. And thus it should first be noted what the subject of the work is when taken according to the letter, and then what its subject is when understood allegorically. The subject of the whole work, then, taken literally, is the state of souls after death, understood in a simple sense; for the movement of the whole work turns upon this and about this. If on the other hand the work is taken allegorically, the subject is man, in the exercise of his free will, earning or becoming liable to the rewards or punishments of justice. . . .

[15] The end of the whole and of the part could be multiple, that is, both immediate and ultimate. But without going into details, it can be briefly stated that the end of the whole as of the part is to remove those living in this life from the state of misery and to lead them to the state of happiness.

[*LCD*, pp. 99, 101–2]

This fourfold division derives in large part from the fourfold method of Biblical interpretation that originated with Clement and other Alexandrian fathers, and remained one standard ecclesiastical procedure for scriptural exegesis well into the seventeenth century. This is not the place to discuss the development of this style of Biblical exegesis, or all the perplexities Dante's allusion to it has caused his commentators. Edgar de Bruyne's *Etudes d'esthetiques medievale* and Beryl Smalley's *The Study of the Bible in the Middle Ages* are the best sources (precise and copious) for anyone eager to pursue the problem and its bearing on Joyce's figural schemes.[2] I have only one claim to make concerning the letter to Can Grande: that its appearance in *Ulysses* suggests that Joyce challenged comparison to Dante's epic in his own, that his inclusion of the Biblical verse in the "Ithaca" episode urges readers to understand *Ulysses* as Dante instructed Can Grande to understand his *Commedia*: as a work structured to reveal several senses in which universal laws of being operate in a particular life.[3] Strict application of Dante's quartet of meanings is impossible in his own epic; it would be vain ingenuity at best in Joyce's. In fact, although Dante uses the quartet from Biblical exegesis in his letter, he primarily asserts a double meaning, the literal and figural, for his poem, with the figural genus displaying three species. Joyce's epic displays the same basic division between a highly detailed, documentary narrative and a figural order that has many different symbolic techniques and subjects (parody, allusion, quotation, analogy). A full account of how I think Joyce appropriated Dante's announcement of his epic's polysemous allegory will emerge after comparison of specific scenes from the two works and general, synthetic remarks about other structural similarities between the poem and the novel. The subject now is Dante's figural poetics, and few critics have established the relations of the several senses, especially of the status of the letter's meaning vis à vis the other three, more clearly than Dante himself.

Having defined the literal, allegorical, and moral levels of a text Dante writes:

[6] The fourth sense is called the anagogical, or the "sense beyond." This sense occurs when a spiritual interpretation is to be given a text which, even though it is true on the literal level, represents the supreme things belonging to eternal glory by means of the things it represents. It may be perceived in that song of the Prophet which says that, in the departure of the people of Israel from Egypt, Judea was made holy and free. [7] For even though the literal truth of this passage is clear, what it means spiritually is no less true, that in the departure of the soul from sin, it is made holy and free in its power. [8] In bringing out this meaning, the literal sense should always come first, it being the meaning in which the others are contained and without which it would be impossible and irrational to come to an understanding of the others, particularly the allegorical. [9] It would be impossible because, in the case of anything which has an outside and an inside, it is impossible to come to the inside without first coming to the outside. Thus, since in a text the literal meaning is always the outside, it is impossible to come to the others, particularly the allegorical, without first coming to the literal. . . . [12] . . . And so, since the establishment of meaning is something constructed by systematic study, and since the establishment of the literal meaning is the foundation of the other meanings, particularly the allegorical, it is impossible to arrive at the others before the literal. . . .

[13] Furthermore, even were it possible, it would be irrational, that is, out of the proper order, and therefore a tiring and erratic process. For, as the Philosopher says in the first book of the *Physics*, Nature wishes our procedure of discovery to be orderly, proceeding from what we know well to what we know not so well. I say that "nature wishes" it because this mode of discovery is an innate gift of nature. [*LCD*, pp. 113–14]

I have quoted this explanation of the primacy of the letter, or literal meaning, for understanding polysemous texts so extensively to display Dante's emphatic insistence that poetry, especially allegorical poetry, provides knowledge and must be studied according to procedures common to all rational disciplines. Dante is so intent on this justification of poetry's rationality that he feels compelled to gloss his figural attribution of "wishing" to nature in the last sentence of the excerpt, as if someone might object to his saying something not literally true, and so not informative. Although Dante does not do so, a clear analogy can be drawn between his poetics and Aristotle's ideas of the soul's existence in the body. Just as the soul can only be understood through observation of its functions in the material world from which it emerges, in which it actualizes its potential, and to which it is inextricably bound, so the allegorical, moral, and anagogical levels of a figural poem must be understood as they emerge from its literal level. No more than the soul can these spiritual senses of the letter operate independently of their material container. The letter, the ineluctable narrative modality of Dante's allegory, is narrow and precise when Dante has specific symbolic meanings to display, boundless when he has grand spiritual subjects to present (such as the vision of beatitude, the union of all matter and form in God). Precise or infinitely extended, the narrative occasion never drops out of the *Commedia*: every moment in the poem is concretely presented as one moment of the pilgrim's journey. All human history may bear on the narrative fact (Dante crawling on Satan's belly, Dante declaring his faith in Paradise) but the text remains a story primarily, even in its most philosophically and metaphysically audacious, packed lines (*Inf* 34).[4] The poem ends where it does because Dante could not make direct mystic knowledge of God part of his story, since that experience exceeds human capacity for understanding, and so for retelling.

Dante's claim for the vernacular's fitness to transmit the classical and Christian wisdom hitherto preserved in Latin (especially understanding of the soul, the highest object of knowledge next to God) required exemplary works to be more than brazen theorizing. When Dante made his case for Tuscan Italian in *De Vulgari Eloquentia* (1304–1309) there were no vernacular works in that dialect, or any other continental tongue, comparable in scope even to Statius's epics, let alone Virgil's *Aeneid*, the secular bible of the Middle Ages (and the Renaissance) and the unassailable standard for literary excellence. By 1321 Dante had given Italy the *Commedia*, the poem it needed to supplant Rome's cultural hegemony. Incorporating Vir-

gil's *Aeneid* extensively in *L'Inferno,* and incorporating Virgil himself up through *Il Purgatorio,* and then exceeding them both in *Il
Paradiso,* Dante proved that Latin culture, Christian as well as classical, could not only be preserved in the language of a modern civilization, but developed as well. Robert S. Haller, in his useful introduction to *Literary Criticism of Dante Alighieri,* gives an excellent
summary of the cultural ambitions Dante's epic displays.

> When Dante saw in the accession of Henry VII as Emperor the
> opportunity to unify Italy and revive Augustan glories, and
> when he conceived a poem of heroic stature equal to his politi-
> cal vision, he chose to devote his energies to politics and po-
> etry, and to leave his lesser cultural works unfinished. [Haller
> refers here to *Il Convivio* and *De Vulgari Eloquentia.*] . . .
> Dante must have been confident that, with the simultaneous
> creation of a new poem and a new society of equal magnitude
> and sublimity, there would be others to do the lesser work of
> cultural consolidation. . . .
> . . . By giving Virgil the functions of guide, stylistic model,
> and precedent for an underworld journey, and by letting Statius
> explain the natural mode of transition between ancient and
> medieval culture, it makes ancient poetry the model and
> source of the excellence of a new poem, as if the epic scope and
> allusions of the *Comedy* itself had not demonstrated this
> point.   [*LCD,* pp. xxv–xxvi]

Joyce in 1914 also set out to adapt classical culture to the new
conditions of life in the vernacular in Ireland. Dante presents the
soul's progress according to a Christian conception of history; Joyce
presents new, secular circumstances for the soul's unchanged, unchanging functions. Both writers needed to justify the identities
their epics established between tradition and innovation in literature, between classical authority and personal genius in analysis of
the universal meanings of a particular life. Dante did so explicitly
in theoretically formulated poetics, Joyce did so implicitly in his
book and obliquely in letters to sympathetic readers. Both men
wrote in cultures that had recently undergone literary resurgence
and political crisis, and both emerged, in exile, as magisterial survi-
vors, victims, and critics of their nation's foment.

These coincidences were not lost on Joyce, who identifies Stephen and Bloom, his personae in *Ulysses*, more than once with Dante the pilgrim (and Stephen also with Dante the epic writer dependent on Aquinas and Aristotle for knowledge of his epic subject—the soul). In "Scylla and Charybdis" Stephen, hiding his literary ambitions from the hostile literati in the National Library, runs their conversation through his mind in a bitter, resentful montage.

> Listen.
> Young Colum and Starkey. George Roberts is doing the commercial part. Longworth will give it a good puff in the *Express*. O, will he? I liked Colum's *Drover*. Yes, I think he has that queer thing genius. Do you think he has genius really? Yeats admired his line: *As in wild earth a Grecian vase*. Did he? I hope you'll be able to come tonight. Malachi Mulligan is coming too. Moore asked him to bring Haines. Did you hear Miss Mitchell's joke about Moore and Martyn? That Moore is Martyn's wild oats? Awfully clever, isn't it? They remind one of Don Quixote and Sancho Panza. Our national epic has yet to be written, Dr Sigerson says. Moore is the man for it. A knight of the rueful countenance here in Dublin. With a saffron kilt? O'Neill Russell? O, yes, he must speak the grand old tongue. And his Dulcinea? James Stephens is doing some clever sketches. We are becoming important, it seems. [*U*, 9.300–313]

This summary of Ireland's prominent writers, from which Stephen's name is conspicuously absent, bears a strong familial resemblance to Dante's summation of his own literary contemporaries made in *Purgatorio* 26 and *Inferno* 10 and 15. Dante has more respect for some of his contemporaries than Dedalus does for his, but Dante avoids proclaiming his superiority to them directly. Like Stephen, he withholds his name. Stephen of course acts out of his cherished sense of being wronged, while Dante's reticence displays formal humility. But the inference of the authors' anonymity in both these literary histories is the same. When Stephen ironically recalls the lines "Do you think he has genius really?" and "Our national epic has yet to be written," the context makes it clear that Joyce, not Colum, not Moore, is Ireland's epic poet of genius. Literary history has so far borne out Joyce's self-appraisal. No work by anyone mentioned in Stephen's paragraph has yet challenged *Ulysses* as modern Ireland's national epic.

Dante also obliquely announces his status as national epic writer when, in *Inferno* 5, he is taken into the company of Lucan, Ovid, Virgil, and Homer with smiles, and told things his modesty forbids repeating. Like Joyce, Dante was writing his nation's first modern epic when he announced its status, and his, as a world classic: the action in both cases is one of extravagant faith, not unmixed with arrogance and pride, which the world has since vindicated. The immediate comparison in Stephen's montage is of *Ulysses* to *Don Quixote*, not the *Commedia*, or the *Odyssey*. Joyce's title challenges comparison with Homer: his multiple references to Dante's epic and Cervantes's suggest that he wanted *Ulysses* to do for Ireland what Homer's work, Cervantes's and Dante's did for their countries—bring it into the first rank of cultural authority for all men in all times.

This, the most general meaning of Dante's presence in the novel, has been apparent to scholars and most readers since *Ulysses* first appeared. But Joyce put the medieval epic to more than rhetorical use. The references to Dante also establish conceptual and technical continuity between Bloom's wandering and the pilgrim's, just as the novel's title unites the adman's struggles to the Greek king's. One aspect of this continuity is Joyce's use of vernacular culture (and an often "vulgar" tongue) to represent the soul's status as particular universal. What Dante did with vernacular speech in his epic—set the values of classical culture in a natural, contemporary medium—Joyce did with vernacular art forms in his; especially with songs, but also pantomimes, junk books, advertisements, popular theater, light opera, operetta, street and barroom ballads, and dirty jokes and quips. This last material made *Ulysses* a succès de scandal and, more importantly, opened new ground for literature after the American Supreme Court decision of 1933 that legally named *Ulysses* "somewhat emetic" but not "aphrodisiac."[5]

Early in his career Joyce repudiated the attempt to establish Gaelic as Ireland's vernacular, dismissing it as purblind nationalism. Gaelic was not the vernacular of Ireland in Joyce's day and had not been for a hundred years. Substituting it for English would be exalting an artificial medium that was once native over the de facto native medium of the Irish or, to put it differently, dressing the artificially resuscitated language in swaddling clothes to prove its manly independence. When the voices in Stephen's montage insist that Moore must star O'Neill Russell as Don Quixote in Ireland's national epic, and do it in "the grand old tongue" (Gaelic), they sound out clearly all the preposterous vanity Joyce found in the Gaelic revivalists. Unable to follow Dante in exalting a national vernacular speech, Joyce chose to write his nation's epic in the language of their oppressor because, despite all ugly political overtones, that language was his people's national speech. He could follow Dante though, and use the vernacular to establish parity between ancient and modern cultures, by making Dublin's Odysseus the most vernacular of men, an adman, who works in the most vernacular literary form, the daily newspaper.

Joyce's vernacular art would certainly have disquieted Dante, who sought the most illustrious form of the vernacular, and who illustrated it in his epic not by quoting forms of trashy drivel, or middle-class entertainment, as Joyce does throughout *Ulysses*, but by quoting only the most elegant lines and presenting only the noblest practitioners of *vulgaris eloquentia*. The soul's accomplishments appear with elegance in excelsis in Dante's vernacular epic, except for the vilest sinfulness of Hell, which at many moments appears in harsh jagged language, the only suitable medium for presentation of deformity. The *dolce stil nuovo*, that burnished, high-minded style that Dante inherited from his predecessors and developed to his own ends in the *Commedia*, is mentioned in *Purgatorio* 26 and praised for the grace and honor it bestowed on Italian and Dante's literary career. In *Ulysses*, the vernacular contains no sweet new style for devotional, abstruse analysis of love's nobility. Dublin's vernacular forms were commonplace Edwardian diversions that either excited lust or tranquilized mass audiences with sentimental obfuscations of love, instead of analyzing its actions in noble hearts. Not courtly love in the sweet new style, but the domestic bliss of "Love's Old Sweet Song" plays through Joyce's presentation of the soul's progress. *Don Giovanni* and *Hamlet* are produced in Bloom's Dublin, but these and other first-class items of eloquent art are extensively implicated symbolically in lesser forms: *Hamlet* in the transvestite production of *Vice Versa* and in Kipling's ballad "The Absentminded Beggar"; and *Don Giovanni* in *Martha* and *The Wife of Scarli*, to name just a few of the many texts clustered around these and other "classics." Their eloquence, consequently, is a silk purse turned into a sow's ear. This cultural difference from

Dante is partly a result of the downward drift in the social classes serious art could represent, a drift that moved to a crashing collapse in the last two centuries intervening from 1321 to 1922. More significantly, the difference is the necessary result of Joyce's comic sense, his anarchic send-up of any human experience, especially noble, tender experience, and his cheerful, equally anarchic discovery of life's value in the simplest, sorriest places.

Dante's poem has an explicitly ethical purpose: "to remove those living in this life from the state of misery and to lead them to the state of happiness." Dante hides this purpose in several senses and multiple structures, convinced that spiritual matters could only be approached through struggle—as his poem presents it, a one-week struggle through Hell, Purgatory, and Heaven. In *Ulysses* that journey is condensed into struggling through one day. Joyce includes in his own epic the text Dante used to explain how progress might be made through the multiple structures and several senses of the *Commedia*—"*In exitu Israel de Egypto*" (*U*, 17.1030). The simplest inference to be drawn from this is that Joyce's epic might also have a meaning enclosed in multiple structures and several senses. Where Dante's comedy is a solemn, ecclesiastical affair (despite his differences with the church) in which happiness lies in freedom from sin, Joyce's is an anarchic bash in which the church is pounded into rubble and human happiness emerges in verbal high jinks that reveal the soul's freedom and universality, apart from any God, apart from sin, apart from the metaphysical authority Dante mystically adored. Like the different uses of the vernacular in each epic, these different attitudes toward human happiness highlight the common subjects of the two works—the power and destiny of the soul.

The *Commedia* in *Ulysses*

In canto 27 of *Il Purgatorio* Dante passes through the fire that purges lust and so purifies himself of the last of the seven mortal sins that keep him, and the dead souls, from entering into Paradise. When he first learns he must pass through the fire Dante resists, as paralyzed and despondent as a man condemned to death. Virgil's reasoned encouragement and promise of safety do nothing to unlock the pilgrim's will. Only his promise that Beatrice awaits beyond the fire persuades the pilgrim to enter the flames. Successfully emerging from this last perfection of the will at dusk, Dante sleeps, dreams of Leah and Rachel, and then wakes just before dawn to hear the following commencement address from Virgil: "That sweet fruit which the care of mortals goes seeking on so many branches, this day shall give your hungerings peace."[6] As they swiftly climb to the mountaintop (Eden) where Dante will be released from the long spiritual effort that began in Hell, Virgil continues his last address to the pilgrim.

> The temporal fire and the eternal you have seen, my son, and are come to a part where I of myself discern no farther onward. I have brought you here with understanding and with art. Take henceforth your own pleasure for your guide. Forth you are from the steep ways, forth from the narrow. See the sun that shines on your brow, see the tender grass, the flowers, the shrubs, which here the earth of itself alone produces: till the beautiful eyes come rejoicing which weeping made me come to you, you may sit or go among them. No longer expect word or sign from me. Free, upright, and whole is your will, and it would be wrong not to act according to its pleasure; wherefore I crown and miter you over yourself.   [*Pur.* 27, pp. 299–301]

This is a crucial moment in the poem. Dante has regained Adam's Edenic privilege of acting entirely according to his own pleasure, since his will is free, upright, and whole as a consequence of its casting off sin and taking on God's law. He is now free to enter Eden, where he will soon encounter Beatrice.

In *Ulysses* Stephen walks in the early morning discussing faith and free will with Haines, a man who is not a Roman Catholic. Mulligan's blasphemous "Ballad of Joking Jesus" provokes the following exchange between Dedalus and the Englishman:

> —You're not a believer, are you? Haines asked. I mean, a believer in the narrow sense of the word. Creation from nothing and miracles and a personal God.
> —There's only one sense of the word, it seems to me, Stephen said.   [*U*, 1.611–13]

Stephen's refusal to deny Catholicism yields only enough for him to make this self-description: "You behold in me, Stephen said with grim displeasure, a horrible example of free thought" (*U*, 1.625–26). Deciding to exile himself from Mulligan's tower, shared with Haines, Stephen adopts for himself the terms of Dante's exile, prophesied to the pilgrim by his ancestor Cacciaguida in canto 17 of *Il Paradiso*: "Now I eat his salt bread" (*U*, 1.631). The following exchange picks up the Dantesque context ironically, switching from *Paradiso* 17 to *Purgatorio* 27. Here Joyce sets the pilgrim Dante's first experience of freedom and self-possession in faith against Stephen's servitude to Mulligan, Haines, and to his own loveless, faithless bitterness.

> —After all, Haines began. . . .
> Stephen turned and saw that the cold gaze which had measured him was not all unkind.
> —After all, I should think you are able to free yourself. You are your own master, it seems to me.
> —I am a servant of two masters, Stephen said, an English and an Italian.
> —Italian? Haines said.
> A crazy queen, old and jealous. Kneel down before me.
> —And a third, Stephen said, there is who wants me for odd jobs.
> —Italian? Haines said again. What do you mean?
> —The imperial British state, Stephen answered, his colour rising, and the holy Roman catholic and apostolic church.
> [*U*, 1.633–44]

Stephen brings Dante's poem silently into this scene. Joyce, also silently, highlights two items in the scene to identify precisely which event from that poem—Virgil's commendation of Dante's free will as the pilgrim enters Eden—he is working into the early morning Dublin conversation.[7] Haines's remark that he sees Stephen as master of himself, able to liberate himself, recalls Virgil's confirmation of Dante's new-won powers of self-determination: "Free, upright, and whole is your will; and it would be wrong not to act according to its pleasure." Stephen's response bitterly reverses the conclusion of Virgil's praise: "wherefore I crown and miter you over yourself." Where Dante may be crowned and mitred ruler of himself, Stephen must serve the crown and mitre on foreign heads, the British king's and the bishop of Rome's. Worse yet, Dante's self-rule is presented with symbols of temporal authority he honored; Stephen's enslavement is to temporal authorities he fears and despises. Dante's will is freed by perfected faith; Stephen's will is trapped by an imperfectly rejected faith in the church on the one hand, and a perfectly developed faith in his own worthlessness and helplessness on the other. When he says to Haines, "You behold in me . . . a horrible example of free thought," he confesses his entrapment in doubt and guilt.

The final irony of Stephen's confession is, of course, that he is not free, in thought, or will, or desire, or in any way at all. Disgust with his ruined vocation as messiah to the continent, despair over the future of his artistic life in Ireland, guilty fear of his mother's death and ghost—these have all crowded Stephen's soul into impenetrable isolation, which he metaphorically thinks of as tyranny. He sees the same enslaving isolation in Sargaent when the young boy stays after class to show Dedalus his sums. "Secrets, silent, stony sit in the dark palaces of both our hearts: secrets weary of their tyranny: tyrants, willing to be dethroned" (*U*, 2.170–72). The regal oppressors are not only external, then, not only the crowned king and mitred Roman bishop, but internal despots, psychological as well as political and cultural despots. Stephen drives the points home when he says in "Circe": "But in here it is I must kill the priest and the king" (*U*, 15.4436–37). The resolution recalls Blake's similar depiction of the two authorities as tyrants, and it focuses from a distance of over four hundred pages the issue of free will and faith introduced in the conversation with Haines. Dante, because he is king and priest over himself, through the purification of his will, is free to do as he pleases. Since no desire can be wrong when the soul is moved by God's love, no authority binds Dante in Eden, no power but his own pleasure guides his actions.

Stephen's situation is precisely the opposite of Dante's in this regard. Dedalus cannot, like Dante, take his own pleasure for a guide precisely because he has no pleasure—his soul has imprisoned itself as much as foreign powers have imprisoned Ireland. Where the pilgrim has perfected his will through the auspices of reason moved by love, love for Beatrice and for God in her, Stephen's will, like that of his counterpart, Hamlet, is sicklied o'er with reason's indeterminacies, not sturdied by certain truths. Free thinking is not immediately possible for Stephen because he has no faith in himself or life, and because he has no love (Dante's salvation). In the same chapter as this talk with Haines, a few pages before it, a narrative voice says of Stephen, who is brooding on his mother's death, "Pain, that was not yet the pain of love, fretted his heart" (U, 1.103). Again, in "Proteus," Stephen's lovelessness appears, now in the young man's own mind and voice: "Touch me. Soft eyes. Soft soft soft hand. I am lonely here. O, touch me soon, now. What is that word known to all men? I am quiet here alone. Sad too. Touch, touch me" (U, 3.434–36).

Love was the only force that could free the pilgrim from his paralysis before the final purgation that perfected his will: Beatrice's name moved him to the ultimate self-development, the last earthly preparation for the vision of God. Stephen lacks such a love and so remains paralyzed before the only test by which life makes artists, in Stephen's own view as it is expressed in "Scylla and Charybdis"—sexual enthrallment of men to women. No character in literature is so illustriously enthralled erotically as Dante is to Beatrice. That devotion is the starting point of all his accomplishments as a Christian and a poet. That devotion has gained him self-determination in Eden, as the canto recalled in Haines's remarks makes clear. The pilgrim's achievement, and his expectation of bliss on the day Virgil pronounces him emperor and bishop over himself, sound very somberly over Stephen's situation on the morning of June 16.

Haines, like Virgil, is a rationalist and nonbeliever who proclaims during a morning walk the freedom and self-determination of his religious artistic companion. From this point on the identity between the passages is ironic, a union of opposites. Virgil praises Dante for achieving freedom through faith, accurately; Haines, with British understatement, chides Stephen on the subject, ignorantly assuming that Stephen has nothing more to free himself from than an imaginative weakness for superstitious fairy tales. Dante is free when Virgil says so, in great part because he says so, Virgil being Dante's analyst, trainer, and judge throughout Hell and Purgatory; Stephen is not free when Haines presumes he should be, and he never could be in the way Haines suggests. Dante can expect bliss that day, permanent satisfaction of the soul's hunger. At this point in "Telemachus" it seems hardly likely that bliss awaits Stephen on June 16, 1904, or that the achievement of self-determination will come on that day. Joyce of course found his Beatrice on that day in that year. Setting Stephen's helplessness where love is concerned against Dante's strength, Joyce depicts his own condition before and after meeting Nora Barnacle. The autobiographical point also repeats one fundamental effort of Dante's *Commedia*: the confession of the artist's spiritual failure and the celebration of his heroism in love, both projected as universal norms for human experience.

There is no Beatrice for Stephen in *Ulysses* to call him through the flames paralyzing the will, but there is for Bloom, Joyce's other persona and Stephen's double. Stephen's symbolic status as Telemachus and Dante the pilgrim, both men who recover happiness from existential crises, suggests that despite his despair, Stephen can be master of himself after this day. None of these possibilities occur to Stephen: they are all implanted in his narrative situation, but elaborated above his head in the several senses Joyce built out of the novel's story. Joyce's first inclusion of Dante's epic in the narrative of *Ulysses* provides an example of the soul's perfect mastery over itself and all it encounters. The example indicates that Stephen Dedalus is not such a soul, but it also indicates how he might become one. By picking a crucial scene from Dante's poem to portray his character's situation, Joyce indicates at the beginning of *Ulysses* the novel's significant connection to the epic poem. No matter how impossible it may seem, Stephen and Bloom will somehow accomplish what Dante does. By the rule of unified opposites that organizes the symbolism of *Ulysses*, the novel will recreate for a Jew and an infidel in twentieth-century Dublin, living under the sway of a Protestant empire, the achievement of Dante's medieval, Catholic pilgrimage to the empire of death: removal from the state of misery to the state of happiness. How Stephen's happiness, and Bloom's, recapitulate Dante's comes clear most in "Ithaca" when Stephen leaves Bloom's house chanting to himself the psalm that Dante has penitents chant in Purgatory, and that he used to explain his epic's structure to Can Grande, "When Israel left Egypt." Before turning to that scene I want to analyze a moment in "Circe" when another crucial scene from the *Commedia* enters *Ulysses*, this time through Bloom.

In canto 18 of *Il Purgatorio*, Dante circles the fourth tier of the mountain, where sloth is purged. Night overtakes the pilgrim on this tier, and he sleeps. In the next canto, 19, the pilgrim dreams the second of three prophetic predawn dreams in Purgatory (the first is in canto 9, the last in canto 27). A stammering, squint-eyed, crippled hag with maimed hands and sallow skin appears to the pilgrim, who transforms her, with love's look, into a beautiful woman. Chanting, she tells Dante she is the siren who lured Ulysses from his voyage, the beautiful woman who so richly satisfies men that they rarely leave her embrace once in it. Before she finishes the song, another lady appears, calling Virgil to identify the disguised chanteuse. The poet appears and, gazing at the second lady, tears the singer's clothes, uncovering to Dante her belly, from which a stench emerges that wakes him.

It is dawn, and the pilgrim and Virgil, guided by an angel, climb up to the fifth tier where avarice and prodigality are purged. During the climb, Virgil sees that Dante is preoccupied, and when the pilgrim confesses his anxiety about the dream, Virgil explains its meaning to him as follows. " 'You have seen,' he said, 'that ancient witch who alone is now wept for above us: you have seen how man is freed from her. Let it suffice you, and strike your heels on the ground: turn your eyes to the lure which the eternal King spins with the mighty spheres' "(*Pur* 19, p. 205). That lure, ironically juxtaposed against the siren's, is God's whirling of the starry heavens, compared in the next lines of the canto to a falconer's whirling lure. God's lure draws the soul up, unlike the falconer who draws his bird down with a spinning enticement (and the siren, who draws men away from true satisfaction, and so debases them). Virgil urges Dante to climb up the mountain by recalling the stars to him, the constant symbol in the journey of its end in God. The encouragement works, and Dante enters the final third of purgation, the top of the mountain where souls redeem sins of the flesh—avarice, gluttony, and lust—consequences of the bad love symbolized by the Siren in the dream.

In "Circe" Bloom and Stephen encounter many varieties of bad love that they struggle with and, for the most part, overcome. Some of the confrontation is conscious on their part, but most of it is dramatized in magical transformations of the realistic situations Bloom and Stephen find themselves in: wandering through the whore-filled lanes of Nighttown, sitting in a brothel's parlor, scuffling with English soldiers eager to pommel any Irishman, especially one so incapacitated as Dedalus is by midnight. One of these "hallucinations," as Joyce calls them, is a reconstruction of Dante's dream, with Bella Cohen and the nymph/nun standing in for the Siren exposed and disguised. Like Odysseus, like Dante, Bloom escapes the shape-shifting spells of bad love through the force of his own reason, which not only eludes the magical power of the Siren but also wrecks it.

The fifth extended spell cast on Bloom in "Circe" begins with Bella Cohen's first entrance, in the parlor of her brothel—"My word! I'm all of a mucksweat" (*U*, 15.2750). From this point until he unveils a hypocritical nymph posing as a nun, Bloom is put through excruciating sexual pain and humiliation by dominatrix Bella, who turns into a man and turns Bloom into a woman for much of the spell. When the nymph's veil is pulled away, Bello becomes Bella once more, Bloom reviles her instead of being reviled by her, and the spell expires (*U*, 15.3449–992). Joyce ends this, the longest and most powerful spell cast in "Circe," by identifying Bloom's magical release from Bella with Dante's dream-deliverance from the Siren. Like most of Joyce's analogies, this one works underground. Pulling a veil off a deceptively virtuous beauty, revealing her depravity by unloosing her stench, Bloom sets resonances of *Purgatorio* 19 moving in a crucial episode of Joyce's epic. The conceptual and narrative force of Dante's poem extends beyond this trivial point of contact, operating in the fundamental structures of *Ulysses*, but that enlarged function, like the function of Homer's epic in the novel, originates in tiny, easily missed details cunningly set out in dark corners.

The nymph appears at the end of Bloom's suffering under Bello. Poldy is condemned to death by Bello after being told Molly's sexual needs have finally been met by Boylan, who has permanently ousted him from Eccles Street. Useless, houseless, wifeless, Bloom goes to a funeral pyre, mourned by his former Jewish friends. Once he is consumed, the pyre's smoke disperses and reveals the sylvan scene and nymph that hang over his bed at home. The nymph steps out of her photo-scene (which has emerged, through transmigration, from the yew fronds and glades on the wallpaper in Bella Cohen's parlor), resurrects Bloom, and then in a series of reminiscences and questions takes up Bella's role, haranguing Bloom, forcing him to confess and justify past sins of the flesh by which he has offended her respectability, her modesty. Her last incarnation as outraged virtue comes when she assumes the guise of a nun. This form is her undoing, since in it she reenacts Bloom's previous suspicion of women who seem chaste.

Here is the nymph as nun in "Circe": "(*eyeless, in nun's white habit, coif and hugewinged wimple, softly, with remote eyes*) Tranquilla convent. Sister Agatha. Mount Carmel. The apparitions of Knock and Lourdes. No more desire. (*she reclines her head, sighing*) Only the ethereal. Where dreamy creamy gull waves o'er the waters dull" (*U*, 15.3434–38). And here are Bloom's skeptical musings from "Lestrygonians" and "Lotus Eaters" that the nun brings back to him. Thinking of his former job with the stationer Wisdom Hely, Bloom recalls:

> Devil of a job it was collecting accounts of those convents. Tranquilla convent. That was a nice nun there, really sweet face. Wimple suited her small head. Sister? Sister? I am sure she was crossed in love by her eyes. Very hard to bargain with that sort of a woman. I disturbed her at her devotions that morning. But glad to communicate with the outside world. Our great day, she said. Feast of Our Lady of Mount Carmel. Sweet name too: caramel. She knew I, I think she knew by the way she. If she had married she would have changed. I suppose they really were short of money. Fried everything in the best butter all the same. No lard for them. My heart's broke eating dripping. They like buttering themselves in and out. Molly tasting it, her veil up. Sister? Pat Claffey, the pawnbroker's daughter. It was a nun they say invented barbed wire.   [*U*, 8.143–54]

Bloom also thinks about religion's chicanery while he observes communion in "Lotus Eaters": "Now I bet it makes them feel happy. Lollipop. It does. Yes, bread of angels it's called. There's a big idea behind it, kind of kingdom of God is within you feel. . . . Thing is if you really believe in it. Lourdes cure, waters of oblivion, and the Knock apparition, statues bleeding" (*U*, 5.359–66). The nymph also brings back to Bloom his previous thoughts of another woman who was pretending to be sexless. In "Lestrygonians" Bloom sees A.E. pass with a young woman, perhaps Lizzie Twig. Their conversation, and the woman's carelessness about stockings, convince Bloom she is a highbrow. Again in this example fraudulence, art, and food are linked.

> Her stockings are loose over her ankles. I detest that: so tasteless. Those literary etherial people they are all. Dreamy, cloudy, symbolistic. Esthetes they are. I wouldn't be surprised if it was that kind of food you see produces the like waves of the brain the poetical. For example one of those policemen sweating Irish stew into their shirts you couldn't squeeze a line of poetry out of him. Don't know what poetry is even. Must be in a certain mood.
> > *The dreamy cloudy gull*
> > *Waves o'er the waters dull.* [*U*, 8.542–50]

The nun's remark, "Only the ethereal, where dreamy creamy gull waves o'er the waters dull," completes the symbolic association of butter and cream with: poetry, music as a Siren's song, female seductiveness (covert and overt), and sham religious sacrifices. Nuns may be virgins, Bloom thinks in "Lestrygonians," but that does not stop them from flirting or hold them to vows of poverty, since they indulge the flesh luxuriously where food is concerned, even when that indulgence causes economic hardship to others (for instance, to Bloom the bill collector in the Tranquilla convent case). Dreamy religion that makes sacrifice pretty, that sanctifies slaughter by spiritualizing bloodshed; dreamy art that nullifies the material world through ethereal symbolism; and fraudulent female chastity that disguises mortal lust—these are all associated with dreamy creamy butter, and are all part of the nymph's deceitful, unjust chastisement of Bloom. Religion, art, and love, this nymph would have Poldy believe, are all too ethereal for someone as bestial as he to experience—they delight high-minded women who have "no more desire" for things of the world, and whose exalted love can never be anything but painful scorn to men.

The nymph succeeds in this pose until she becomes a nun and repeats to Bloom phrases from his own rational discovery of religious and sexual hypocrisy. Poldy's button snaps after the nun's

speech, freeing him from the delirium of her hauteur. Coldly, he
says to her, "You have broken the spell. The last straw. If there were
only ethereal where would you all be, postulants and novices? Shy
but willing like an ass pissing" (*U*, 15.3449–51). This is strong language for Bloom, stronger even than his dressing down of the Citizen in "Cyclops," and it suggests how thoroughly fraudulent Joyce
wanted to make the feminine ethereal pose in *Ulysses*. Bloom's
comparison of the nymph's coyness to an ass pissing passes immediately from a figure of speech to a fact: "*a large moist stain appears on her robe*" (*U*, 15.3457). The scabrous comedy mounts to
hilarious frenzy as the nymph responds to this desecration by trying
to castrate Bloom. With a blasphemy that scalds the heart of any
true believer Bloom counterattacks with words—"What do you
lack with your barbed wire? Crucifix not thick enough?"—and
deeds—"(*he clutches her veil*). . . . THE NYMPH (*with a cry flees from
him unveiled, her plaster cast cracking, a cloud of stench escaping
from the cracks*)" (*U*, 15.3464–65, 3469–70). The nymph's undoing
is also Bello's. As she flies calling "Police," Bella Cohen appears,
female once more, and is unmasked by Bloom: "(*composed, regards
her*) *Passée*. Mutton dressed as lamb" (*U*, 15.3483).

Unveiling the nun, Bloom unveils the destructive fraudulence of
lust that he has succumbed to in this hallucination, almost to the
point of disaster. The situations of Bloom and the pilgrim, from
which reasoned observation deliver them both, are just short of
identical. Dante is dreaming when the Siren comes to him, Bloom
is under a spell; both are deprived of their rational powers and so
extremely vulnerable to the claims of the body. Dante is about to
confront the perversion of love by concupiscence, Bloom is trying
to rescue Stephen Dedalus, and himself, from whoredom. The Siren, who first appears hideous, is transformed by Dante's dreaming
eyes of love into a beauty, indicating sexual desire's immense capacity to enmesh the soul in delusion. The tawdry nymph Bloom
associates with Molly in "Calypso" was advertised falsely in *Photo
Bits* as a "splendid masterpiece in art colors" (*U*, 4.370). Bloom
succumbed once to the false representation, finding, through his
love for Molly, beauty in the magazine's mendacious splendor,
enough beauty to put the image over his bed: "Not unlike her with
her hair down: slimmer. Three and six I gave for the frame. She said
it would look nice over the bed" (*U*, 4.371–72). Bloom, being

Bloom, probably also thought he was getting a deal spending only three and six to frame a "splendid masterpiece." The aesthetic error is a comic example of Bloom's insensitivity "to artistic impressions . . . plastic or pictorial," and of the modern Dubliner's debased Odyssean prudence—thrift in search of beauty—but the erotic motive for discovering beauty in a soft-core porno photo links Poldy clearly to Dante, the eager devotee of Beatrice's eyes (*U*, 17.20–21). The nymph's psychological authority over Bloom in "Circe" derives from the transformation his loving eyes have made of her. This naked porno girl pretending to be a nymph and then a nun endangers Poldy with fraudulent innocence and beauty, as Dante's Siren endangered the pilgrim. In both cases loving men, deceived by their imperfect love, mistake their summum bonum.

Dante escapes the Siren not through his own efforts, but through the intercession of two figures. A lady representing judgment calls upon Virgil, who depicts will at this moment, to identify the imposter. Together they unveil her. When Virgil tears the Siren's garments a stench emerges, revealing her true nature—a stench so noisome it wakes the dreamer. Requiring analysis of the dream from Virgil, Dante learns how the Siren symbolically predicts the purgation of bad love that he must complete in the last three tiers of Purgatory. Bloom has no Virgil and no symbolic lady of reason to help him; he acts himself as will and judgment, provoked to his own deliverance through the agency of a snapped button. Adding Virgil to his role as pilgrim, Bloom tears the Siren nun's veil and then analyzes the stench her broken body gives off: "Fool someone else, not me. (*he sniffs*) Rut. Onions. Stale. Sulphur. Grease" (*U*, 15.3477–78). Joyce could not rest with stench as a symbol of the nun's vice but had to specify Dante's detail even further by having Bloom break the stench up into component parts, thus giving reason a more precise and practical role in deliverance from concupiscence.

Bloom's triumph over the nun, like Dante's over the Siren, displays the soul's freedom to love rightly, even after near mortal error. The pilgrim goes on to find God, with Beatrice as guide after his exit from Purgatory. Bloom makes his way home to Molly and conquers the humiliation of cuckoldry through his equanimity about sexual failure. Having cast off Bella's dominion and the nymph's, Bloom is free to contemplate Molly's "plump melonous hemisphere" silently, to joy in the flesh without suffering from it, to come as close as he can to delight with her in "a proximate erection" (*U*, 17.2242, 2246). With that restoration of good love Joyce departs from Dante's goal, the love of God, locating human happiness in a much humbler end. Bloom's freedom leads him to proximate consummation, the most sexual love can be in the world of *Ulysses*, and, given the book's truth-telling mission, the most Joyce thought it could be in the world *Ulysses* depicts, ours.

There is some difference between the sexual satisfaction of a proximate erection and the sexual satisfaction of being "fucked yes and damned well fucked too up to my neck nearly" as Molly puts it (*U*, 18.1511). But even Boylan's rendering of what Bloom calls "complete satisfaction" to Molly cannot permanently appease that "constant but not acute concupiscence resident in a bodily and mental female organism" (*U*, 17.2159–61). Complete satisfaction cannot be found in sexual love even if the male flesh, unlike Bloom's, is entirely willing. Boylan leaves Molly resentful and slightly battered, having lavished no tenderness or mind at all on her for all his brute strength. The imperfection of sexual love is of course a major topic in the *Commedia* where it indicates the superior perfection of God's divine love. Such satisfaction is withheld from Bloom, from humanity, by Joyce. He depicts Poldy's conquest of concupiscence—its torments and fraud—by reference to Dante's in *Purgatorio* to indicate that Bloom dramatizes, as the pilgrim does, the soul's struggle with the body and reason's triumphant part in that struggle. In the next, final Dantesque transposition analyzed in this chapter, both Bloom and Stephen are delivered from their long day's effort—the young man to love's possibility, and thereby according to Joyce's aesthetics and Dante's, to art; the older one, like Moses, like Virgil, to the melancholy contemplation of bliss almost but never finally achieved.

In the first canto of *Purgatorio* Dante and Virgil meet Cato, the pagan ruler of the purifying mountain. At Cato's request for a justification of the unorthodox presence of a damned soul and a living man in this second realm of the afterlife, Virgil tells how Beatrice came to him in Hell and urged him to rescue Dante, whose folly had led him to the extremity of spiritual danger. "He goes seeking freedom" is Virgil's justification for Dante's presence at the mountain's base, freedom in the pilgrim's case being deliverance from sin

(*Pur* 1, p. 7). Satisfied with the account, Cato instructs Virgil to wash Dante's face in rushes that grow at the island base (a ritual humiliation that befits Dante for penance), where they will discover their path up the mountain. Canto 2 begins at oceanside after dawn. Dante has been cleansed of Hell's soot when he and Virgil see an angel gaining shore at the rudder of a boat holding more than one hundred souls, all singing "*In exitu Israel de Aegypto*" (*Pur* 2, p. 15). These are the souls assigned to Purgatory, singing Psalm 113 in the Vulgate, 114 in the King James Version, the psalm of deliverance that commemorates Passover and Exodus, in Catholic biblical exegesis the typological promises of the soul's final deliverance, Christ's Exodus, Easter. Dante recognizes among the newly arrived souls Casella, a contemporary musician, and lapses with him from the immediate purpose, penance, long enough to hear Casella sing "*Amor che ne la mente mi ragiona*," (Love, who discourses in my mind), the first verse of one of Dante's *dolce stil nuovo* love poems (*Pur* 2, p. 20). But psalms are to be the music of Purgatory, and hymns that are set to other Bible verses and church prayers, not canzone in which reason glorifies mortal love, as Dante and Virgil discover when Cato chastises them for stopping to sing what on Purgatory's mountain are frivolous, degraded ditties. Frightened, startled, the hundred-plus souls fly to the mountain cliffs, with Dante and Virgil, to pursue their unknown penance and so win their promised exodus.

The first scene of "Ithaca" finishes with Bloom and Stephen exiting from the kitchen, where they have been chatting until the dead of night, into Bloom's garden in back of 7 Eccles Street. Here are Joyce's words for the exit:

> In what order of precedence, with what attendant ceremony was the exodus from the house of bondage to the wilderness of inhabitation effected?
>
>
>
> Lighted Candle in Stick
> borne by
> BLOOM
> Diaconal Hat on Ashplant
> borne by
> STEPHEN
>
>

With what intonation *secreto* of what commemorative psalm?

The 113th, *modus peregrinus: In exitu Israel de Egypto: domus Jacob de populo barbaro.*   [*U*, 17.1021–31]

Stephen's ecclesiastical parody sends up one narrative detail, and in the process suggests a method for dealing comically with the novel's structural, conceptual identification of narrative facts and symbolic ones. Stephen's mock church procession echoes Dante's serious parody of church music as celebration of spiritual freedom. Dante begins that parody in *Purgatorio* 2 with the psalm Stephen chants to himself in "Ithaca" and continues it through the end of the second *cantica*. Dedalus's joke also displays the verse Dante chose to explain his epic's "polysemous" structure to Can Grande. Obliquely (as usual) Joyce invites comparison with Dante in this double-layered allusion, urging readers to think about how freedom in the medieval epic applies to life in Bloom's world and how Dante's integration of one meaning's many senses might bear on a modern epic of the soul.

Starting, after Dante's instructions to Can Grande, at the literal level—the story—the first thing to notice is that Stephen alludes to Dante's poem for the sake of an erudite, snide joke in which he belittles himself as much as Bloom. The line displays mental habits Stephen alternately frets over and indulges in all day: unkindness; a sharp, nervous metaphorical ingenuity; and guilty, nostalgic, compulsive reference of any and all facts to the hated church for interpretation. Since Stephen is leaving Bloom's house for good, the young man must be thinking of himself as Israel and Bloom's house as Egypt, the land and people of strange language. He ridicules the kindness of Bloom's unsolicited aid and hospitality, perhaps also condemning Bloom's discreet but clear plans for a sexual liaison between the resident soprano of Eccles Street and the youth who might teach her Italian. Stephen sardonically connects both these snares, and his boredom with Bloom's rambling good citizen scientific speech (a language thoroughly strange to Dedalus, who cultivates instead the obscure verbal pomps of artistic alienation), with epical tyranny. Everything Bloom has to offer Stephen amounts to oppression identical to that suffered by Jews in Egypt as far as our

Byronic hero is concerned, who thinks of his departure from the loquacious, many-minded Bloom as the momentous Exodus of the Israelites from slavery, and the deliverance of man from death at the new, improved Exodus, Easter.

But Bloom is the exiting Jew, not Stephen, and the two leave Egypt together, despite the young man's nasty verbal play. This unification of the two men in the symbolic (and narrative) pattern of the episode is the final presentation of their consubstantiality in the novel. The Christological metaphor identifying the Father and Son has as one analogue in *Ulysses* the cultural religious equivalence the Irish (and every Christian nation) made between themselves and Israel long before Joyce came on the scene. In Ireland's case the comparison emerges from a heritage of political, cultural, religious, and economic oppression common to both nations, and the reliance of both on rich traditions and memories of a glorious past to preserve spiritually the freedoms destroyed by political and financial oppression. Like so many other themes in *Ulysses*, the connection of father and son and the solemn, lamentable identity of the Jews and the Irish take their final bow in a comic, small allusion in "Ithaca."

Dante's epic puts the inevitable counterpoint into this comic citation of church ritual. Stephen refers to the psalm in part as a burlesque celebration of his escape from entanglement in Bloom's plans for alleviating domestic captivity. To some extent Dedalus, more than Bloom, is the prudent one in this scene, the many-minded Odyssean hero who sees through plots and slips nooses even when they are amicably suspended near him. Stephen's sarcasm toward Bloom seems slightly less ugly when he is viewed as a man struggling to free himself from nomination as a cuckold's resident violator. Poldy in this reading has no chance of escape from Egyptian Molly once his victim flees; he steps out of Egypt, but only Stephen passes over its borders. Bloom goes back to Molly's bed when Stephen disappears into "the wilderness of inhabitation"—which is "no habitation" according to the distorting precision Joyce achieves with Latin prefixes in this chapter (*U*, 17.1022). Packing Dante's dramatic citation of the psalm into Stephen's flight, Joyce unfolds the contrary version of Stephen's parody, its revelation of the freedom Dedalus has gained in keeping Bloom's company (as well as fleeing it), and the freedom Poldy finds with Molly, the *nostos* that makes him, more than Dedalus, Odysseus.

In Dante's poem the psalm expresses the hope of redeemed sinners who have been promised freedom but have not yet achieved it. Like the Israelites, the souls in Purgatory journey to an unknown reward that they must struggle to attain. Stephen's behavior with Bloom in "Ithaca" shows him ushered into a similar pursuit unawares. The allusion to the *Commedia* implies that Stephen's departure from Bloom is the beginning of the young man's freedom to pursue the life that will make him an artist. Up until June 16 Dedalus has sought out beauty in metaphysics and isolation. He feels both as tyrannies in *Ulysses* and calls them "Egypt" in "Oxen of the Sun." Thinking of the legacy of Mother Church, and of his own mother, Stephen complains (in a passage already quoted), "And thou hast left me alone for ever in the dark ways of my bitterness: and with a kiss of ashes hast thou kissed my mouth" (*U*, 14.378–80). Continuing, he derives from his own psychology a universal principle: "The adiaphane in the noon of life is an Egypt's plague" (*U*, 14.385–86). Such isolation belongs, to paraphrase the rest of Stephen's remark, to the dark void before and after life, not to noon, the middle of the soul's bodily journey. He disguises here an identification of himself with Dante, who also found himself in the darkness of spiritual nullity in the noontime, "nel mezzo del camin," of his life. Dante's freedom comes to him through grace operating in Virgil, Beatrice, and Bernard, who guide him out of Egypt into the Promised Land of Paradise in the afterlife. Quoting Psalm 114 when Stephen leaves Bloom, Joyce implies that somehow Stephen has gained comparable freedom by associating with Poldy, who plays Moses to his Israel, Virgil to his Dante. Stephen's unnecessary cruelty to Bloom (singing the antisemitic ballad *Little Harry Hughes*) and his aloofness make it hard to see how the exchange has improved him, but Joyce's symbolic extensions of the meeting reveal the saving grace that Dedalus's rudeness obscures.

Bloom has been wandering back from the consequences of Molly's betrayal to reconciliation with her all day, and achieves it that night soon after Stephen leaves. At Dedalus's departure Bloom is just short of the sanity (in the Latin sense of wholeness) that enables him to move through equanimity back to unviolated love for his violated, violating wife. After facing the inevitable Joycean crisis (female perfidy) and surviving, Poldy lives as Stephen says Shakespeare finally did, and any male artist must—accepting the tyranny of nature that women embody. Stephen has been ushered into that life (if only as a spectator) in his conversation with Bloom, not in his theorizing about Shakespeare, but he does not recognize the Joycean advance toward artistic productivity implicit in the conversation. That recognition is preserved for the reader, who sees symbolic identities the characters can not in the offhand allusion to Dante's epical poetics and to Psalm 114.

Dedalus and Bloom are identified throughout *Ulysses* in many different intersecting symbols. The union of these men appears most persistently in "Ithaca," the homecoming episode. Their coincidence begins in the first sentence where they take "parallel courses" and moves through their mutual "like and unlike reactions to experience," that is, their pleasures and dislikes (not their dissimilar tastes, but their similar dissatisfactions), and through dozens of unifying phrases and configurations (*U*, 17.1, 19). Grammar joins the two as much as any symbol, as this game with pronouns indicates.

> What, reduced to their simplest reciprocal form, were Bloom's thoughts about Stephen's thoughts about Bloom and about Stephen's thoughts about Bloom's thoughts about Stephen?
>
> He thought that he thought that he was a jew whereas he knew that he knew that he knew that he was not.
>
> [*U*, 17.527–31]

This simple reciprocity confuses Bloom with Stephen, or forces even the sharpest readers to, by attempting to distinguish them so precisely. The clarity grammar should bestow also invokes the inevitable comic opposite here; mishmash, one form taken by unified contraries. Once they have left the house and Stephen has chanted the psalm, the ironic grammatical clarity makes one final merger of the two.

> Both then were silent?
> Silent, each contemplating the other in both mirrors of the reciprocal flesh of theirhisnothis fellowfaces. [*U*, 17.1182–84]

Dante's *Commedia* enters this systematic unification of the two men when Dedalus chants the commemorative psalm. Together with the chapter's trinitarian metaphors, the Biblical verse, with its medieval exegetical function as prophecy, indicates that Dedalus will experience Bloom's lot as the Son manifests the Father's nature, as sons inherit their fathers' destinies, as Christians recapitulate, in worship of the Resurrection, the deliverance of Israel from Pharoah. These symbols do not contradict the narrative, in which the two men are not freely intimate; instead they exaggerate one element of the scene, the tranquil acceptance each makes of the other. This tranquil recognition of shared experience between Bloom and Stephen in "Ithaca," and Bloom's union with his wife, make up the chapter's Homeric action, and are, for that reason, presented with magnifying symbolism.

Concerning the male union: Dedalus spends more time in Bloom's company on June 16 than in anyone else's, from midnight in "Circe," through 1:00 A.M. in "Eumaeus," to 2:30 A.M. in "Ithaca"—almost three hours. Bloom is the only man in Dublin who esteems Stephen's genius without mocking or criticizing him. That bestowal is the Joycean analogue for Odysseus's empowering Telemachus, as Mulligan's sarcasm is the Dublin analogue to Antinous's usurpation of the royal son's privilege and power. Stephen has his only *conversation*, that is, exchange of mind, with Bloom in "Ithaca"; the other encounters are all ingenious performances in which Dedalus shields resentment, guilt, and fear and fortifies compulsive alienation. Conversation may seem a trivial event from which to draw such symbolic conclusions about identity as those implied by trinitarian monotheism and the *Commedia*, but conversation for a soul so perilously close to extinction as Stephen's not only justifies such magnification, but could not be accurately rendered in any humbler terms. The conversation is a major event in Bloom's life as well. As one learns earlier in the same episode (*U*, 17.58), Bloom has not had a friendly, rambling conversation with another man since 1893 (for roughly the same period he's been exiled sexually from Molly). He feels his life has been impoverished by the absence of male friendship, a fact that makes his hope that this conversation will initiate regular symposia with Dedalus reasonable and poignant; courageous as well as ridiculous. The novel's comedy depends on this kind of apparently indecorous identification of triviality and its opposite, grandeur. If Bloom's cigar in Barney Kiernan's pub is Odysseus's stake in the Cyclops's cave, the only tranquil interchange Stephen and Poldy have with another male deserves rendition as the deliverance of the stricken soul into Purgatory, the difficult wandering through Sinai to Canaan, the procession of the Son from and to the Father through the Holy Spirit.

These are some of the narrative meanings the allusion to *Purgatorio* 2 and the Can Grande letter via Psalm 114 uncovers in Bloom's story and Stephen's. Although the happiness Joyce bestows on his heroes is not Dante's, the issue in both stories remains identical: what means insure freedom to live correctly in this world? Casting Poldy as Moses, the original lawgiver of Christendom, and Stephen as Israel, the original law-breaking, law-abiding nation, Joyce has his own say about a system of ethics that was already ancient when Dante made it a fundamental conception of his *Commedia*, with Virgil as Moses, and himself as Israel. The ethical experience of any Christian soul had been understood from the earliest days of the church as a recapitulation of the Exodus story. Augustine's commentary on Psalm 114, the most illustrious response to that text before Dante's, shows what moral, historical conclusions the analogy made possible.[8] That commentary was known to Joyce, who heard part of it every year on Good Friday in the Tenebrae service, his favorite church production, which celebrates man's salvation through the new Passover, Christ's Passion. Fitting the first verse of Psalm 114, a central text in the church's intellectual development, into *Ulysses* ironically, Joyce makes June 16 Passover and makes his novel, like the *Commedia*, an epic of the soul's deliverance.

That event requires no transcendent cause in Bloom's world and insures no permanent satisfaction, unlike the deliverance of the penitents in Purgatory. Freedom's end in Dublin is not God but human love, which has both fatal and vivifying consequences. Christ is not superior to Moses in Joyce's view, or Dante to Virgil, since the son comes to the same end as the father—liberty to accept nature's humiliating restrictions with equanimity. Manageable disappointment and shabby accommodation of imperfection are the conditions of happiness in Joyce's world. They may not seem encouraging, but they are not as severe as the conditions Dante and the church imposed with their conception of the world as a Sinai in which the best happiness is anticipation of escape through death. Christians of course have God to justify all suffering and make severity "light," as Isaiah has it. That fact makes Dante's depiction of the soul's escape from Egypt in *Inferno*, and struggle through Sinai in *Purgatorio*, end in *Paradiso's* joyous Canaan. *Ulysses*, on the other hand, shows how man can be happy without God, and consequently the novel sacrifices the permanence and perfection God affords Christians after death, placing a higher value on mundane success than the church says He allows.

Psalm 114 explains the poetics as well as the ethics of the *Commedia* and bears on the same topics in *Ulysses*. The polysemous structure Dante spells out to Can Grande with Psalm 114 is a justification of symbolic narration, an insistence that the soul, which lives by integrating the various forms of nature relevant to its salvation, cannot be accurately presented in poetry that has only one dimension. Just as the soul lives in two worlds at once, in nature and by anticipation in the empyrean, so a poem presenting it must operate in multiple forms, must symbolically align spiritual truth with whatever narrative action fictive characters perform. Dante's specification of four levels is not so relevant to his purpose as the letter to Can Grande suggests. The point of his explanation is not to send readers looking, in the narrative fact that there are four rivers in Hell, for church history, or personal moral information, or precise prediction of how the festivities at the Last Judgment will occur. "Polysemous" does not mean encoded secrecy of this kind in Dante's poem, but amplified significance for its story, an assurance that truth about the most valuable topic, the soul's progress, can be found in the invention of a literary place.

Joyce insinuates in Stephen's chant that his novel is polysemous in this way, that its fiction is informative, that its subject is the soul, itself polysemous, since as the form of forms the soul integrates multiple subjects. In Catholicism, instruction about the soul reaches every believer through the catechism. "Ithaca," whose technique Joyce named "catechism (impersonal)" in the working schema he gave Stuart Gilbert, instructs readers in the mysterious powers of the soul that Joyce depicts throughout the novel.[9] Readers of *Ulysses* experience a literary "form of forms," a story identical, in a Joycean manner, to all that is, from the first page of the novel. Crucial moments in the story link this novel to Dante's epic of the soul. In "Ithaca," the hour of answered and unanswered questions, Joyce flashes Dante's explanation of his polysemous epic to readers through Stephen, who introduced thought about the soul's powers into the novel in "Nestor."

The organ Joyce depicts in "Ithaca," liberally extending that word's meaning, is the skeleton, according again to Gilbert's schema.[10] The episode provides many of those hard facts that hold together the characterization and action of Stephen and Bloom, cataloguing in more abundant detail than any other episode the personal history and the temperamental makeup of the two men. With the allusion to Psalm 114 the episode also provides a technical and conceptual theory of literature (Dante's "polysemous" epical narration) that supports all the symbolic equivalences Joyce builds around those narrative facts.[11] The bare bones of the faith come under analysis in the church's catechism; the bare bones of symbolic narrative shine through the "tranquilising spectrality" of Joyce's in "Ithaca" (*L*, 1:176). In both interrogatory systems every answer somehow reveals the soul's vital capacity for integrating multiple and opposed realities. Dante structured his poem around that revelation; Joyce altered the revelation by omitting God, but retained the same structure, eager to master the grand form Dante had mastered, the universally informative epic defining all the values of human experience.

Recasting an Epic Journey of the Soul

In *Ulysses* Joyce appropriated more than scenes from the *Commedia's* epic narrative. He reworked the principle structures of that narrative into his own epic, telling Bloom's story very much the way Dante tells the pilgrim's. The imitation consists in writing through Bloom's day symbolically, in arranging the mundane experiences of that day as Dante arranged the extramundane experiences of his week-long visionary journey—to indicate universal principles of being in one life. The facts of both stories (what Bloom encounters in Dublin, how he reacts; what Dante encounters among the dead, how he reacts) are set out in multiple symbolic magnifications, in analogies, parodies, and allusions that emerge from character and action but that never exceed them. In both epics the symbols originate in a narrative pretending to be literally true, one made up of graphic representation of material and historical facts.

Joyce makes this physical grounding clear in his novel by systematically aligning narrative events with anatomical ones throughout the book. Under the heading "IN THE HEART OF THE HIBERNIAN METROPOLIS" that begins Bloom's episode in the newspaper office, the trams that rattle back and forth depict the blood running through the heart (the junction at Nelson's pillar) across systematically organized veins and arteries (tram tracks) to bring and carry off material (Dubliners) necessary for metabolism (commerce) in various parts (Blackrock, Kingstown, Dalkey, etc.) of the body (Dublin). The mail cars, described under the headline "THE WEARER OF THE CROWN," are the nerves receiving various impulses (flung sacks of post) from the brain (the wearer of the crown) for transmission (delivery) to the rest of the body (the globe in this case) (U, 7.1–2, 7). All this starts off a chapter stylistically focused on rhetoric, the product of the lungs, the body's Aeolian caves of wind. Across the whole novel Joyce manages to depict in various places various systems of the body (digestive, reproductive, etc.) together with its organs. Dante expressed the primacy of narrative in his poem not with anatomical metaphors for his action but with the analogy to Biblical interpretation that Joyce quotes in "Ithaca." The story is to the symbolism in his epic as the literal level is to others in Biblical exegesis—the foundation of all understanding. Any conclusion about how Joyce developed Dante's epic presentation of the soul in *Ulysses* needs to start with how Joyce developed Dante's literal level, his invention of a place, characters, and plot.

One of the pleasures Dante scholars all discover working on the *Commedia* is mapmaking. The afterworld has geography, a climate, population distribution, flora and fauna, everything from mundane existence that can be measured, catalogued, and drawn to scale. The reason is simple: two thirds of the afterlife takes place on the same earth the souls occupied when alive, although in places inaccessible to the living (Hell's subterranean inverted cone and the Purgatorial mountain in the southern, watery hemisphere). Paradise lies outside the created universe in the empyrean, but even there the degrees of blessedness are depicted with scientific measurements of the physical heavens enclosing the earth, and each state of rapture is symbolically presented to the pilgrim as he passes through the nine spheres with Beatrice to her place (his also, eventually) outside space and time. To a large extent, Dante makes his poem an expedition, a scientifically accurate account of unexplored regions of the created world. The cosmological explanations in Paradise, comprised of astronomy and physics as much as they are of theology, and the meteorology and geology of Hell and Purgatory all give Dante's poem the aura of a universal natural history. The cosmic travel book also defines and describes the civilizations of all three realms and so makes Dante a universal cultural historian as well. Since the civilizations of the dead reward the behavior of the living, Dante's account of them refers to secular human history as well, depicting the perfected results of all worldly endeavors when it depicts the conditions death has brought souls to.

The detailed physical setting of the *Commedia*, its thoroughly concrete presentation of an actual culture in a real place, conforms to Dante's insistence that poetry must inform men truthfully when it invents fictions. By naming real names throughout his epic Dante justifies his Biblical poetics and establishes a literal meaning for his characters that makes plausible the invented actuality of his setting. Timing the pilgrim's journey with constant references to constellations, immense indicators of God's order, Dante achieves the same effect. He gives the unrepeatable journey through an uncharted place credibility by conducting it under the divine authority of the charted heavens. No one can be sure whether Dante thought Hell and Purgatory were real places on the globe, but this much is certain—he could not have made them more immediately present to his pilgrim's senses, and his readers' imaginations, as physical places had they been as native to him as Dublin was to Joyce. Dante's fictiona substantiality has the following result in Joyce's *Ulysses*: as Dante unfolds the soul's progress in a setting of physical specificity and density unprecedented for its time, so Joyce sends Bloom, his image of the soul, through the most massively detailed physical setting English literature had yet produced.

The action of *Ulysses* owes as much to Dante's epic as it does to Homer's. The *Commedia's* plot shows Dante recuperating from the most dangerous crisis of his life. After Beatrice's death, his faith almost utterly lost, Dante collapsed into ruin, the wood of error where the poem begins. At the last possible moment he recovers enough rationality to realize his peril—he finds himself: "mi ritrovai" (*Inf* 1, p. 2). Revived from the somnambulism that led him to the wilderness, Dante immediately tries to escape. He follows the rising constellation Venus, "the planet that leads men aright by every path," to a hill at the edge of the wild valley (*Inf* 1, p. 3). This escape fails when he discovers the hill's slope impeded by three beasts, a leopard, a lion, and a she-wolf, all embodiments of his unexamined sinfulness. At this desperate moment Virgil appears, explaining that he must take another route out of the savage valley—a route through Hell, Purgatory, and Paradise. Only that detour will provide the knowledge necessary for regaining the spiritual high road he has abandoned.

Such long-delayed deliverance is forced on Dante by the extremity of his error. As Beatrice tells Virgil, whom she sends to guide Dante and who repeats the interview to the pilgrim in *Inferno* 2: "my friend—and not the friend of Fortune—finds his way so impeded on the desert slope that he has turned back in fright; and, from what I have heard of him in Heaven, I fear he may already have gone so astray that I am late in arising to help him" (*Inf* 2, p. 17). Again in *Purgatorio* 30, this time in front of Dante, she explains the necessity of his lengthy way out of error's wood: "He fell so low that all means for his salvation were now short, save to show him the lost people" (*Pur* 30, p. 335). Along the journey Dante himself has understood its purposeful indirection. In *Inferno* 15 he says to Brunetto Latini, "There above, in the bright life . . . I went astray in a valley, before my age was at the full. Only yesterday morning I turned my back on it. He appeared to me, as I was returning into it, and by this path he leads me home" (*Inf* 15, p. 157). The errant journey home comes up again when Dante says to Casella in *Purgatorio* 2, "My Casella, to return here once again where I am I make this journey," that is, to be saved and enter Purgatory after death I have come here alive; to win the race I have first walked the whole course before taking my place with the other runners at the starting line (*Pur* 2, p. 19). The reformation of the will, the action of Dante's epic, starts at square one and requires retrospective analysis, in every tier of Hell, Purgatory, and Heaven, of the pilgrim's sins. This medieval psychotherapy is metaphorically rendered as a detour in the *Commedia*, a long circular return to the liberation Dante could not pursue directly on the strength of his first cliff-hanging repentance. On that journey Dante learns everything the soul can merit and how to merit for himself the bliss that his genius and God's love clearly declare he deserves.

Ulysses also displays its heroes recovering from the most dangerous crises of their lives, pulled back from catastrophe at the extreme moment. Bloom has not had complete sexual intercourse with Molly for "10 years, 5 months and 18 days," or complete mental intercourse for "9 months and 1 day" (*U*, 17.2282, 2289). The separation results in Molly's adultery on June 16, the worst psychological blow Bloom has yet encountered. Like Odysseus, Bloom never forgets his spouse or stops loving her; like Dante, who did forget Beatrice's example, Bloom is himself responsible, as Odysseus is not, for the trouble he's in vis-à-vis his isolated lady. Odysseus's ten-year struggle to return to Penelope results from accidental interference, not from unwillingness on his part, whereas Bloom's ten-year-plus (trust Joyce to improve all his analogies by detailing them so specifically) alienation from Molly, while it is brought on by the accidental death of Rudy, contains no struggle for sexual reunion and is in fact acquiescence, symptomatic of a drifting will as calamitous as Dante's. While Bloom's wandering Dublin on June 16 recapitulates Odysseus's errant detour home, it also reenacts Dante's purposeful doubletracking through the afterlife. Bloom's reconciliation to Molly, like Dante's to Beatrice and the Divine love she leads him to, is a reeducation of the will, unlike Odysseus's homecoming, which depends not on his moral education along the way, but entirely on his prudence and perseverance. Homer's hero returns because he has faith and reason marshaled; Joyce's Bloom possesses these virtues, but he also needs to face, as Dante does, the failure in his soul that has put him at such a distance from happiness.

Bloom cannot stay home to forestall his cuckoldry; things have gone too far, as he knows, for that to prevent the inevitable result of his middle-aged failure. His return, like Dante's, starts with recognition of the desperate situation he is in, realization of the full sundering he has brought about between himself and his love. Unable to move simply, directly out of the wilderness he has drifted into, Bloom must wander in circles all over Dublin, analyzing himself and those he encounters, identifying the failures and successes of a world in which he is as alien as the living Dante is in the afterlife. In Dante's poem a living soul learns its nature from the dead; in Joyce's crisis narrative two living souls, Bloom and Stephen, are sent out to recover themselves by observing the world of generation alien to them. In both epics the heroes recover only after they travel through a world more real than the one their mistakes have trapped them in. Dante sees the absolute, permanent life of the dead; Bloom and Stephen see the perpetual transformations of generation and decay, from which they are cut off through sexual isolation. Dubliners, like the dead, are good and evil, and like the dead they show Bloom and Stephen truths that fit the two Irish pilgrims for the symbolic deliverance Dante earned on his Odyssey—the chanting of Psalm 114.

Stephen's error is simple to identify: he's loveless and so lifeless. June 16 finds him in extremis, with no home, no job, no direction, no hope until Bloom comes on the scene. The older man's kindness can retrieve Dedalus from the fatal consequences of the adolescent funk that he has been nurturing and can direct his artistic genius to mundane affairs, the only satisfying subject for artists, the only possible one. Stephen is found by Bloom as Dante is by Virgil, help-less, aware of his mistakes but ignorant of their remedy. He faces his danger in this passage from "Scylla and Charybdis": "Fabu-lous artificer. The hawklike man. You flew. Whereto? Newhaven-Dieppe, steerage passenger. Paris and back. Lapwing. Icarus. *Pater, ait*. Seabedabbled, fallen, weltering. Lapwing you are. Lapwing be" (*U*, 9.952–54). The answer to Stephen's cry "Pater, ait," comes in Bloom's goofy solicitude, in the practical rescue of Dedalus from Nighttown, and in the symbolic proferring of personal and artistic maturity to Stephen during the late-night conversation in "Ithaca." As guardian and instructor of an artist recovering himself, Bloom recapitulates Virgil's assistance to the pilgrim. And Stephen repeats Dante's circling through the afterlife to recoup moral and creative force, as he circles through Dublin retrospectively analyzing his own will's errors by observing humanity at large.[12]

Bloom's error is more difficult to pin down, since he is, as Joyce wanted him to be, a good man, the normative man, Odysseus. The adulterous violation of his marriage is the last consequence of the error, the event that forces him to discover what has been wrong for ten years and what needs to be done for any reconciliation with

Molly to be possible. The mistake of course is abandoning Molly sexually; what caused the deprivation is never entirely clear. Rudy's death is the efficient cause, but Bloom's personality, his response to the loss, is the material and final cause, and Joyce is not explicit about what went wrong in Poldy. The most plausible explanation, psychologically, is that Bloom fell into guilty despair when Rudy died, believing he was responsible for his son's death. Two passages from the novel suggest this. In "Lestrygonians," Bloom thinks, "Could never like it again after Rudy" (*U*, 8.610). In "Hades," after seeing a child's hearse pass, Bloom remembers his son. "A dwarf's face, mauve and wrinkled like little Rudy's was. Dwarf's body, weak as putty, in a whitelined deal box. Burial friendly society pays. Penny a week for a sod of turf. Our. Little. Beggar. Baby. Meant nothing. Mistake of nature. If it's healthy it's from the mother. If not from the man. Better luck next time" (*U*, 6.326–30). Having failed nature's fundamental requirement (reproduction) by creating a diseased, preempted extension of himself, Bloom simply drops out and gives up his natural privilege as sire, convinced he cannot enjoy it. Life has demonstrated his insufficiency, Bloom feels: there is no point in challenging the hideous evaluation nature made of him when Rudy died. Unwilling to deprive Molly utterly of sexual life, the options for Bloom are to substitute annoying peculiarities or to force her into adultery, both of which he takes, neither of which satisfy her.

Bloom has wandered for ten years in the chronic delusion that his marital responsibilities ended with Rudy's death. Until June 16, Bloom has been acting as if serving Molly breakfast in bed suitably substitutes for what nature requires she should receive there. Boylan's presence shocks Bloom into understanding that such an arrangement will not do and forces him to discover how he might put his house in order. Unlike Odysseus, Bloom recovers his wife psychologically without ousting her lover from their bed. In the course of his wandering Bloom redefines the meaning of husband, which he has distorted for ten years, so that it denotes not sexual possessiveness (a hopeless aspiration, as the passage from "Ithaca" about the series of violators indicates), but intimate understanding and delight with a lifelong companion. That discovery does little for Bloom's sexual inertia. He still has nothing better than a proximate erection at the end of this day, and that after kissing Molly's unfertilizable, diversionary bottom. She will continue seeing Boylan, plans the liaisons that night in "Penelope," but those plans do not affect Bloom's superior place in her affections, the place Bloom has resecured for himself that day by understanding the importance and insignificance of her infidelity. Given this shift in their emotional balance, given Bloom's continued sexual appetitiveness, and the confidence he has gained by surrogate fatherhood with Stephen, the possibility that Bloom could renew a full sexual life with Molly, and try for another son, seems not inconceivably remote. In that possibility Bloom enacts Odysseus's recovery of his patrimony. The difference between the two accomplishments makes for the comedy, joy, and acute psychological realism of Joyce's art and thought.

Bloom's psychological mastery of adultery is not an evasive rationalization of the crisis he has brought on but the only possible successful resolution of it. Bloom nullifies the suitor's assault on his happiness when he reaches equanimity about Molly's adultery, and in the process undoes the worst effects of his despair, the cause that forced that violation. Before Boylan, Bloom did not need to understand what his failure meant to Molly, and so compounded its damage, behaving all the while as if his marriage was safe. After Boylan, Bloom knows what his failure has meant, and what it hasn't, and through that knowledge ends the drifting anxiety he has been lost in for the entire day (and, one assumes, for ten years previous to it). Walking through Dublin, reevaluating himself and his love for Molly as those subjects are recalled to him by the chance encounters of the day, Bloom puts his house in order by reforming his will, understanding his negligence vis-à-vis his wife, and accepting its consequences (finally in "Ithaca") without evading or exaggerating them. The long sundering is reconciled that day, although the sexual alienation that has been its chief symptom persists.

Like Dante, and unlike Odysseus, Bloom returns to his lady after educating his will, because he has changed himself. The return, like Dante's, is more psychological than physical. Beatrice is dead, after all, and Dante's love for her cannot be more than spiritual. The marriage Bloom saves, like Dante's to Beatrice, lives in spiritual devotion more than in bed, where it has been lost for over a decade (the time Dante has been separated from Beatrice, according to *Purgatorio* 32, the time Odysseus has been wandering home to Penelope). Bloom's error and Dante's are sexual failures brought on by the deaths of loved ones. Whereas Dante's sin was licentiousness and promiscuity (so the *Commedia* suggests in *Purgatorio* 29–31), Poldy's is sexual negligence. Both heroes recover their happiness not by direct assault on their problems, but by understanding how they came to be through observation of the full range of the soul's actions, Dante on a detour through the next world, Bloom on a detour through Dublin. Bloom, like the Greek king, regains his marriage couch, but its fullest pleasures are not immediately (or even certainly) restored to him, as Odysseus's and Penelope's were.

Stephen, talking of Shakespeare, analyzes the playwright's career in a way that accounts nicely for the narrative structure of the *Commedia* and *Ulysses*. "He [to Stephen, Shakespeare; to Joyce, Dante, Bloom, any person] found in the world without as actual what was in his world within as possible. . . . Every life is many days, day after day. We walk through ourselves, meeting robbers, ghosts, giants, old men, young men, wives, widows, brothers-in-love, but always meeting ourselves" (*U*, 9.1041–46). Dante, of course, meets someone from all of these categories while he undertakes the journey of self-knowledge and reformation, as Bloom does in his. Bloom repeats Stephen's observation in "Nausicaa," thinking of his first meeting with Molly: "Curious she an only child, I an only child. So it returns. Think you're escaping and run into yourself. Longest way round is the shortest way home" (*U*, 13.1109–11). This last sentence improves on Stephen's metaphorical rendition of life as travel, adding to it the Dantesque idea that a detour could be the most direct, the only direct way home.

Ulysses is filled with such insinuating analyses of circular motion as self-discovery, as narrative structure. Dante of course travels in circles throughout his reformation because the circle is a Christian symbol for God, the object of Dante's pilgrimage. Bloom ends the day where he began it, at 7 Eccles Street, after wandering through Dublin. He does not go in circles repeatedly, as Dante does, but his journey has the same purpose: to discover how the crisis he has brought himself to may be successfully resolved. And Bloom thinks of his life, of all lives, as circular more than once in the novel. The excerpt from "Nausicaa" cited above continues with Bloom's calling human experience "Circus horse walking in a ring" (*U*, 13.1111–12). This bitter remark has more hopeful connotations than Bloom intends. He may feel like a mindless slave entertaining

Fate on his weary round, but Bloom's long way round also identifies him (true to Joyce's unification of opposites) with the grand success of Dante.

Here are two examples of the Dantesque action (circular detour) used as literary symbols of a metaphysical principle governing human experience. In "Circe" Stephen expatiates, through drunkenness, on the harmonic structure of renaissance church music.

STEPHEN

... The reason is because the fundamental and the dominant are separated by the greatest possible interval which. . . .

THE CAP

Which? Finish. You can't.

STEPHEN

(*with an effort*) Interval which. Is the greatest possible ellipse. Consistent with. The ultimate return. The octave. Which. . . .

STEPHEN

(*abruptly*) What went forth to the ends of the world to traverse not itself, God, the sun, Shakespeare, a commercial traveller, having itself traversed in reality itself becomes that self. Wait a moment. Wait a second. Damn that fellow's noise in the street. Self which it itself was ineluctably preconditioned to become. *Ecco!*   [*U,* 15.2005–16]

Here is an encapsulated explanation of the literary structure of Joyce's epic, a circle that absorbs contrary forms, an octave stretched over six hundred plus pages in which "the greatest possible ellipse" (Bloom's long walk) ends in "the ultimate return" (the reconciliation with Molly). The musical terms "fundamental" and "dominant" stand for Bloom and Molly, Bloom and Stephen, Bloom and Stephen before and after the crucial day, Odysseus and Bloom and Stephen, any and all of the opposites united in the novel. The travels of God, the sun, Shakespeare, etc., through which the travelers become their predestined selves, recall Bruno's idea of experience as the progressive, cyclical unfolding and implication of universal particularity in the world-soul, and Dante's spiraling journey down the pit of Hell, up the Purgatorial mountain, and through the widening nine spheres, during which he becomes himself again.

The "commercial traveller" in Stephen's passage is, of course, Bloom, whose life is rendered with the same metaphor of circular return and self-creation in "Ithaca." Poldy has been thinking of leaving Molly. Odysseus even in his fantasies, he also thinks of his subsequent return to her. The journey he imagines recapitulates his experiences in Dublin that day, and Dante's trip out to the farthest fixed points of the created universe and back, and of course, Odysseus's voyage among various people.

> Would the departed never nowhere nohow reappear?

> Ever he would wander, selfcompelled, to the extreme limit of his cometary orbit, beyond the fixed stars and variable suns and telescopic planets, astronomical waifs and strays, to the extreme boundary of space, passing from land to land, among peoples, amid events. Somewhere imperceptibly he would hear and somehow reluctantly, suncompelled, obey the summons of recall. Whence, disappearing from the constellation of the Northern Crown he would somehow reappear reborn above delta in the constellation of Cassiopeia and after incalculable eons of peregrination return an estranged avenger, a wreaker of justice on malefactors, a dark crusader, a sleeper awakened, with financial resources (by supposition) surpassing those of Rothschild or of the silver king. [*U*, 17.2012–23]

Bloom travels like Dante (another sleeper awakened for a return voyage), selfcompelled and suncompelled, choosing to recover the self which, as Stephen puts it, he "was ineluctably preconditioned to become." His errors have made the journey necessary and determined its course; his sun, the center of his universe, Molly, and his son Rudy, who caused the voyage, compel Bloom's return as well as his departure, as Dante's sun, Christ, the light of the world, compels Dante's reformation. Dante and Bloom (even Stephen, as he will discover) choose to become what they must be. They are not run out through life like trains on rails, as Stephen imagines, or like entirely mindless circus horses in a ring, as Bloom thinks, but create their happiness by willing what is necessary. This is the distribution of responsibility for experience in Bloom's selfcompelled, suncompelled trip, one Dedalus has not yet understood or assumed, one Dante spends a week among the dead to discover. Like all circles (and reconciling oppositions) freedom and necessity begin and end in the same place. As Joyce depicts it, following Dante's example, and the arguments of Aristotle and Bruno, that place is the soul.

Like the *Commedia* (unlike the *Odyssey*), *Ulysses* makes the physical wandering of its hero correlative to his psychological transformation. As in any novel, the action of *Ulysses* moves through characters who are confronting each other on some common ground and responding to each other in some dynamic way. Joyce elaborates the dense psychological and social matrix of events more than any writer in English and exhausts that strategy of representing life in telling Bloom's story. Bloom's tale also perfects the novel's other plot mechanism, episodic digression. Here the action results not so much from the transformation of long-standing relationships between various characters in a common setting, but from isolated, arbitrarily sequential events and encounters between the protagonist and many other people, some he may know, others whom he briefly encounters only once or a few times. The sequence may be integrated into the main action, as happens in Dickens's later novels, *Our Mutual Friend* for instance, or it may be left a string of diversions or occasions that reveal some quality of the protagonist without determining the story's outcome, as is true of *Pickwick Papers* and *Nicholas Nickleby*. From the beginning of the English novel in Fielding and Richardson, the two styles have been combined in plots, usually with one style dominant.

The action of *Ulysses* owes at least as much to Dante's revision of the classical epic's action as to types of plot in the novel. Like Bloom and Stephen, Dante confronts various people on his journey (many more than the Dubliners do), most of whom he has connections to. Still, his development is not a social one that these people cause, but a psychological one, a spiritual one to be more precise, for which they are the occasion. Bloom and Stephen have been made what they are by the kind of social interaction Dante analyzes but does not dramatize in his poem. *Ulysses* does not dramatize the long-term formation of their characters in Dublin on June 16—that is relegated to memory, or conversation about the past. Like Dante's poem, Joyce's book shows two men meeting, judging, and leaving acquaintances and strangers. The social and psychological interactions that would have occupied Henry James, for instance, in such situations are reduced to a minimum, and instead Joyce gives us both protagonists in the process of summing up the moral character of whomever it is they meet, evaluating their usefulness or danger, and moving on. As Dante does in the afterworld, these two have adventures in Dublin, but the adventures are corollaries for psychological events, occasions for the heroes to understand themselves, not, as in the *Odyssey*, primarily external determinations of the protagonist's behavior. To be sure, Odysseus's mind figures prominently in the action of his story. Joyce's fascination with Homer came about, to a great extent, precisely because the Greek poet presented the first intellectual hero in European art. But the Ithacan king's response to adventures, while it plays a crucial role in his deliverance, is less important in his story than the responses of Dante, and Bloom and Stephen, are in theirs. Odysseus learns many things on his voyage, and survives it because of what he knew before it started, but his education is a result of the events in his story, whereas in Dante's narrative and Joyce's the education of their heroes is the story—the cause, the content, and the result of their pilgrimage.

The double subject of Dante's *Commedia* (one man's miraculous journey, the soul's reformation and salvation) required, as Dante put it to Can Grande, a polysemous form that could present multiple topics as one. In Dante's case the polysemous form keeps the multiple senses of the journey integrated but stratified. At various points during the exploration of the three dead worlds Dante tells readers to look beneath the veil of his allegory, but he never switches allegorical and literal levels, never stops putting the pilgrim in some concrete physical setting in order to present some moral or anagogical meaning. The amplified senses of the narrative are always secondary or tertiary matters during the pilgrim's education. The primary sense is always the literal one: where the travelers are now, how much of his reformation the pilgrim has accomplished. Joyce suggests, quoting Psalm 114 in "Ithaca," that Dante's polysemous structure bears on *Ulysses*, and even one reading of the novel indicates, generally, what the influence is: Bloom's traveling has expansive moral and psychological senses for him and for humanity at large, as well as a literal (that is, literal within the fiction) narrative sense, an irreducible set of fictional facts that the symbolic senses amplify. But Joyce exceeded Dante's polysemous structure with its stratified levels of meaning when he recast the Italian epic in his own. What Dante made polysemous Joyce made polymorphous; he kept multiple senses in his epic and also multiplied their formal relations one to another.

In *Ulysses* at many points whole pages of purely symbolic writing take over the narrative, reversing the order of Dante's epic, burying the story line. "Oxen of the Sun," "Cyclops," and "Circe" are the primary examples of this. And locally in every chapter there are moments when the narrative goes under, when readers are no longer in the minds or actions of characters or any recognizable storyteller, but set loose in some amplified sense of the literal level. The effect inverts the normal function of allusions: instead of being grace notes that emphatically punctuate some narrative detail, Joyce's references to other texts or artworks, or to other places in *Ulysses*, often replace local narrative occasions.

There are other differences between Dante and Joyce that are as deliberate on Joyce's part as the resemblances. Despite the symbolic presentation of Bloom's story and the pilgrim's as the Exodus of Israel from Egypt led by Moses, and the wandering to solutions of personal problems that this metaphor represents in both epics, Joyce's action differs fundamentally from Dante's. Bloom's recovery goes on in commonplace circumstances, whereas Dante's salvation is miraculous from the first to last step; and Bloom's goal is the restitution of a very secular marriage, not the rediscovery of God's love through love of an idealized Lady. Dante's comedy is largely a matter of moral and spiritual victory, a recovery of the highest solemnity the mind could rise to; Joyce's comedy has no solemnity at all, ranges from whimsey to burlesque, and is largely a matter of reconciliation to the imperfections of experience. Mary Reynolds makes the point deftly:

> Joyce carried out his new purpose, I believe, by creating a second figure of Dante. Bloom as well as Stephen could carry the image and likeness of Dante, author and protagonist of the *Divine Comedy*, man as well as artist. The sardonic humor of Stephen Dedalus balances, in *Ulysses*, with the humanely comic perspective of Leopold Bloom. Comedy is the attribute of maturity. Joyce's comic mode (which sharply differentiates *Ulysses* and *Finnegans Wake* from the manner and atmosphere

of the early works) came into his epic when he realized that the mind of Mr Bloom (in addition to all the other artistic chores performed by this character for his author) could portray the humanistic equivalents for Dante's sense of unity, his vision of perfection, and his affirmation of life.[13]

Both authors insist that their heroes are unique figures, and both make these unique figures Everyman. Both heroes are the best men of their civilizations who have some near-mortal error to correct through prolonged self-examination "in a retrospective kind of arrangement," but Bloom's recovery, unlike Dante's, is not ostentatiously heroic, or accomplished in a direct progress through rationally ordered steps that lead to perfect knowledge of all things (the vision of God). Instead, like Odysseus, Bloom goes hither and yon, encountering people in the welter of historical circumstances—not, like Dante, observing the absolute, sequestered ranks of the good and the bad. Bloom's deliverance is not a climactic one. He slips into bed, badgered by the woman he's traveled for, with only so much glorious triumph as an unguaranteed demand for breakfast supplies.

Dante's pilgrim is normative, Everyman, because he has seen the end of all human wishes and learned what serves and ruins happiness. Bloom is also normative, but with an Odyssean difference that signals an essential departure from Dante's *Commedia* in Joyce's epic. The Ithacan king who appears in Dante's poem in *Inferno* 27 is an evil genius, the mad scientist figure of the Middle Ages, bequeathed to Dante from Virgil (Homer being unknown, except in distorted synopsis, to the Middle Ages). This villain destroyed Troy, the righteous forebear of Rome, with an intellect unmindful of any divine restrictions or human ethical standards, and he suffers in Hell for that hubris in the *Commedia*. Joyce's Odysseus is the resourceful, brainy man who survives by his free intellect, who submits everything he learns with it to the rule of civic responsibility. This Ithacan king's intellectual wherewithal is not hubris, but dignified, liberating curiosity.

Dante's classical precedent for his pilgrimage is the life of Aeneas, whose piety and general virtue, normative in the Middle Ages, Dante ascribes to himself in the *Commedia*. Joyce's hero is not pious (the equivalent of stupid in *Ulysses*); unlike Odysseus he is not even paganly religious, but empirical and atheistic. What he learns comes only by reason and sympathy; it requires no grace, no miracle. Dante conceives of the normative person as someone saved, someone who has chosen to become normal by accepting transcendent laws of being that distinguish her or him absolutely from people who have not made that choice. Normality is not elected in Joyce's book; it is what people are without choice, effort, or decision. Being ordinary in *Ulysses* does not mean discovering and willing your place in the order of being through faith, as it does in Dante's poem, nor does it mean vegetating in fatalistic or unconscious despair, as it did to Thoreau. Bloom is ordinary as Odysseus is ordinary: he has gone through the whole order of experiences necessity ordains for humanity, surviving with skills common and natural to all human minds—reason, and the persistent devising of stratagems to secure happiness. God has nothing to do with this in *Ulysses*, in fact his Roman Catholic presence in Dublin offends reason and frustrates happiness. In Dante's poem, of course, exactly the opposite is true.

Bloom does have one quality that Odysseus lacks. The Jew not only loves his wife but has kindness for humanity at large. Bloom's pacifism and sentiments of universal brotherhood go far beyond the Greek warrior's courtesy and sense of justice; they are the secular variety of the universal love Dante develops on his journey, *caritas*. Medieval Christianity, following Augustine, defined *caritas* as the love one soul feels for all others united in Christ, a religious mystery that exceeds *cupiditas*, sexual desire and all other pleasures that end in use and possession of the loved object. Bloom does not display Dante's *caritas*, since Poldy's kindnesses to Mrs. Purefoy and Mrs. Dignam are the result of interest in humanity, not divinity, but the fellow feeling that prompts him to altruism is in all other respects consistent with the Christian commandment "Love ye one another," and is a radical departure from the pagan heroism of Odysseus. In ethical matters, Poldy is the twin of Dante's pilgrim, and the opposite of the Greek king, who slaughters enemies with impunity, who is capable of charity but not *caritas*, not even its secular variety.

Bloom's fellow feeling is one narrative form that Joyce's concept of universality, of the soul's identity with all things, takes in *Ulysses*. Homer's epic gives the book its classical pedigree as a universalizing work, but in Homer the hero's universality is primarily an intellectual and empirical matter, Odysseus having seen and learned all a person can. Dante's epic gives *Ulysses* a Christian source for universality in which love makes the soul, in a manner, all that is. The *Commedia* ends with a rapturous depiction of the soul's end—loving rest in God. Dante writes of this mystical culmination to his journey:

> O abounding grace whereby I presumed to fix my look through the Eternal Light so far that all my sight was spent therein.
>
> In its depth I saw ingathered, bound by love in one single volume, that which is dispersed in leaves throughout the universe: substances and accidents and their relations, as though fused together in such a way that what I tell is but a simple light. The universal form of this knot I believe that I saw, because in telling this, I feel my joy increase.   [*Par* 33, p. 377]

Replace God (the "Eternal Light") with Everyman, with Poldy, in this passage and it becomes a comically accurate synopsis of the conceptual order of *Ulysses*, especially of the novel's last episode. This claim might give some pause. Aristotle's terminology specifying how one soul knows its relation to all that is, the Neoplatonic idea of universal particularity that eventually spawned Bruno, and the encompassing metaphor of the universal book that increases joy—these concluding philosophical terms for an exultation of love in the *Commedia* seem entirely unrelated to the love scene that closes *Ulysses*, Molly's nostalgic masturbatory fantasy. Or if they are related at all (through the fact that both Dante and Molly remember exaltation rather than directly experiencing it, and through the rose symbolism of Molly's reminiscence, for instance), it could only be through intellectual and tonal oppositions so irreconcilable that either Molly or Dante is ridiculed in the comparison.

There is some skeptical lip curling in the tone of the last pages of *Ulysses*. On Molly's part: "here we are as bad as ever after 16 years" she complains, thinking of Bloom's ineptitude as a provider, and of his gullibility where their mock-Odyssean old Cohen's bed is concerned (*U*, 18.1215–16); "as well him as another" is the deflating rationale she recalls from her final sexual choice of Bloom on that voluptuous Howth Hill afternoon (*U*, 18.1604–5). On Joyce's part: Molly has been thinking of picking up the first man she meets at the morning market immediately prior to this ending (*U*, 18.1501); she's in a shabby bed, afraid Bloom will kick her in the teeth during the night because he sleeps so oddly, annoyed that she can't even fart in comfort because of her husband's proximity (*U*, 18.905–7). Insofar as Dante figures in the finale of the book these ironic details compromise his exultant intellectualized rapture as well as Molly's sensual one. But the prickly scorn comes in scattered patches in a scene that provides unmatched exuberance and joy in human sexuality and natural beauty. The lyric intensity Joyce and Dante gave their books' last pages, the recollection of prior beauty and love's joy made to sustain a mundane, reduced present—these similar epic conclusions suggest that Joyce must have had more in mind than simply making Molly appear salacious or Dante fatuous when he coupled them as the concluding voices of Bloom's story.

Dante sees love as a book that gathers in all dispersed texts and stories, all philosophical and material oppositions, fusing them in one joyous light. Molly's womanly experience of that joy omits the philosophical rigor Dante gave it. Bloom's ethical experience of that love is reflected in the following parody of love's universality, which recapitulates Dante's joy in Paradise and reduces its divine cause to a platitude. In "Cyclops" Bloom tells the thugs in Barney Kiernan's his belief that life is love, the opposite of hatred. After Bloom leaves, the Citizen responds sardonically: "—A new apostle to the gentiles, . . . Universal love" (*U*, 12.1489). He is more right than he knows, but he can see no more truth in Bloom's remark than his next statement indicates: "He's a nice pattern of a Romeo and Juliet" (*U*, 12.1492). A parody of universal love takes over next that transforms the Citizen's mockery of Bloom into persuasive, although gruesome, whimsey.

Love loves to love love. Nurse loves the new chemist. Constable 14 A loves Mary Kelly. Gerty MacDowell loves the boy that has the bicycle. M.B. loves a fair gentleman. Li Chi Han lovey up kissy Cha Pu Chow. Jumbo, the elephant, loves Alice, the elephant. Old Mr Verschoyle with the ear trumpet loves old Mrs Verschoyle with the turnedin eye. The man in the brown macintosh loves a lady who is dead. His Majesty the King loves Her Majesty the Queen. Mrs. Norman W. Tupper loves officer Taylor. You love a certain person. And this person loves that other person because everybody loves somebody but God loves everybody. [*U*, 12.1493–1501]

That "God loves everybody" is inexpressibly true in the *Commedia* and authorizes all Dante's literary and intellectual efforts. The idea is not true in *Ulysses*, at least not a relevant issue. God aside, Bloom's reformation ends where Dante's ends, and is possible only because Poldy has at the outset what Dante only receives in Paradise—love that loves to love love.[14]

This universalizing capacity of the soul is what Dante lays out tier by tier, heaven by heaven, throughout Hell, Purgatory, and Paradise. Love has bound all the souls to their reward, love, as Virgil explains to Dante in *Purgatorio* 17 and 18, is the cause and effect of all activity in the universe. The poem's narrative and symbolic structures display the loving soul's object; their interdependence displays, as the pilgrim's journey does, the loving soul in action. The aesthetic unity of the poem's multiple senses is an image of the unity maintaining the soul's integrity through all its ingathering— the persistence of love ceaselessly maneuvering toward satisfaction. The long-suffering Odysseus, the long-suffering Dante—both are heroes whose success after perseverance glows in the reduced circumstances of Bloom's day, making the recovery of love for a lost lady an action of conceptual as well as emotional magnitude.

If the inclusion of Dante's poem has any meaning in *Ulysses*, besides puffing for Joyce's comparable genius and prophetic ambitions, it is as a precedent for the Irish infidel's philosophically copious presentation, in a multidimensional literary form, of the soul's universality. In Joyce, as in Dante, the realization of that universality comes through love, what Molly and Bloom live with imperfectly, what Dedalus needs so badly. Dante's theological exposition of the soul's universality in the *Commedia* takes sexual love as a starting point. Joyce's antitheological exposition of the soul's universality originates in analysis of carnal love, but unlike Dante's account, never exceeds it. Whether the soul is depicted through

Odysseus and Penelope, Dante and Beatrice, Bloom and Molly, or Jumbo and Alice, its universality in human affairs has the same mundane actuality for Joyce. As *Finnegans Wake* puts it: "Well, you know or don't you kennet or haven't I told you every telling has a taling and that's the he and the she of it" (*FW*, p. 213).

JOYCE *&* ARNOLD

U *lysses* opens with a confrontation between Stephen Dedalus and his host Buck Mulligan in which Mulligan criticizes Stephen's morose alienation and proposes to correct it by making Dedalus live up to the Greek pedigree his name declares. After Mulligan claims that his name too has "a Hellenic ring" because of its "two dactyls," he proposes a trip with Dedalus to Athens and then brings Swinburne into the discussion: "—God! he said quietly. Isn't the sea what Algy calls it: a great sweet mother? The snotgreen sea. The scrotum-tightening sea. *Epi oinopa ponton.* Ah, Dedalus, the Greeks! I must teach you. You must read them in the original. *Thalatta! Thalatta!* She is our great sweet mother. Come and look" (*U*, 1.77–81). The conversation moves awkwardly through a reference to Wilde's aesthetic manifesto prefacing *The Picture of Dorian Gray* until, in one last effort to win Stephen over, Mulligan again reverts to Greece: "God, Kinch, if you and I could only work together we might do something for the island. Hellenise it" (*U*, 1.157–58). This is the first reference to Matthew Arnold in *Ulysses,* and it comes from the fourth chapter of his *Culture and Anarchy,* "Hebraism and Hellenism." Don Gifford's gloss in *Ulysses Annotated* gives a clear account of how this allusion functions in the context of the late Victorian literature Mulligan and Stephen have been fencing with for the first five pages of a book named after one of the two primary Greek epics.

> The verb *to Hellenise* was coined by Matthew Arnold (1822–88) in his attempt to distinguish what he regarded as the two dominant impulses of Western culture. *To Hebraise* (by which he meant to *do* in the light of the "habits and discipline" of a revealed dogmatic truth) and to *Hellenise* (to *know* in the light

of a "disinterested" and "flexible" humanism) are concepts central to Arnold's *Culture and Anarchy* (1869), particularly Chapter 4, "Hebraism and Hellenism." Arnold argued that the English had Hebraised to excess and should Hellenise in pursuit of "our total perfection." Arnold's essentially intellectual distinction underwent a series of modulations as it was popularized in the closing decades of the nineteenth century, modulations informed in part by Swinburne's poetic development of the opposition between the sensual-aesthetic freedom of the pagan Greek world and the repressiveness of late-Victorian "Hebraism." By 1900 *Greek* had become Bohemian slang for those who preached sensual-aesthetic liberation, and *Jew* had become slang for those who were antagonistic to aesthetic values, those who preached the practical values of straightlaced Victorian morality. [*G,* 1.158n]

Mulligan's cynical reduction of Arnold's coinage, and his stagey championing, at the very start of the novel, of things Greek are both ironical flourishes introducing Joyce's fundamental metaphor in *Ulysses*: the identity of two opposites, Greek and Jew, in the book's hero, Bloom. The Buck, with his sensualism and affected animality, may wish to Hellenise Ireland, but it is Bloom, the Jew, who does that in *Ulysses*, bringing to Stephen and Dublin the values of intellectual clarity and the striving after inner perfection, the now infamous "sweetness and light" that Arnold meant by "Hellenism." Ireland is already all too Greek, in Mulligan's terms, for Stephen, as it was for Joyce, at least that part of Ireland represented by the Dublin intelligentsia who boldly sport Wilde's "decadence" as the *summum bonum.*

Mulligan's ideas of things Greek come up repeatedly in *Ulysses*, always as vain burlesques of the serious value of classical attitudes. In "Wandering Rocks," slandering Stephen to Haines, Buck says: "—They drove his wits astray, he said, by visions of hell. He will never capture the Attic note. The note of Swinburne, of all poets, the white death and the ruddy birth. That is his tragedy. He can never be a poet" (*U,* 10.1072–75). In "Scylla and Charybdis" his idea of the new paganism, complete with Wilde's sexual deviation, surfaces, connected this time in an insinuating way to cynicism about Bloom's Jewishness:

—Jehovah, collector of prepuces, is no more. I found him over in the museum when I went to hail the foamborn Aphrodite. The Greek mouth that has never been twisted in prayer. Every day we must do homage to her. *Life of life, thy lips enkindle.*
  Suddenly he turned to Stephen:
—He knows you. He knows your old fellow. O, I fear me, he is Greeker than the Greeks. His pale Galilean eyes were upon her mesial groove. Venus Kallipyge. O, the thunder of those loins! *The god pursuing the maiden hid.*   [*U*, 9.608–17]

Bloom's mixed status as a homosexual Greek-Jew comes up soon after in the same chapter: "—The wandering Jew, Buck Mulligan whispered with clown's awe. Did you see his eye? He looked upon you to lust after you. I fear thee, ancient mariner. O, Kinch, thou art in peril. Get thee a breechpad." (*U*, 9.1209–11).
  Against this gaggle of homosexuality, faithlessness, and libertinism that Dedalus scorns, Joyce poses in the person of Bloom another set of literary, moral, and intellectual values that Dedalus needs to discover. In the course of *Ulysses* Stephen and Bloom reveal that they are both both Hellenic and Hebraic in Arnold's terms, with Hellenism dominant in the Jew and Hebraism in the Greek-named gentile. The coincidence of contraries in each character, and the coincidence of the contrarily composed characters themselves, move throughout *Ulysses*, consistently casting the novel as a dramatization of Arnold's concept of the gradual accomplishment of human excellence. A brief account of Arnold's argument, and citation of its second degraded appearance in *Ulysses*, should establish the relevance of the terms "Hellenic" and "Hebrew" for analysis of the double comparison of Bloom to Moses and Odysseus that stretches across the whole epic, unifying it more consistently than any other analogy, including the Homeric one considered separately.

Arnold's *Culture and Anarchy*

Arnold begins his argument in Chapter 1, "Sweetness and Light," by dismissing those definitions that render culture arcane intellectual achievement (knowledge of Latin and Greek, especially scanty knowledge) and dandyism relevant only to the intelligentsia, to critics and pedants, chief residents in the lotus land of belles lettres. His aim is to show the political necessity of culture for any nation whose aspirations include realizing human excellence. "Political" should not mislead here. Arnold has no systematic plan for distribution of economic, legal, or military power in mind when he talks of culture's political value. He means instead to indicate why culture is necessary in political life, what its function is, and what self-evident reasons there are to believe in its efficacy.

To remove culture from the stink of amateurish academics, Arnold first analyzes the two constitutive motives of all cultural pursuits. The first is curiosity, by which he means "a liberal and intelligent eagerness about things of the mind."[1] This curiosity is the "scientific passion," in his terms "a desire after the things of the mind simply for their own sakes and for the pleasure of seeing them as they are" (CA, pp. 472, 473). The second motive, which he calls "the main and preeminent part" is "the moral and social passion for doing good" (CA, p. 473). As natural as the scientific passion, this motive aims at perfecting humanity, which ultimately means making "reason and the will of God prevail" (CA, p. 473). God here is not in any sense a transcendental being, or even a theological one. Instead of piety, Arnold's religious term denotes a rationalist's sense of the natural social order. The scientific passion seeks natural satisfaction in drawing "towards a knowledge of the universal order which seems to be intended and aimed at in the world" (Arnold's definition of the will of God); the moral passion seeks the same satisfaction in making this order prevail, and so ensuring man's happiness by creating the only conditions conducive to his perfection (CA, p. 475). Wanting to know what is true, and so, valuable, and wanting to do what is truly valuable; these are the contrary motives that must coalesce for culture to exist and advance.

In Arnold's argument, culture originates in the personality for the sake of personal happiness. Since the passion and the satisfaction of curiosity and duty are both immaterial, and culture itself nothing except a spiritual condition, it would not be unfair to say Arnold thinks of it as a state of the soul. Although he never uses that term, he does write:

Religion says: *The kingdom of God is within you;* and culture, in like manner, places human perfection in an *internal* condition, in the growth and predominance of our humanity proper, as distinguished from our animality. It places it in the ever-increasing efficacy and in the general harmonious expansion of those gifts of thought and feeling, which make the peculiar dignity, wealth and happiness of human nature. As I have said on a former occasion: "It is in making endless additions to itself, in the endless expansion of its powers, in endless growth in wisdom and beauty, that the spirit of the human race finds its ideal. To reach this ideal, culture is an indispensable aid, and that is the true value of culture." Not a having and a resting, but a growing and becoming, is the character of perfection as culture conceives it; and here, too, it coincides with religion.   [*CA*, p. 476]

Personal as culture is, it cannot exist in isolated individuals. Because people are by nature sympathetic to one another and recognize each other as "members of one great whole," they must pursue the perfecting aims of culture generally (*CA*, p. 476). They will not experience the internal presence of culture if others around them do not. Arnold takes eloquent pains to insist that the spiritual and therefore individual benefits of culture only result from social aspiration toward equality for all citizens.

The great men of culture are those who have had a passion for diffusing, for making prevail, for carrying from one end of society to the other, the best knowledge, the best ideas of their time; who have laboured to divest knowledge of all that was harsh, uncouth, difficult, abstract, professional, exclusive; to humanise it, to make it efficient outside the clique of the cultivated and learned, yet still remaining the *best* knowledge and thought of the time, and a true source therefore, of sweetness and light.   [*CA*, p. 499]

Just as all individuals must be included for one individual to experience culture, so "*all* the powers which make the beauty and worth of human nature" will be developed by a cultivated citizen; none in isolation, but all in "harmonious expansion" (*CA*, p. 477). This assertion of culture's general presence in society brings Arnold to a statement of its function. Culture, "which consists in becoming something rather than in having something, in an inward condition of the mind and spirit, not in an outward set of circumstances, " exists to free humanity, particularly the British in Arnold's case, from civilization's mechanisms—industrial and institutional— which substitute material possession, or public esteem and political authority, for internal longing after truth and goodness (CA, p. 477). Culture offers a "spiritual standard of perfection" characterized in part by "sweetness and light" (beauty and intelligence) (*CA*, p. 483). Loving these, an individual becomes human; ignoring them he or she reverts to mechanized animality, becomes a Philistine. The political value of culture, put most simply, is to make perfect people, or at least people who study perfection, and will therefore move to free Britain, or any nation, from the tyranny of mechanized values. Knowing and advancing the authority of "sweetness and light," people of culture will bring the universal order into being, the order Philistines impede, disrupt, and ignorantly scorn.

The next two sections of Arnold's argument are mostly analysis of the specific social conditions culture must battle against in England and do not advance the book's conceptual structure much. Two points do bear on the idea of culture however, specifically on what the struggle to make perfection prevail involves psychologically, and who is most likely to endure that struggle. Arnold divides English society into the aristocracy, the middle class, and the populace. The aristocracy, impervious to new ideas because it exists by enshrining the old ideas that have gained it privilege, has no yearning for light, the pursuit of truth, and so it cannot advance culture. The middle class, determined to reach a certain level of material prosperity without interference or help from the state, relying solely on individual initiative to attain and maintain a fixed level of comfort, is indifferent, in fact hostile, to the first law of culture, which requires that perfection take place not in satisfied being, but in perpetual striving for more human excellence. The populace, uneducated, has no notion of the spiritual standard of perfection and is too busy trying to secure material well-being to learn anything about it. Who then will make culture prevail?

Each class includes a certain number of people Arnold calls "aliens," "persons who are mainly led, not by their class spirit, but by a general *humane* spirit, by the love of human perfection" (*CA*,

p. 538). This alien indicates the best self hidden in the ordinary self of any member of any class. Culture will only prevail when general conditions encourage the alien best self to struggle for its perfection. Although Arnold insists that the aliens come from all classes, one part of his argument implies, indirectly, that the middle class aliens have the best chance to make culture prevail. Each group's characteristic excellence has a defect. The aristocrats, extreme in the protection of their elegant status quo, are prone to grow precious. When their world is challenged they cannot defend it but collapse, like wedding cakes in a rainstorm. The middle-class defect is lack of satisfaction in the condition that it has come to through great effort. The defect of the populace, which acts with thoughtless ferocity and solidarity when it is strong, is selfishness and desperate hedonism, paralysis in the obverse mode of that helplessness which overcomes aristocrats. Arnold offers himself as an example of the defective middle class, in terms that suggest but do not proclaim that this defect might go farther than the strengths or defects of the other classes toward creating the conditions under which aliens could bring culture, a nation's best self, into being. Describing his longing for sweetness and light Arnold writes: "The line, again, of a still unsatisfied seeker which I have followed, the idea of self-transformation, of growing towards some measure of sweetness and light not yet reached, is evidently at clean variance with the perfect self-satisfaction current in my class, the middle class, and may serve to indicate in me, therefore, the extreme defect of this feeling" (*CA*, p. 528). Having established that only the alien, best self can make culture prevail, Arnold needs to explain the cause of this split between ordinary and cultural mentality in order to show how perfection, limited by human mortality and weakness, might come to be. This he does in part four, "Hebraism and Hellenism."

He begins by arguing that the English prefer action over thought, and so readily adhere to unexamined standards of value, mistaking the ordinary self for the best one, too often making the ordinary self the only one. This ready adherence comes from the preeminent power of duty and effective common sense in the English. Against this power, Arnold sets its necessary partner, intellectual analysis and assertion of which ideas should govern duty and the urge to its practical achievement. The two forces, which Arnold says divide "the empire of the world between them," are Hebraism, character-

ized by obedient conduct, and Hellenism, characterized by purely
intellectual curiosity (*CA*, p. 558). Both aim at human perfection,
Hebraism through rigid adherence to unchanging, simple prescrip-
tions of human excellence, Hellenism through constantly adjusted
analysis of any and all indications of human excellence, through a
refusal to settle for a program fixed by tradition or any authority
except the desire to gain objective insight into the conditions that
encourage human happiness and the development of the best self.
As Arnold summarizes it: "The governing idea of Hellenism is
spontaneity of consciousness; that of Hebraism, *strictness of conscience*" (*CA*, pp. 560–61). These contrary urges are the ground for
the impulse to know and to do the good, the impulses that combine
to create a cultivated spirit.

These two impulses together make up the development of human history. They are both natural attempts to make the universal
order prevail. Their ideal relationship would be symbiotic; their
real connection has been a waxing and waning mutual antagonism,
with dominance oscillating between them from historical period to
period, neither force ever vanquished utterly. The vacillation is dia-
lectical, or to use Arnold's phrase, "evolutionary." What evolves is
the human spirit. Arnold ends his book by arguing that Hellenism
started this evolution, prevailed until Christianity, a form of Hebraism, conquered it, and reasserted itself in the Renaissance, where it
was again superseded by the Protestant Reformation, a period not
free of Hellenic qualities, but dominated by the idea of duty, strictness of conscience, and a distrust of the free play of the intellect.
This last movement has led England, in Arnold's view, to rely
solely on the ordinary self, whose activity has degenerated into
sterile, mechanical adherence to materialistic values that are bringing England to chaos. The absence of Hellenism has meant an absence of cultivated people, which has caused anarchy—isolated in-
dividualistic pursuit of mechanical happiness—to threaten the nation's political life. The remedy Arnold proposes is a resurgence of
intellectual questioning and a consequent purification of England's
conception and pursuit of happiness, a combination, as his conclusion indicates, of the two laws "Hebraism" and "Hellenism."

Four propositions from *Culture and Anarchy* are especially relevant to Joyce's *Ulysses*. First: that culture is a spiritual condition—

not material possession, social status, or privilege. A cultured soul strives after the perfection of the universal order apparent in nature, and in so doing strives for the fullest development of the best self, the greatest happiness that mortality and prevailing circumstances will allow. Second: that culture's struggle has two contrary forces that must function harmoniously for happiness to flourish— the desire to know what is truly valuable for its own sake (Hellenism) and the desire to do what is truly valuable for its own sake (Hebraism). Together these forces direct human history. Third: that the cultured individual cannot be isolated but must pursue true knowing and good doing for all. The aliens, who more than anyone advance sweetness and light because they are dissatisfied with the ordinary virtues of their class, can never achieve their best selves or reform their society if they are utterly alienated from it. Fourth: that this inward state is continuously progressing, never at rest or satisfied with the development of isolated capacities, but always eager to achieve complete well-being by developing the complete set of resources for happiness that nature's universal order displays as humanity's best fate. Together Stephen and Bloom bring these ideas into Dublin. To Stephen first.

"Hellenism" and "Hebraism" in *Ulysses*

Arnold's *Culture and Anarchy* puts in a second appearance in *Ulysses* in "Circe," again connected to Stephen Dedalus. In a sequence where Stephen thinks about the ruination of his artistic career and ways to salvage his future, the whore Florry asks him to sing to her.

(*The Siamese twins, Philip Drunk and Philip Sober, two Oxford Dons with lawnmowers, appear in the window embrasure. Both are masked with Matthew Arnold's face.*)

PHILIP SOBER

Take a fool's advice. All is not well. Work it out with the buttend of a pencil, like a good young idiot. Three pounds twelve you got, two notes, one sovereign, two crowns, if youth but knew. Mooney's en ville, Mooney's sur mer, the Moira, Larchet's , Holles street Hospital, Burke's. Eh? I am watching you.

PHILIP DRUNK

(*impatiently*) Ah, bosh, man. Go to hell! I paid my way. If I
could only find out about octaves. Reduplication of personality.
Who was it told me his name? (his lawnmower begins to purr)
Aha, yes. *Zoe mou sas agapo*. Have a notion I was here before.
When was it not Atkinson his card I have somewhere. Mac
Somebody. Unmack I have it. He told me about, hold on, Swin-
burne, was it, no?   [*U*, 15.2512–27]

This comic pair, ancestors of the good and bad angels or advisors
who appear in so many cartoons tempting and guiding a faltering
hero or heroine (and derived from a legendary story of Alexander
the Great's father, Philip of Macedon), present themselves to Stephen as spokesmen for Hebraism (Philip Sober) and Hellenism
(Philip Drunk). The first keeps an eye on Stephen's money, as
Bloom does, and implies that Dedalus is wrecking his talent by
squandering resources on drink. (See Bloom's conversation with
Stephen in "Eumaeus," especially 16.62, where Bloom is called
"disgustingly sober." See also 16.85–95, 1138–71, and especially
1819–65, where Bloom plans a singing career for the youth who
would not please the whores with a song.) Philip Sober speaks with
the voice of duty, practical efficiency, moral severity, and chastity
that belong to Arnold's Hebraism. He wants Stephen to do the right
thing. Philip Drunk, quoting Byron's Greek (which translates to
"My life, I love you," and "My Zoe"—one of the whores present—
"I love you"), and referring to Swinburne in his eagerness to know
arcane intellectual details for their own sake (the relationship of
octaves to duplication of personality), identifies himself unmistakably as the degraded mimic of Arnold's Hellenism. He carries on
the reduction of that concept of intellectual and moral freedom
introduced by Mulligan in the novel's first scene, the place where
Arnold is first imagined as a gardener with a lawnmower by Stephen (*U*, 1.172–75). The twins offer Stephen, ironically, two ways
back to an artistic career—knowing the good and doing it, the two
forces Arnold says determine the growth of the soul toward culture.

As Siamese twins, one of whom is groping through an alcoholic
brain-fog to remember something about twinning in music and in
human personality, Philip Sober and Philip Drunk dramatize, with

gruesome comedy, Arnold's insistence that Hellenism and Hebraism act best together. Appearing to Dedalus they indicate how much this young man needs to develop the real spontaneity and zeal of conscience that their zany antics distort. To become an artist Dedalus must acquire intellectual flexibility, scientific objectivity, and some sense of responsibility to the talent that is threatened by his desperate hedonism on the one hand (degenerate Hellenism), and his fanatical obssession with Catholicism's cruelty and authoritarian vengeance on the other (degenerate Hebraism). Bloom practices those virtues the twins ape, and it is through his acquaintance with Bloom that Dedalus is exposed to their saving grace.

Stephen's symbolic association with the Hellenic-Hebraic pair is not merely attached to him by various narrative voices. Dedalus thinks of the connection of these forces himself, twice, and so establishes a realistic source for the symbolic analogies. In "Proteus," thinking of the origin of life, he mocks mystic returns to the beginning of all things by casting such illumination as a telephone call to Eden. "Will you be as Gods? Gaze in your *omphalos*. Kinch here. Put me on to Edenville. Aleph, alpha: nought, nought, one" (*U*, 3.38–40). The Hebraic elements here are variations on the Eden story and the coupling of "aleph," the first letter in the Hebrew alphabet, with "alpha," the first letter in the Greek one. In addition to this polyglot phone number, Dedalus recalls Mulligan's Greek term for the tower, "omphalos" (navel) while he plays with ideas of origin (*U*, 1.544). Mysticism is ridiculed in this combination of Hellenic and Hebraic elements, but Arnold's idea that these forces are the origin of all human activity holds in *Ulysses*, despite the slur Stephen incidentally casts on them at this point.

The next time Dedalus thinks of the connection, it is mocked again, but now he is more ambiguous about the concept's validity. In "Circe" Stephen starts a philosophical disquisition about harmonics when he plays the piano, which provokes the following surrealistic episode. Lynch has been the audience for the speculations, and his cap returns this acknowledgement of them to Dedalus: "(with saturnine spleen) Ba! It is because it is. Woman's reason. Jewgreek is greekjew. Extremes meet. Death is the highest form of life. Ba!" (*U*, 15.2097–98). Dedalus responds: "You remember fairly accurately all my errors, boasts, mistakes. How long shall I close my eyes to disloyalty? Whetstone!" (*U*, 15.2100–2101), and then he proceeds to offer, resentfully, hoping to be scorned, a Neoplatonic analysis of the octave (Philip Drunk's mock Hellenic topic) as an image of the soul's procession from and return to the One (*U*, 15.2104–21). This speech returns Stephen to the realistic narrative, ending with Lynch, not, as in the first case, Lynch's cap, mocking Dedalus.

Certainly Arnold's *Culture and Anarchy* cannot be cited as the only source for Stephen's idea of opposites coinciding, but the terms "Jewgreek" and "greekjew" have their origin in that book in Stephen's world. Even if Dedalus has never read it—which seems unlikely given his fantasy involving Arnold at Oxford that follows Mulligan's introduction of the term Hellenism into the novel (*U*, 1.165–75)—the argument for the coincidence of Hellenism and Hebraism obviously bears on those recent intellectual and artistic heroics that he despairs over in this scene, in the schoolroom scene, and throughout the day.

Despair, in short, is Stephen's problem in *Ulysses*. Like Telemachus, like Hamlet, this son of an absent father feels compelled to act and equally unable to act. His failed mission to the Continent, which was to have made him the creator of his race's conscience, its moral and intellectual soul, haunts, mocks, paralyzes him. Back in Dublin for a year (the time elapsed since his mother's death cut short his self-imposed exile and initiated his resentful, guilt-ridden inertia), Stephen exhibits all the defects Arnold saw in English society. He is helpless to fight against the brutal worldly circumstances that have curtailed his exquisite dream because, like the aristocrats, his temperament is too delicate, too refined; he is utterly dissatisfied with himself and his lot, like the failed middle-class spirits in Arnold's argument; and like the populace of Arnold's England, he falls into hedonism and defeatism after his return to what he views as hostile and invincible authoritarian Dublin. Ironically, his mother's death, forcing him to face reality (the artist's only subject) in a way he has never had to, qualifies Stephen for his messianic literary career more powerfully than his romantic aspirations to satanic exile ever did. But Dedalus cannot view things this way: for him, the death is God's attack on his rebellion, the family's attempt, and the church's, to enslave, once more, his artist's soul. The moral and intellectual values of the conscience he was to create for Ireland have vanished from his own life. In Arnold's terms, he cannot see things as they are for their own sake, and so can do nothing to make sweetness and light prevail.

Two characters describe Stephen's problem as defective Hellenism or Hebraism in the novel. Buck Mulligan tells Dedalus that his religious sense of duty is perverted: "You wouldn't kneel down to pray for your mother on her deathbed when she asked you. Why? Because you have the cursed jesuit strain in you, only its injected the wrong way" (*U*, 1.207–9). Professor MacHugh, the Hellenophile, diagnoses Stephen's alienation this way: "—You remind me of Antisthenes, the professor said, a disciple of Gorgias, the sophist. It is said of him that none could tell if he were bitterer against others or against himself. He was the son of a noble and a bondwoman. And he wrote a book in which he took away the palm of beauty from Argive Helen and handed it to poor Penelope" (*U*, 7.1035–39). This link of Dedalus to a Greek reviser of Homer comes just after Stephen's parable, which, soon after the reference to Antisthenes, receives the Hebrew subtitle "A Pisgah Sight of Palestine" (*U*, 7.1057–58). The connection of Greek and Hebrew elements in Stephen's second literary effort of the day, and the quality of those elements—sophistry and riddling ambiguity, both caustic, both at extreme distance from the sweetness and light, the moral clarity and zeal of Hellenism and Hebraism as Arnold defined them —all this, together with the other examples cited above, clearly sets the terms from *Culture and Anarchy* as relevant items for understanding Stephen's spiritual collapse in the novel. Urgent to free his best self for the intellectual and moral action a writer must perform to bring beauty into the world, Dedalus flails about, trapped by defective Hebraism—guilt, shame, zealous self-hatred— and defective Hellenism—carousing, anarchic intellectual sniping, obsessive retreat from any responsible action. Dedalus does not need to kill anyone to recover from this situation, unlike his symbolic double Hamlet, who shares the same symptoms. As Joyce presents him, Dedalus will only be relieved from adolescent anguish as Telemachus is, by the superior moral and intellectual power of a father, the preeminent Greek father Odysseus, as he is reincarnated in the Jew Bloom (minus, of course, the violence of Odysseus's vengeful restoration of culture to Ithaca).

In the course of *Ulysses* Bloom exhibits Arnold's Hellenic and Hebraic impulses continually. In their degraded and their original form, sweetness and light and zeal for duty emerge repeatedly, usually comically, as controlling forces of Bloom's Odyssey and Exodus on June 16. Very often they converge in the symbolic or narrative detailing of scenes, but they also appear separately when one of Bloom's two natures momentarily eclipses the other. Since Bloom's sexuality governs so much of *Ulysses*, it seems reasonable to begin arguing for the relevance of Arnold's terms with analysis of Jewish Poldy's degraded Hellenism, particularly the sexual licentiousness and domestic instability of *la vie de bohème* espoused by the fast set in which Stephen moves so precariously.

When, in the passage from "Scylla and Charybdis" already quoted above, Mulligan charges Bloom with being "greeker than the greeks" for spying out the nonexistent anus of a statue representing Aphrodite, he makes the right identification of Bloom's sexual life for the wrong reason (*U*, 9.614–15). Poldy in the museum is not covertly indulging homosexual fantasies, as Mulligan warns Stephen, but trying to satisfy scientific curiosity about paganism through observation: Did Greek anthropomorphic religion extend to messy details? The experimental observation of course does have a sexual component, but it is not the inversion Mulligan means when he says "Greek."[2] Bloom (like his creator) favors female bottoms, to the extent of favoring what passes through them as well, and he approaches the goddess with both sexual and scientific curiosity.

This identification of licentiousness and things Greek also extends to a living object of Bloom's lewd ardor, Gerty MacDowell. His partner in masturbation in "Nausicaa," Gerty is first introduced in that chapter this way: "The waxen pallor of her face was almost spiritual in its ivorylike purity though her rosebud mouth was a genuine Cupid's bow, Greekly perfect" (*U*, 13.87–89). This sentence clearly links her to the Aphrodite Bloom has nosed about, both by making her a statue with characteristics of Aphrodite's son Cupid, and by naming her "Greek"; but it also links her to a Jewish beauty, the Virgin, through the terms "waxen pallor" and "ivorylike" that give off the light of Mariolatry (wax for the candles around the statue, ivory for Mary's liturgical identity as tower of ivory) as clearly as they do the glossy sheen of sentimental painterly appreciation, this chapter's version of Arnold's bright Hellenic sweetness. Finally, the words "spiritual" and "purity" perfect the identity of this spiteful, pathetic, wasted girl (who wears Mary's blue) with the Virgin. Naughty sex, fruitless sex, free sex may all be termed "Greek" in Bloom's world thanks to Arnold, but the Victorian's conception of the soul's growth toward culture requires that Hellenism meet Hebraism, and consequently, even in its degraded form, the Greek impulse has a Jewish component in Bloom.

Poldy's other sexual infidelity, with Martha Clifford (more accurately, his titillating flirtation—he seems not to want any actual carnal knowledge of her, as his response to her letter in "Lotus Eaters" indicates), also has Greek elements (*U*, 5.270–72). The epistolary romance (partly a realistic narrative device, partly a parody of epistolary fiction, and partly an item in the encyclopedic account of literary forms Joyce wanted *Ulysses* to be) goes on in secret, with at least Bloom, and probably Martha Clifford, using an alias and sending correspondence to P.O. boxes. Under the name Henry Flower, Bloom has advertised in *The Irish Times* for an amatory pen pal and has chosen Martha out of forty-four respondents (*U*, 8.323–26). Bloom's list of Molly's possible adulterous companions only includes twenty-five names (*U*, 17.2132–42). In the critical rush to make Molly appear the licentious violator of a timid spouse, this discrepancy between the Blooms' potential infidelities has gone unnoticed. They both actually cheat on each other on June 16, Molly heartily in the official Catholic sense, and Bloom in furtive masturbation with Gerty, but when it comes to psychological straying, Bloom, who loves his wife entirely, exceeds her wandering lust by almost two to one. Why he chose Martha over the other forty-three respondents is never entirely clear. One, Lizzie Twigg, disqualified herself as a blue stocking (*U*, 8.330–33), but no other cause for Martha's success is given. Her readiness to be angry and punish Henry is the closest Joyce gets to offering an explanation for Bloom's choice, Poldy being inclined to submissiveness, to put the matter politely, where the struggle of the sexes is concerned (*U*, 5.273–74).

To return to the Greek connection. In "Sirens" Bloom, dining with Richie Goulding in the Ormond Hotel, replies to Martha's note, which he thinks of in "Nausicaa" as "her silly I will punish you letter" (*U*, 13.787). At the moment he so characterized the letter, Bloom was congratulating himself on not wasting masturbation's joy on Martha but saving it for what Joyce calls the "Greekly perfect" charms of Gerty. In the Ormond Hotel things Greek emerge in Bloom's sexual life again, as he reminds himself to continue the habitual secrecy of his correspondence by disguising his handwriting with "Greek ees" (U, 11.860). After he has left the Ormond Hotel, Bloom makes a special detour to mail his letter of epsilons, during which he dodges "round by Greek street" (U, 11.1181). All the Hellenic paraphernalia obviously pertains because Bloom is Odysseus carrying out one of the many-minded mariner's schemes, but it pertains apart from this symbolic decorum as well, since "Greek" in Bloom's day, thanks ironically to Arnold via Swinburne and crew, meant exactly the kind of sexual frankness and license to which Bloom aspires in his epistolary espionage. Of course the fact that this frank license is hemmed in by secrecy, disguises, and a resolution on Bloom's part to have no sexual involvement with Martha makes a burlesque of Poldy's "Greek" prowess, which is exactly fitting to Joyce's mock-epic purpose. Since Bloom's nobler Greek virtues, Odyssean prudence, savvy, resourcefulness, get such a rough ride in *Ulysses*, depiction of his shabbier Hellenism naturally calls for the genial derision Bloom's doubly unheroic infidelities inspire.

Greek Henry's Martha, like his Gerty, also has a connection to a Jewess, to Martha the sister of Lazarus and Mary of Bethany. When he finishes reading Martha's letter in "Lotus Eaters," Bloom associates the pin enclosed in it with women's clothes in general and with a song he heard sluts sing once, "O, Mary lost the pin of her drawers" (U, 5.281). This leads him to think of Martha and Mary paired as Christ's friends in a picture he once saw, partly since Christ has a redemptive connection to prostitutes, as well as to women named Mary and Martha. Bloom makes the association equivocally, in a way that indicates he is not entirely familiar with the Biblical story.

Martha, Mary. I saw that picture somewhere I forget now old master or faked for money. He is sitting in their house, talking. Mysterious. Also the two sluts in the Coombe would listen.
To keep it up.
Nice kind of evening feeling. No more wandering about. Just loll there: quiet dusk: let everything rip. Forget. Tell about places you have been, strange customs. The other one, jar on

her head, was getting the supper: fruit, olives, lovely cool water out of a well, stonecold like the hole in the wall at Ashtown. Must carry a paper goblet next time I go to the trotting-matches. She listens with big dark soft eyes. Tell her: more and more: all. Then a sigh: silence. Long long long rest.

[*U*, 5.289–99]

Joyce has conflated Homer's *Odyssey* and the New Testament here, characterizing Christ's friendly ease at Bethany, one of the only domestic moments in Christ's ministry, as Odysseus's dangerous stay in the land of lotus ("No more wandering about. Just loll there: . . . let everything rip. Forget. . . . Long long long rest"). He has Bloom unknowingly superimpose the Greek text on the Jewish one in order to carry out the symbolic design of opposites united. But there is also something crucial being conveyed about Poldy's narrative situation here. In this excerpt Bloom apparently thinks Martha is the listener and Mary the homebody. As "Ithaca" indicates, there has been no mental intercourse, no listening, between Molly and Bloom for "9 months and 1 day" (*U*, 17.2289). The correspondence with Martha has been undertaken largely for Bloom to have an affectionate female audience to replace Molly. In his fantasy Bloom recreates the New Testament story with himself as Christ and his correspondent Martha as the listener whose dark soft eyes have replaced Molly's, whose sighing and silence offer the rest Molly's domineering and badgering have taken from him. The joke here is that Bloom recreates the Biblical scene in reverse; he remembers that one sister was active and one contemplative, but associates his Martha with the Jewish listener when in fact Martha is the active one gently rebuked by Christ for her impatience with contemplative Mary. Arnold's definition of Hellenism and Hebraism as thought and action applies perfectly to the gospel story, which is constructed on that opposition, and in which Christ, like Arnold, ultimately calls contemplation the better portion of the two necessary impulses in human life (Luke 10:38–42).

One of the slang connotations of "Greek" in Bloom's world derives from a slang meaning of "Jew." "Jews" maintain straightlaced Victorian morality; they are solid citizens with permanent residences and permanent jobs, they *provide* in stable measure with stable means the economic security that keeps the family solvent and in one place. "Greeks" are fancy-free, live as they can, move about, do not have jobs that restrict their sensual or aesthetic liberty, do not commit themselves to familial stability. The distinction Joyce makes in *Finnegans Wake* between the "Ondt" and the "Gracehoper" is the distinction Edwardian England and Ireland made between the prudent "Jew" and the imprudent "Greek," a distinction exploited extensively in *Ulysses*. It has become a critical rule to distinguish Stephen as the penniless Greek opposed to the faulty champion of middle-class values, Jewish Bloom. The rule applies, but like almost every rule for analysis of this book, its opposite also does. Bloom's domestic and financial life has been shaky from the start, and it is by no means a fixed entity on the day Stephen meets him and presumably observes the benefits of providence in the middle-class. Two kinds of evidence (in addition to the sexual irregularities of both spouses) display the "Greek" laxity of Bloom's domicile: the number of times he has changed it, moved, and the number of jobs he has changed, often because he has been removed from them.

In sixteen years of marriage Bloom has lived in eight houses, none of which he has owned, and for at least three of those years he cannot be located at any address at all. His residence, or residences, for the seven years preceding his marriage are also left a mystery. In any novel the characters' homes are crucial factors. For Joyce, fixated on realistic narrative details, not to locate his protagonist anywhere for at least ten of the man's thirty-eight years, almost one quarter of his life, some crucial issue must be at stake, something very telling about Bloom. Why all the shuffling, why the narrative gaps? In *The Chronicle of Leopold and Molly Bloom* John Henry Raleigh details extensively the conditions of life for Bloom, single and married, at all his various addresses, but he does not specify, because Joyce did not, exactly why Bloom moves so much.[3] Money is one clear reason. Single or married Bloom has never had enough capital to buy a house. How his father collected enough to buy the Queen's Hotel is a mystery, but there is no mystery about the fact that the property never descended to Poldy. Surely Bloom could have stayed in one rental for more than four years in his adult life if he had wanted to. At the narrative level his wandering could be put down to restlessness and dissatisfaction with the various accommodations, but Joyce provides scant evidence for either conclusion.

The cause for this set of realistic facts shows up more clearly in the book's symbolic structure. Odysseus Bloom is a Greek Jew: on one hand a libertine Bohemian wanderer (Arnold's "Greek") in search of a forsaken patrimony (Homer's heroic Greek); on the other hand a struggling, cursed exile who cannot find entrance in a strange land (biblical Jew) and an industrious but perpetually unsuccessful provider of middle-class comfort (Arnold's Jew). Poldy's domestic situation, like his sexual one, emerges from his mock-heroic stature, a coincidence of contrary identities persistently displayed in the paradoxical union of opposed meanings for "Greek" and "Jew."

Bloom's domestic wandering is outdone by his economic hegira. There is some narrative account for at least two of Bloom's dismissals: he played the know-it-all with Cuffe and was therefore fired, according to Molly's recollection in "Penelope" (*U*, 18.510–12), and lost his second job with Hely for the same reason (*U*, 8.131–42). The same symbolic meanings for his homelessness apply to his chronic joblessness: Bloom as "Greek" is improvident (slang Arnold) and, according to his Homeric pedigree, wily. This second quality, Odyssean prudence, should keep him solvent, but Joyce bends the virtue into a comic disability by having it appear too often in Poldy's life as insensitive one-upmanship over his employers. Scheming at least keeps Bloom in the running: after every lost job some stratagem lands him a new one. But stratagems, most likely, will cost him whatever economic security he gains. And they are not always successful—recall his Royal Hungarian lottery fiasco in 1893.

The prudent stratagem supplanting a steady career in one field also has its Jewish aspect. In "Cyclops," recalling the lottery, the narrator lets go one of many antisemitic blasts in that chapter and characterizes Bloom as insolvent because he is inept at being Jewish, that is, he is a failure as a crook. "He was bloody safe he wasn't run in himself under the act that time as a rogue and vagabond only he had a friend in court. Selling bazaar tickets or what do you call it royal Hungarian privileged lottery. True as you're there. O, commend me to an israelite! Royal and privileged Hungarian robbery" (*U*, 12.775–79). Joyce also works the ritualistic exclusion of Jews from respectable professions into Bloom's life, making him a denizen of the economic demimonde—a debt collector, a kind of bookie, a salesman of cheap religious trinkets—as well as a minor functionary in more solid enterprises (a newspaper, a stationers, political campaigns, the cattle industry, etc.). There are Jews in *Ulysses* who make a go of it as small businessmen—Mesias, Bloom's tailor, and Dlugacz the butcher—but Poldy is not one of them. He certainly lacks none of the intelligence or industry necessary to keep secure economically, but his personality and his luck somehow drive him away from every possibility of long-term solvency. In biblical terms, Bloom is the cursed Jew who will not prosper because, like Odysseus, supernatural forces are set on punishing him for offenses. In Arnold's terms, slang and serious, Bloom is a burlesque of the values of "Hebraism," a parody of the practical solid citizen devoted to providing security against the penury that ruins happiness and so ruins culture.

On June 16 Bloom is by no means poor: if all his efforts of the day pan out he will be, as he himself puts it, "on the pig's back" (*U*, 8.1060). And there is Molly's concert tour with Boylan, a successful entrepreneur, immediately pending. But the gains here are uncertain, as is all of Bloom's economic future. His greatest economic stability lies in mysteriously acquired holdings in Canadian securities, £900 at 4 percent interest, free of tax duty, which earns him £36 annually. None of this adds up to prosperity, none of it relieves Molly's disgust with enforced frugality in her wardrobe and household expenses. The stocks are there if disaster comes, but they are supplementary funds and could not hold out long if, as is highly likely, Bloom continues losing every job he narrowly lands to replace the last lost one. When it comes to money, when it comes to housing, Bloom is more "Greek" in the worst sense of Arnold's term than his Homeric association suggests. The failures of his Jewish worldliness locate him more solidly in the Bohemian world of "Greek" improvidence than has previously been noticed.

The authentic value of Arnold's Hellenism applies to Bloom as well: the scientific passion to know things as they are. Odysseus Bloom often comes close to making a shambles of scientific curiosity in his imperfectly empirical ruminations, but his errors do not nullify the virtue of his inner struggle to see the true order of things. Joyce's comedy habitually renders every good ludicrous in some way, both to display human freedom over any prescriptive code of happiness, and to test the permanent value of whatever people pursue. Mulligan's ideas of Hellenism are never more than ludicrous in *Ulysses*, but Arnold's, in great part because Bloom displays them with the unconscious ease that guarantees frequent error, persistently emerge in the novel as one half of the soul's creative vitality, one face, in literary terms, of epic heroism. Poldy makes technically scientific queries and experiments throughout *Ulysses*— so many that citing them all would bloat this section of my argument. I offer a small portion of them as evidence for the case that whenever Joyce is satirizing Bloom's scientific investigations—for example, when in "Cyclops" he mocks the Greek Jew's intellect and German scientists by distinguishing his hero as "the distinguished scientist Herr Professor Luitpold Blumenduft" (*U*, 12.468)—he is also exalting the spiritual ambition Arnold earlier termed Hellenism.

> Numbers it is. All music when you come to think. Two multiplied by two divided by half is twice one. Vibrations: chords those are. One plus two plus six is seven. Do anything you like with figures juggling. Always find out this equal to that. Symmetry under a cemetery wall. He doesn't see my mourning. Callous: all for his own gut. Musemathematics. And you think you're listening to the ethereal. But suppose you said it like: Martha, seven times nine minus X is thirtyfive thousand. Fall quite flat. It's on account of the sounds it is.   [*U*, 11.830–37]

The connection of Arnold's Hellenistic spirit, eager to know the truth of things, to Homer's story is clear here. The Siren in the Ormond Hotel is music's sentimentality, which hides the fact of experience from the singers and listeners, and lures them into moral indifference or luxuriant mendacious palliation where suffering is concerned. Bloom's hesitant participation in the maudlin music and his accurate analysis of its fraud in this scientific passage recapitulate the scene in which Odysseus hears the siren while lashed to the mast and survives the blandishments others have perished in. The catgut thong Bloom wraps around his fingers while listening to Simon Dedalus sing (*U*, 11.704) stands in for the ropes lashing Homer's hero to the mast of reason; Bloom's scientific analysis of harmony stands in for the Greek hero's new knowledge of the siren's evil. The Greek king's curiosity appears here as the scientific curiosity Arnold called a fundamental impulse in the soul's Hellenistic urge to master happiness through understanding.

Bloom displays that curiosity to explain the pain of love in "Nausicaa." After his encounter with Gerty, trying to understand sexual attraction and Molly's adultery with Boylan, Bloom thinks:

Very strange about my watch. Wristwatches are always going wrong. Wonder is there any magnetic influence between the person because that was about the time he. Yes, I suppose, at once. Cat's away, the mice will play. I remember looking in Pill lane. Also that now is magnetism. Back of everything magnetism. Earth for instance pulling this and being pulled. That causes movement. And time, well that's the time the movement takes. Then if one thing stopped the whole ghesabo would stop bit by bit. Because it's all arranged. Magnetic needle tells you what's going on in the sun, the stars. Little piece of steel iron. When you hold out the fork. Come. Come. Tip. Woman and man that is. Fork and steel. Molly, he. Dress up and look and suggest and let you see and see more and defy you if you're a man to see that and, like a sneeze coming, legs, look, look and if you have any guts in you. Tip. Have to let fly.

[U, 13.983–96]

Here the scientific spirit gives Bloom a universal picture of the laws governing nature that allows him to do what Arnold said Hellenism does—free the mind from rigid moralism and direct it to the truth that justifies moral codes. In this analogy of macro- and microcosms, Bloom not only rationalizes sexual misdemeanors, he also thinks about how sex operates outside of moral codes so that he can evaluate accurately the emotional situation passion constructs for human creatures. Thinking about the natural facts that should govern morality, Bloom displays the force of Arnold's Hellenism.

Bloom's urge to see things as they are in themselves unmasks social pretensions as well as amatory and aesthetic ones. In "Lestrygonians" he thinks he would like to be a waiter serving delicacies to aristocratic ladies, until this speculation curtails the daydream: "Still it's the same fish perhaps old Micky Hanlon of Moore street ripped the guts out of making money hand over fist finger in fishes' gills can't write his name on a cheque think he was painting the landscape with his mouth twisted. Moooikill A Aitcha Ha ignorant as a kish of brogues, worth fifty thousand pounds" (U, 8.891–95). He makes the same kind of leveling observation about aristocratic pretensions, this time on sex, during an attempt at voyeurism (slang Hellenism) that is frustrated in "Lotus Eaters."

> Mr Bloom gazed across the road at the outsider drawn up before the door of the Grosvenor. The porter hoisted the valise up on the well. She stood still, waiting, while the man, husband, brother, like her, searched his pockets for change. Stylish kind of coat with that roll collar, warm for a day like this, looks like blanketcloth. Careless stand of her with her hands in those patch pockets. Like that haughty creature at the polo match. Women all for caste till you touch the spot. Handsome is and handsome does. Reserved about to yield. The honourable Mrs and Brutus is an honourable man. Possess her once take the starch out of her.   [*U*, 5.98–106]

Both these examples are partly comic presentations of Bloom comforting himself for sensual deprivation, but the comfort in both cases comes from accurate and exact observation of things as they are in themselves and carries a gain on truth as well as less dignified rewards—tepid resentment in the case of the fishmonger, and burlesqued seducer's savagery vis-á-vis the haughty lady. Mixing these temperamental qualifiers into Bloom's enactment of Arnold's Hellenism, Joyce keeps symbolic concepts within the narrative bounds of character in his fiction. Whatever qualities of the soul *Ulysses* presents, it presents this way. Arnold's Hellenism, Bruno's universal particularity, Dante's "retrospective arrangement" through an epic journey—they all happen in and through the events of all-too-normal life.

Technically scientific thoughts occur to Bloom repeatedly as he wanders through Dublin observing events and speculating about their causes. Poldy's characteristic response to any item he encounters is scientific in the largest sense. He thinks: What do I see, what do I already know about this, what new information am I receiving, what conclusions, based on all the evidence, are now possible? His formal education and his experience of the world have given him a scientific vocabulary (concepts and terms) that, considering his class and professional knocking-about, is copious and fairly impressive.

In "Lestrygonians," to rid himself of the despair a meditation on the futile cycles of history has brought on, Bloom searches for a restaurant, observing, "Hope they have liver and bacon today. Nature abhors a vacuum" (*U*, 8.498). This last statement, an axiom of chemistry and physics, has probably come down to Bloom from Vance, the high school teacher who more than anyone else established his interest in things scientific. Bloom thinks of Vance's teaching, usually muddling it, often during the day. On gravity: "It's a law something like that. Vance in High school cracking his fingerjoints, teaching. The college curriculum. Cracking curriculum. What is weight really when you say the weight? Thirtytwo feet per second per second. Law of falling bodies: per second per second. They all fall to the ground. The earth. It's the force of gravity of the earth is the weight" (*U*, 5.41–46).

Bloom thinks of gravity, specifically of the thirty-two feet per second per second computation, four times in the novel, without ever correcting the initial confusion (*U*, 8.157; 15.1605, 2781, 3374). He also recalls Vance on the spectrum of light, twice: in "Nausicaa": "Some light still. Red rays are longest. Roygbiv Vance taught us: red, orange, yellow, green, blue, indigo, violet"; and in "Circe": "*he performs juggler's tricks, draws red, orange, yellow, green, blue, indigo and violet silk handkerchiefs from his mouth)* Roygbiv" (*U*, 13.1075–76; 15.1603–5). The relation of gravity to acoustics also occupies him: "Acoustics that is. Tinkling. Empty vessels make most noise. Because the acoustics, the resonance changes according as the weight of water is equal to the law of falling water" (*U*, 11.980–83). And he puzzles over the problem of heat's conductivity three times after its first appearance in "Calypso": "Be a warm day I fancy. Specially in these black clothes feel it more. Black conducts, reflects (refracts is it?) the heat" (*U*, 4.78–80; 11.446; 13.1013–15; 15.401). For the record, the answer to Bloom's query, which he never discovers, is that black absorbs heat. He also considers the properties of light: "Clearly I can see today. Moisture about gives long sight perhaps" (*U*, 5.112–13), and "Confused light confuses memory. Red influences lupus. Colours affect women's characters, any they have. This black makes me sad" (*U*, 15.2737–39). And to put an arbitrary end to this list, the ancient experimental philosopher Archimedes also figures in his thoughts: "Howth a while ago amethyst. Glass flashing. That's how that wise man what's his name with the burning glass. Then the heather goes on fire. It can't be tourists' matches. What? Perhaps the sticks dry rub together in the wind and light. Or broken bottles in the furze act as a burning glass in the sun. Archimedes. I have it! My memory's not so bad" (*U*, 13.1137–42).

Bloom's pleased "I have it" when he remembers that "what's his name" is Archimedes is a nice example of Joyce's comedy. Archimedes, of course, is famous for his Greek exclamation of intellectual discovery, "Eureka" ("I've found it" literally), which is a far cry from Bloom's satisfaction in remembering. Archimedes called out when he discovered specific gravity (precisely, displaced water—the topic Bloom thinks of when he speculates about Molly's tinkling chamberpot), not the properties of light Bloom thinks of here. The story of Archimedes's setting an enemy fleet on fire by concentrating the sun's rays on it with mirrors, which Bloom recalls here, is a perfect example of the quality of the adman's scientific expertise. The story is apocryphal and so displays the nonprofessional, popular interest Bloom takes in science; it is mismatched with the surrounding allusions to Archimedes (which are more relevant to Bloom's earlier thoughts), indicating some confusion on the part of the Dublin phenomenologist, and it puts theoretical science to practical use, indicating the most crucial function of science in Poldy's mind—its application to worldly affairs.

In "Ithaca," where Bloom's scientism takes hold as one dimension in the narrative voice (another is Stephen's theological catechistic learning), and where Poldy thinks most consistently about science (astronomy, geology, biology, physics, mathematics, hydraulics, mechanics, etc.), Joyce ostentatiously presents Bloom's Hellenistic impulse to pure knowledge of things as they are in themselves as being subject to his Hebraic impulse to turn such knowledge toward improving human life, toward making the true order of nature, which brings about happiness, prevail.

What two temperaments did they individually represent?
The scientific. The artistic.
What proofs did Bloom adduce to prove that his tendency was towards applied, rather than towards pure, science?
Certain possible inventions of which he had cogitated when reclining in a state of supine repletion to aid digestion, stimulated by his appreciation of the importance of inventions now common but once revolutionary, for example, the aeronautic

parachute, the reflecting telescope, the spiral corkscrew, the safety pin, the mineral water siphon, the canal lock with winch and sluice, the suction pump.
Were these inventions principally intended for an improved scheme of kindergarten?
Yes, rendering obsolete popguns, elastic airbladders, games of hazard, catapults. They comprised astronomical kaleidoscopes exhibiting the twelve constellations of the zodiac from Aries to Pisces, miniature mechanical orreries, arithmetical gelatine lozenges, geometrical to correspond with zoological biscuits, globemap playingballs, historically costumed dolls.

[U, 17.559–75]

Long before this point, Joyce shows the Hebraic spirit mingled with the Hellenic one in Ulysses, as part of both the symbolic structure and the realistic narrative. The law of gravity is expressed with Elijah, a somewhat eminent Hebrew, as its object twice (U, 8.57; 15.3374–75). Out of sympathy for a blind stripling Bloom conducts comical experiments on himself to discover what difficulties and compensations the stripling's life brings (U, 8.1135–39), and finally, again comically, his kindly interest in humanity's well-being leads him to the following observation in "Sirens," made immediately after his debunking analysis of music as mathematics: "Time makes the tune. Question of mood you're in. Still always nice to hear. Except scales up and down, girls learning. Two together nextdoor neighbours. Ought to invent dummy pianos for that" (U, 11.841–43). Happiness would certainly be improved through such an invention, although musical expertise would most likely be reduced, a fact that escapes the compassionate scientist, as so many facts do.

The point here is that Bloom's Hellenism in the best sense—his independent scientific curiosity for knowledge and truth—like his Hellenism at its worst—license and domestic ruin—has an equal and opposite component of Hebraism, compassion and moral sanity in that term's authentic meaning, and plodding affectation of stolid Victorian ethics in its degraded one. Arnold's requirement that knowledge and behavior cooperate in cultivated souls gets dramatized in Bloom's book with enough coarse humor to nullify the Victorian's vague sermonizing, and with enough empirical grit to vindicate his fundamental conception. The books of popular science in Bloom's library—Robert Ball's *The Story of the Heavens*, and *A Handbook of Astronomy*, to name only two (*U*, 17.1373, 1391)—from which he has collected botched information as well as accurate knowledge; Poldy's recollections of Vance; his persistent, sometimes indelicate experimental temper [see the most specifically detailed observation in nonpornographic literature of defecation in "Calypso" (*U*, 4.500–541], and his Utopian inventiveness are all narrative embodiments of the intellectual soul's vigor in *Ulysses*. That Bloom's science always has some beneficial practical purpose or aspiration reflects Joyce's insistence that the soul operates on the material world through the body (to put it Aristotle's way), that the soul and the body are identical opposites (to put it Bruno's), that symbols must emanate from narrative facts (to switch to Dante's literary version of the same idea), or finally, to use the terms from Arnold that Joyce comically magnified in Poldy's history, that Hellenism and Hebraism concur in the spiritual progress of cultivated creatures. The positive and negative extreme meanings of Greek—scientist and philanderer—meet their Jewish counterparts, the dutiful man of conscience and the Tory who upholds society's norms out of nothing more enlightened than habitually rational self-interest.

The Edwardian slang version of Arnold's "Hebraism" made "Jew" a synonym for antagonism toward sensual and aesthetic pleasure and for prudish commitment to utilitarian virtue. According to a more ancient slander, the "Jew" adds to these faults an extremity of practical virtue—selfishness. Prudence in this extremity decays into scheming, and industry into theft. All four belong to Odysseus, as well as to the slandered Jew, a fact that Joyce occasionally elaborates when he has Bloom act or suffer insult as a stage Jew. Bloom never recognizes his own financial schemes as Odyssean or Jewish, but he is tender where anti-Semitism is concerned, so much so that at one point in the novel he tries on the role of Dublin Philistine, commenting on the moneylender Reuben J. Dodd, "Now he's really what they call a dirty Jew" (*U*, 8.1159). Bloom judges both falsely and accurately here (Dodd, a gentile, exhibits no human decency at all in the book), but something more than offended civic honor prompts the judgment. Poldy seems to be proving to himself that he is no Dodd here, and in the process he demonstrates what damage prejudice achieves, since his adoption of the gentile slur can never gain him access to the society that exiles him by means of that slur. Bloom thinks of himself, with some accuracy, as a paterfamilias and upstanding member of the community—precisely the qualities of Arnold's Hebraism in its degraded form. He acts and poses that way partly because he is Odysseus (Homer's epic is about the restoration of Odysseus to that role) and partly because he will not think of himself as a Reuben J. Dodd. In fact, he has enough of Dodd in him for the Victorian and ancient connotations of Jew—solid, dull businessman and schemer—to fit him as a tragicomic shirt of Nessus. The utilitarian implies the conniver in Bloom, as much as it shows him unsuccessfully eager to be a Dublin burgher.

The ad-canvasser habitually concocts schemes for financial gain on June 16, and has been doing so for many days preceding it. In the past there has been the Hungarian lottery scandal. In the present: in 4.107–10 he thinks of profitable positions for pubs consequent on the rerouting of tramlines; in 6.396–403 of the dishonest ways to engage in trading the wasteproducts of slaughterhouses, of a new tramline to take cattle to the quays, and of municipal funeral trams; in 6.772–75 he imagines a business trading in corpses to manure gardens, and so on, ad nauseam. The crescendo of this strain in his mental life comes in "Ithaca" where his schemes for "rapid but insecure means to opulence" are listed for several pages (U, 17.1672ff). The most characteristic of these, and the funniest, is this: "The utilisation of waste paper, fells of sewer rodents, human excrement possessing chemical properties, in view of the vast production of the first, vast number of the second and immense quantity of the third, every normal human being of average vitality and appetite producing annually, cancelling byproducts of water, a sum total of 80 lbs. (mixed animal and vegetable diet), to be multiplied by 4,386,035 the total population of Ireland according to the census returns of 1901" (U, 17.1701–8).

Joyce is not Pound or Eliot, and none of these schemes makes Poldy a Reuben J. Dodd. There is no authorial presentation of Bloom in Ulysses remotely similar to Pound's "kikery" or to Eliot's charmer in "Burbank with a Baedeker: Bleistein with a Cigar," where the financial structure of Europe, symbolized by Venice's bridges, is ruined by Jews: "On the Rialto once. / The rats are underneath the piles. / The Jew is underneath the lot. / Money in furs."⁴ Joyce saw what these other writers saw in Europe, but he did not retreat insanely, as they did, into Jewish conspiracy theories for explanation. Nonetheless, Poldy does scheme for money throughout Joyce's first epic, not only because he is more alert and responsible than his contemporaries (almost without exception he is), but in large measure because Joyce wanted the comic effects such "insecure means to opulence" provided. Jewish greed is not a fact in *Ulysses*, but a burlesqued convention; not a credo, as it was for Pound and Eliot, but a stupidity to be laughed away. Bloom exhibits it so ineptly, that no one could imagine, or has imagined (at least in print) that Joyce presents it to defame Jews. The only race Joyce defames in *Ulysses* with regularity is his own.

In "Cyclops," the scene of much anti-Semitism in *Ulysses*, the narrator, convinced Bloom has won on a horse that day and is hoarding his gain, says of him: "There's a jew for you! All for number one. Cute as a shithouse rat" (*U*, 12.1760–61). Bloom, of course, has bet nothing and does not learn of the race's outcome till hours later, in "Eumaeus," but the nameless barfly, although he is entirely vicious, is not entirely wrong about Poldy. The schemes listed above do show extravagant ingenuity for gain on Bloom's part, and the one examined below shows less than noble aspirations for profit. The irony of the barfly's salvo recoils on him, of course, when one considers that Bloom has stepped out of Kiernan's not to collect money, but to arrange financial matters for Dignam's widow, to whose welfare he has contributed cash that day (something one cannot say for the gonorrhea-ridden barfly). There is much more to say about Bloom's humanitarianism shortly; I mention it here because I am about to discuss a compromised version of it, and do not want to appear ignorant of its value. For all his altruism, Poldy does have ludicrous and dangerous moments of selfishness, pathetic and risible impulses to pull strings for sordid and silly gain.

In the cases listed above Bloom's scheming endangers no one. In the following one a plan for wealth endangers the person Bloom ostensibly wants to help—Stephen Dedalus. Throughout *Ulysses*, of course, Bloom does help Stephen: he tries to shield him from dangerous drinking urged by destructive comrades in the Maternity Hospital; he follows him into Nighttown after those comrades desert him; there, he shields him from Bella Cohen's theft, cares for him once a ruffian soldier has knocked him unconscious, and, through a ruse worked with Corny Kelleher, keeps him out of jail for disorderly conduct. In "Eumaeus" he decides to bring Stephen home and offer him asylum for an indefinite period. All this solicitude springs from Bloom's intuitive conviction of Stephen's superior value, and from Bloom's sad lack of a son and his natural urge to father someone. In one sense Bloom's offer in "Eumaeus" is the final development of that solicitude and lack, and eminently generous. In another sense, the offer is a fair business exchange (less generous, but not for that reason sordid). But for all his conscious effort to act as Stephen's father and business manager, the Jew's offer has its ignoble goal. Bloom wants Stephen to be Molly's lover, and so rid him of his marital responsibility and the disgusted humiliation caused by random adulterers of Boylan's quality.

The offer of asylum forms itself by stages in Bloom's mind during the episode. Justifying his interest in Dedalus's talent, despite the money and danger it has cost him (again we have Bloom the solid citizen, and Bloom the prudent exiled king, weighing risks and benefits), Poldy thinks for the first time of the good Stephen might do him: "Still to cultivate the acquaintance of someone of no uncommon calibre who could provide food for reflection would amply repay any small. Intellectual stimulation as such, was, he felt, from time to time a firstrate tonic for the mind" (U, 16.1219–22). This hope for intellectual stimulation soon evolves into the following scheme that would provide much more.

Bloom, solicitous for Dedalus's future, has already urged him to pursue a literary career to recoup his educational expenses and to serve Ireland (U, 16.1152–59). Discussing Parnell's adultery (which is symbolically connected to Bloom's marital situation throughout the novel, especially in this chapter), Poldy remarks that Kitty O'Shea was Spanish and, apropos of this, shows Stephen Molly's picture, asking if the young man considers her looks Spanish (U, 16.1425–26). The question, designed to expose Stephen to Molly's "fleshy charms on evidence in an open fashion" elicits from him the observation that she is handsome, which is what Bloom wants to hear (U, 16.1428). The following passage shows Poldy's first addition of sexual service to Molly as an added benefit to be derived from Stephen's intellectual stimulation of him.

The vicinity of the young man he certainly relished, educated, *distingué* and impulsive into the bargain, far and away the pick of the bunch though you wouldn't think he had it in him yet you would. Besides he said the picture was handsome which, say what you like, it was though at the moment she was distinctly stouter. And why not? An awful lot of makebelieve went on about that sort of thing involving a lifelong slur with the usual splash page of gutterpress about the same old matrimonial tangle alleging misconduct with professional golfer or the newest stage favourite instead of being honest and aboveboard about the whole business.   [*U*, 16.1476–84]

What Stephen "has in him" is the capacity to please Molly (which Bloom has lacked for ten years), and the subject of Bloom's question "Why not?" is the young man's prospective enjoyment of that capacity. For all Bloom's dismissal of social hypocrisy where adultery is concerned, for all his urging of straightforward presentation of the facts in the business (the mercantile metaphor is not dead here), Bloom is neither straightforward nor aboveboard about his pandering to Stephen, but deliberately sly in comically obvious ways. The arch schemer, Greek and Jewish, who pretends to urge no subterfuge, is about as subtle with Stephen as the scheming Polonius is with Hamlet.

Immediately following the passage quoted above, Bloom draws an analogy between Stephen's projected adultery and Parnell's real one as he remembers returning Parnell's hat in a fracas after the leader fell from political grace. The implication of that comparison is that as Bloom favored Parnell, the adulterer who was nonetheless an accomplished man, so he will help Stephen, the projected adulterer, accomplish his talents and achieve his fame. Soon after this Bloom thinks it a pity that a brainy fellow like Stephen, incapable of insipid courtship with penniless and scheming proper young ladies, wastes his time with whores who might very well give him a lifetime venereal remembrance of themselves. He continues: "To think of him house and homeless, rooked by some landlady worse than any stepmother, was really too bad at his age" (*U*, 16.1565–67). What he really needs is a good home and a good woman, and Bloom of course is more than willing to offer both, though he is cautious (even while bumblingly obvious) in making the offer, sensitive to Stephen's possible embarrassment at seeing the picture (*U*, 16.1464–68). He decides to bring up the plan with a light reference to music: "Because he more than suspected he had his father's voice to bank his hopes on which it was quite on the cards he had so it would be just as well, by the way no harm, to trail the conversation in the direction of that particular red herring just to" (*U*, 16.1658–61).

On leaving the cabman's shelter, as he pockets the bait (Molly's photo) and asks Stephen to Eccles Sreet, Bloom is almost carried away with his project: "All kinds of Utopian plans were flashing through his (B's) busy brain, education (the genuine article), literature, journalism, prize titbits, up to date billing, concert tours in English watering resorts packed with hydros and seaside theatres, turning money away, duets in Italian with the accent perfectly true to nature and a quantity of other things" (*U*, 16.1652–56). Charged up with this latenight zeal, Bloom eventually pops out an invitation to meet Molly, sounding for all the world like a dime-store Lothario: "What's this I was saying? Ah, yes! My wife, he intimated, plunging *in medias res*, would have the greatest of pleasure in making your acquaintance as she is passionately attached to music of any kind" (*U*, 16.1800–1802). Prospective passionate attachment to Dedalus, of course, is not mentioned.

Bloom's last fantasy removes Molly from Stephen's singing career. No longer planning duets for the adulterers, Bloom imagines Stephen a smash success alone, with Molly to look after his wardrobe and teach him the social amenities of concert life. The money would even give him leisure for his literary career. As they make their way to Eccles Street after this fantasy, Bloom urges Stephen to leave Mulligan's company; a horse mires (so much for Bloom's plans), and the two walk off stage *"to be married by Father Maher"* (*U*, 16.1887–88). Married to each other, that is, through a mutual association with Molly, Stephen enacting the matrimonial role of his ghostly father, Bloom recovering his wife through the image of his son—something very like the situation of *Hamlet* as Stephen conceived it in the National Library earlier that day. Lest doubt remain, Joyce provides one final statement of Bloom's sordid adoption plan in "Ithaca." Questioned on the advantages of Stephen's living with the Blooms, the answering voice of that chapter responds: "For the guest: security of domicile and seclusion of study.

For the host: rejuvenation of intelligence, vicarious satisfaction. For the hostess: disintegration of obsession, acquisition of correct Italian pronunciation" (*U*, 17.937–39).

Bloom's offer by now should seem the complex thing it is. He really does imagine himself in it as the paterfamilias who can advance his adopted son's career at the same time as he reestablishes a family for an alienated father, mother, and son. So far so good. Even the grandiose financial obsession of the fantasy can be put down to Bloom's desire, manifested throughout "Eumaeus," to become a prosperous prominent cultural figure. But the sexual scheme, while it is a reasonable expectation given Bloom's problem and Molly's character (she imagines an affair with Dedalus herself in 18.1331–67, and, ironically mistaken about Stephen's cleanliness, she fantasizes, as her husband did, that the liaison will appear in the newspapers), must appear ludicrous given Stephen's disposition (he is quite sexless throughout *Ulysses*), and selfish in the extreme given Stephen's needs. Dedalus despises the beggar's condition that requires him to go about in hand-me-downs from Mulligan, whom he views as an exploitative, usurping benefactor. Would he acquire the confidence and humanity he desperately wants with a hand-me-down wife? Would he be free, as Bloom thinks, to pursue his future independently while educating and satisfying an uneducable and highly venereal mother-wife, or speculating with a misinformed, rambling middle-aged skeptic, singing constantly to support them all?

Dedalus is already struggling with an Oedipal fixation—Molly's love could hardly dispel that grief. And intellectually, while Bloom's range of discourse is exactly what Stephen needs, its quality is hardly suited to the requirements of the young genius Joyce has made Dedalus in the book. Certainly Stephen needs married love, but his own, not Bloom's. *Ulysses* commemorates the day Joyce found that in Nora and celebrates its mature development in portraying the Blooms, and to that extent Molly, who was modeled on Nora almost entirely, is Stephen's intended, and Poldy's offer not only a selfish scheme, but a prophecy. In the narrative, however, these symbolic autobiographical elements enter the scene ironically. There, Joyce presents Stephen's potential assumption of Bloom's adulthood as a trap, a comic danger for Dedalus to escape. In his refusal to accept, Stephen becomes Odysseus himself, using prudence to keep searching for his real home when a false one is offered. Ironically, then, Bloom's offer is effective only when it is refused—Stephen becomes an adult when he rejects the burden of another adult's failed responsibilities. Dedalus has already tried to father himself by abandoning his fleshly father, and failed. It is only when he abandons his ghostly one that he succeeds. This is one meaning of the song Stephen sings for Bloom in "Ithaca," in which a Jew's invitation results in a gentile's murder when accepted (*U*, 17.800–831). Ironically again, when Bloom behaves as a selfish Jew with aspirations toward middle-class respectability, he also enacts the opposite, noble Hebraism of Arnold—unwittingly, altruistically working to bring the natural moral order into being in Stephen's life.[5]

Throughout *Ulysses* Bloom aspires to the middle-class respectability and comfort, the civic pride and worthiness connoted by "Jew" as a degraded form of Arnold's Hebraism. This is nowhere more evident than in "Eumaeus," the chapter whose style presents Bloom's literary apologia, the "orthodox Samaritan['s]" (*U*, 16.3) hypothetical narration of prosperous propriety. He is, of course, acting to save Stephen from ruin and preserve him for use in society (as a writer, a singer, a thinker) in this chapter, and in the process pronounces and speculates on many avenues to middle-class security—economic, domestic, medical, and psychological. Bloom has struck this pose in the preceding chapter, pretending to Mrs. Breen, whom he meets in one of the hallucinations in Nighttown, that he has come to that disreputable locale as the secretary of a charitable institution that seeks to reclaim fallen women (*U*, 15.401–2). He does not need to lie then, since he is in fact on a charitable mission to rescue Stephen, but the opportunity to appear respectable and official in his charity is something Bloom cannot pass up. Part of the deception is a comic Odyssean ruse to disguise and so safeguard the true objective of his presence in an immoral place, but in large part Bloom lies because he needs to think of himself as a moral leader of the society that has spurned him, finding a place in fantasy for the moral intelligence and civic impulses political reality has not accommodated. The ultimate symbolic expression of this quality in Bloom comes in the extended analogy drawn throughout the novel between his life and that of Moses, sometimes a hyperbolic irony, sometimes a comic salutation. The middle-ground of that analogy is Bloom's status as a slang Arnoldian "Jew," a status that the lie to Mrs. Breen and the following plans and actions confirm (by no means exhaustively).

While trying to protect Stephen from thuggish soldiers at the end of "Circe," Bloom warns them that Dedalus is a gentleman, the son of a famous and highly respected citizen of Dublin, and that his arrest or mistreatment would scandalize the community (neither observation being remotely accurate, both faking civic eminence to acquire its privilege) (*U*, 15.4488, 4838–41). In the same vein, he accuses the soldiers of unjustly brutalizing a citizen whose people have fought for the British Empire (*U*, 15.4788–89, 4606–7), and urges Cissy Caffrey, who has started the fracas, on her sacred honor as a female *civis*—"You are the link between nations and generations"—to speak for Dedalus (*U*, 15.4647–48). She will not. So much for civic pride in Dublin, so much for justice.

Once he has rescued Stephen, Bloom makes it his business to talk to him about health, the virtues of family life, the necessity of a living wage and public service, the evils of gambling and especially drink, and the pleasures of sobriety, legality, and material comfort that the responsible citizen may claim and cultivate. Sobriety crowns Bloom's hidebound respectability and gains him suspicious contempt among Dubliners (not a notoriously abstemious group) throughout the novel. The barroom conversation in "Lestrygonians," 8.976–82, is a prime example of their attitude toward Bloom's abstemious habits.

In addition, a perpetual fear of robbery appears in Bloom's thoughts as the comically reduced, timorous domestic counterpart of the Odyssean guile and the burlesqued Jewish greed symbolically attached to his schemes for financial gain. Odysseus, who carries off treasure himself, loses it along the way (fortunately he gets a new horde from Alcinous and the Phaiakians) and almost loses his patrimony to robbers until he acts as his own police force after returning to Ithaca. Bloom, who has also been a robber of sorts (a peddler of religious trash, a con-man in the Hungarian lottery scheme) thinks more than once about the duties, obligations, and abuses of power in the police force. Among many observations appears this one, displaying both Bloom's civic dependence on the protection police offer and his moral indignation at the injustice these defenders of the populace enforce. "Never on the spot when

wanted but in the quiet parts of the city, Pembroke road for example, the guardians of the law were well in evidence, the obvious
reason being they were paid to protect the upper classes" (U, 16.79–
82). And there are soldiers, the cousins of policemen, of whom
Bloom thinks in the same place: "Another thing he commented on
was equipping soldiers with firearms or sidearms of any description
liable to go off at any time which was tantamount to inciting them
against civilians should by any chance they fall out over anything"
(U, 16.82–85).

These serious sentiments of the public man of virtue have their
comic forms as well, descending to the level of bombastic enthusiasm for clichés (Bloom, passing a bakery in "Eumaeus" and inhal-
ing the smells with a great sense of well-being and silly pride,
thinks "our daily bread, of all commodities of the public the primary and most indispensable"), and absurd variations on them,
such as the following qualification that Bloom makes in a plan for
insuring greater public access to Ireland's splendid nature spots in
vacation time: "Howth . . . was a favourite haunt with all sorts and
conditions of men especially in the spring when the young men's
fancy, though it had its own toll of deaths by falling off the cliffs by
design or accidentally, usually, by the way, on their left leg" (U,
16.57–58, 557–62). There are many more examples, each with special meanings for Bloom's character and the novel as a whole.
Those I've mentioned and the uncited cases all indicate clearly that
Bloom, who has some of the stage Jew in him, owes much as a
character to the Victorian reduction of Arnold's Hebraism that depicted Jews as stuffed shirts entrenched in the dull, middle-class
tyranny of respectability (a condition opposite, incidentally, to that
of the stage Jew).

Authentic Hebraism shines through Bloom's groping aspiration
toward citizenship in his humanitarian fantasies of reform. Like
everything else about Bloom, these fantasies emerge comically
compromised by mock-epic irony, now grandiose (and grandiosely
ridiculed), now modest (and winked at coyly). In both cases,
Bloom's effort to make the best order of nature prevail and thereby
bring culture to Dublin and Dubliners survives the comedy, in fact
gains dignity from it. In a remark like "a revolution must come on
the due instalments plan," Joyce displays the authentic Hebraic
spirit in Bloom, whose naive civic discipline and pragmatism con-

stitute what Arnold called the Hebraic sense of duty (*U*, 16.1101).
At his best ethically, Bloom transmutes wiliness, love of reputation, and financial scheming into industrious, altruistic devotion to
the best elements of the public good, to culture, perceived from the
Hebraic point of view. If that devotion and industry are largely confined to his imagination, hostile Dublin is to blame. Hebraism, for
all Arnold's emphasis on dutiful practice when he discusses it, is a
state of mind, an internal condition. It follows that Bloom's reformer's disposition qualifies as "Hebraic" as much as the few acts of
kindness he accidentally accomplishes among the Philistines.
Poldy's mind sends up Hebraism so continually that anyone seeking more evidence for it than I offer here will have a very short
search. I've chosen these particular displays of it for their complex
clarity and their comic pleasures.

In "Circe," during his hallucinatory reign as emperor, Bloom climaxes a public appearance with the following speech:

> I stand for the reform of municipal morals and the plain ten
> commandments. New worlds for old. Union of all, jew, moslem
> and gentile. Three acres and a cow for all children of nature.
> Saloon motor hearses. Compulsory manual labor for all. All
> parks open to the public day and night. Electric dishscrubbers.
> Tuberculosis, lunacy, war and mendicancy must now cease.
> General amnesty, weekly carnival with masked licence, bonuses for all, esperanto the universal language with universal
> brotherhood. No more patriotism of barspongers and dropsical
> imposters. Free money, free rent, free love and a free lay church
> in a free lay state.   [*U*, 15.1685–93]

Because he plays Messiah, and plays it to the Irish, Bloom's stump
speech turns the crowd against him immediately. The "Greek" licentiousness of this new order, in which Parnell's fatal "free love"
occurs, and which Bloom thinks will free Ireland, only helps do
him in. Such Hellenic Hebraism in Roman Catholic Dublin could
never hope to escape the destiny reserved for all previous liberators
there: ritual sacrifice. As Joyce has the mob put it: "Lynch him!
Roast him! He's as bad as Parnell was. Mr. Fox!" (*U*, 15.1762). Reforming the Decalogue to initiate freedom, ease, and delight may
not seem Hebraic at first glance, since duty and reverence are not
stated or implied means or ends of the plan, but the goal Bloom

clearly aims for—achieving the social conditions best suited to human happiness—is precisely the goal that duty and reverence serve
in Arnold's essay.

In the hallucination Bloom's humanitarianism is a delusion of
grandeur as much as a political program, and it fails because it is
hubristic as much as it does because it is messianic. The same
impulse shows up later in the novel, again in Bloom's fantasy life,
this time in "Ithaca," not as an uncontrolled seizure, but a pro-
grammatically indulged wish-fulfillment. After Stephen leaves 7
Eccles Street at 2:30 A.M., Bloom indulges his habitual "Flowerville" fantasy, in which he presides over an Ithaca of his own creation situated "not less than 1 statute mile from the periphery of
the metropolis" (U, 17.1514–15). This "island" home would require
civic and social as well as economic management, and in the following excerpt Poldy imagines the course of action he would pursue
to keep "Flowerville" just, prosperous, and eminent.

> A course that lay between undue clemency and excessive rig-
> our: the dispensation in a heterogeneous society of arbitrary
> classes, incessantly rearranged in terms of greater and lesser
> social inequality, of unbiassed homogeneous indisputable jus-
> tice, tempered with mitigants of the widest possible latitude
> but exactable to the utmost farthing with confiscation of es-
> tate, real and personal, to the crown. Loyal to the highest con-
> stituted power in the land, actuated by an innate love of recti-
> tude his aims would be the strict maintenance of public order,
> the repression of many abuses though not of all simultaneously
> ... the upholding of the letter of the law. ...   [U, 17.1617–27]

The radical reformer of the hallucination has vanished, rectitude
has taken the place of freedom, and strict ordering of society according to law has ousted the Utopian anarchy that Emperor Bloom
envisioned. Happiness is still the goal, but the stakes are lower: an
estate, not a nation, is to be granted stable felicity through the
dutiful reverential government of a civilized country gentleman.
This idea of social order shows as much slang Hebraism as authentic spiritual cultivation, but it preserves the essential element of
that higher state, humanitarian interest in justice, compassionate
enforcement of the laws that insure human excellence is brought
into being together with the order of nature. (Flowerville will also

include a garden managed Hellenistically in the most up-to-date manner, with the latest scientific items. It is intriguing to note in this context that Arnold appears as a garden worker in the first chapter of the novel.) Finally, this excerpt begins with a Greek element, the Aristotelian mean, demonstrating once more that the Hebraic spirit in Bloom acts harmoniously with Hellenism, the spirit responsible for the great flexibility that Bloom imagines his judgment of malfeasance will take.

For all his exile in Dublin, Bloom's humanitarian rectitude has more than an imaginary role in his life. Poldy actualizes the possibilities of Hebraism continually throughout *Ulysses*, displaying kindness to a blind stripling, pitying impoverished children, feeding animals, courteously avoiding arguments (except in the case of the Citizen in "Cyclops," where his anger is righteous indignation, a Christ-like variant of rectitude), rescuing Stephen, visiting Mrs. Purefoy in her three-day agony, compassionating nurse Callan for the death of her medical beau, contributing to Mrs. Dignam's welfare, and so on. Even the Dubliners who otherwise scorn him allow him a reputation for sympathy. In "Wandering Rocks," when Cunningham and company go about soliciting contributions for the Dignams, Martin displays a list of donors that includes Bloom's name and the tendered sum of five shillings, and he elicits by the act this remark from John Wyse Nolan: "I'll say there is much kindness in the jew" (*U*, 10.980). Referring as it does to Shylock's bargaining for a pound of flesh to repay a failed debt, Nolan's comment delivers admiration only through sarcasm. Bloom is not to be freely admired by Dublin even when he acts so graciously, a precondition that renders the sardonic commendation more flattering than Nolan at his most civil could intend. It is interesting to note, in passing, that in this quote Joyce has conjoined opposite meanings of "Jew"—Shylock's pitiless, vindictive greed and the practical *caritas* of Arnold's "Hebraism."

"Moses, Moses, King of the Jews"

So much should substantiate the claim that Arnold's terms for the secret impulses of personality that create culture, Hellenism and Hebraism, are at work in *Ulysses*, ordering the presentation of events and depiction of character. Not only Bloom and Stephen, but Ireland itself, the nation that Bloom as Everyman and Stephen as Everyman's son, Telemachus, represent, is characterized repeatedly by Joyce as a reincarnation of the tragic kingdom of Israel and the glorious, defeated civilization of ancient Greece. The comparison occurs most ostentatiously with Professor MacHugh in "Aeolus," 7.551-70, and in the judicial parody in "Cyclops," 12.1111-40, where Irish legal procedure is compared to an observation of Athena's rites and the convening of the Sanhedrin. The very metaphor that Joyce made the titular key to his novel, Bloom's day as the *Odyssey*, emerged in part from a notion of identity between Greek and Jew in Homer's epic that is parallel to the identity of Hellenism and Hebraism in Arnold. Ellmann writes of Joyce's first work on *Ulysses* in Zurich in 1917: "He came to know, at about this time, the contention Victor Berard first formulated about the beginning of the century, that the Odyssey had Semitic roots, and that all its place names were actual places, often detectable by finding a Hebrew word that closely resembled the Greek" (*E*, p. 408). And Ellmann adds in an endnote, "He frequently consulted in 1918 and 1919 Dr. Isaiah Sonne, now at the Hebrew Union College in Cincinnati, for Greek-Hebrew cognates" (*E*, p. 408n). Hellenism in the narrative of Bloom's day has its symbolic counterpart in Homer's epic; Hebraism has it in Exodus, the second epic that provides a hero—Moses—and a civilization—Judaism—that join in every chapter with Homer's heroic civilization to make Bloom's experience universal (in traditional Western terms). There is no necessity to do more than list the attributes of Odysseus symbolically grafted into Bloom's day, since they have occupied critics for sixty years. The Mosaic analogy needs more attention, since its equivalence to the Homeric one has been too long neglected.

Not all of Odysseus's qualities and accomplishments have analogies in the story of Moses. The prophet is not, for instance, wily, prosperous, courteous, or ready to absorb the thought and customs of strangers in strange lands. Nor is the Greek adventurer an historian, an inventor of moral codes, or the founder of a nation. These differences do not figure in the literary metempsychosis through which Bloom becomes an archetypical composite of the Greek and Jewish heroes. Joyce does elaborate one major opposition in the figures, however. Odysseus and Moses both liberate their people from a military enemy, destroying the enemies' forces in the process. Odysseus and Moses both attempt to restore liberated national remnants to their patrimonies, and both meet resistance from dependents in the attempt. Odysseus loses his followers and returns alone, largely because the sailors disobeyed his warnings, and most significantly because the Greeks were only ambiguously befriended by divine powers (Athena for Odysseus and his men, Poseidon against them). Moses loses only some of his followers for their disobedience (the episode of the Golden Calf) and leads a people unambiguously favored by divine power into their patrimony, only to be denied that reward himself. The Greek liberator redeems himself, his family, and Ithaca, having brought down an honorable foreign enemy (Troy) by guile (and force) and a dishonorable domestic enemy (the suitors) by force (and guile). The Hebrew liberator redeems a nation at last, but not himself, having brought down a thoroughly ruthless, heathen enemy with miracles. The Greek savior wins through courage and craft, the Hebrew one through righteousness and the sacred power of spiritual obedience. Intellect in the first case preserves one man for the restitution of social order; sanctity in the second puts one man's personal fate into the tragic service of establishing a moral civilization.

These oppositions unite in Joyce's portrayal of Bloom's *nostos* in "Ithaca," where Stephen tells his parable "A Pisgah Sight of Palestine" to Bloom (*U*, 17.640–41), and where Joyce magnifies the protagonists' final separation with Psalm 114 (*U*, 17.1030–31), a commemoration of the Exodus from Egypt. The full shaky grandeur of that culminating unity of Moses and Odysseus in Bloom has been under construction from the opening of the novel, patched up comically and poignantly through persistent analogy and symbolism. Tracing that construction requires a quick look at the general similarities of Moses and Odysseus that Joyce operates with, and then a more detailed observation of some moments where the Mosaic analogy emerges in the narrative and draws together the complex ambitions and disappointments of Dublin's Homeric royal family, Mr. Bloom, Mrs. Bloom, and Bloom *fils*, Stephen.

In the course of Homer's epic Odysseus appears as a wanderer and guide; a warrior and military hero who is courageous and lionhearted; a man of sorrows who is long-suffering and pious; an isolated hero with no confidants to aid or advise him in crisis. These of course are all attributes of Moses displayed in his epic, Exodus: he leads the wandering Israelites through their forty-year desert journey to Canaan; he helps defeat their enemies by presiding over forces led by Joshua, infusing them miraculously with military force by holding up his staff; his courage is plain to see in the encounters with Pharaoh and with the rebels who oppose him in the desert. Like Christ, he is a man of sorrows, acquainted with the grief of rejection suffered time and time again at the hands of the remnant he saves; like Christ he is pious, accepting his tragic sacrifices without complaint. He is the first great example in the Bible of the suffering servant who redeems Israel and leads it to a patrimony provided by God's grace. Although Aaron accompanies and helps Moses throughout Exodus, in the most crucial stages of the prophet's life—when he is called, when he receives the Ten Commandments in a mystic encounter with God's hindparts, when he looks over Palestine from Pisgah—Moses, like Christ, like Odysseus for most of his ordeal, suffers and exults alone.

The literary records preserving the exploits of both heroes also have some identical qualities. Both are legendary, have legendary authors, and are too ancient to be dated with any accuracy. Both also have an obviously historical foundation included as their primary narrative structure—the destruction of a civilization and its painful consequences for the victors in Homer's case, and the painful creation of a civilization by an exiled race freed through destruction of their oppressor's military force in Moses' book. And both texts were the essential documents of their civilizations for hundreds of years, providing the primary laws governing religion, politics, and the intellectual disciplines (history, philosophy, literary study), displaying the best values cherished and aspired to by individuals and their state. In *Ulysses*, by writing the adventures of Odysseus and the Mosaic birth of a nation into Bloom's commonly trivial life, Joyce claimed the same cultural authority for his comic epic. Its hero displays modernity's best values, his story provides the standards for human excellence, his history will preserve this epoch as Homer's and Moses' works preserved theirs. An account of those places in *Ulysses* where Odysseus Bloom and his ghostly son Stephen add attributes of Moses to their Greek poses bears out this claim. Separately, and together, both characters appear in all the modes linking Moses and Odysseus listed at the beginning of the last paragraph, especially as heroes exiled, isolated, wandering, and vainly proffering liberation to an abusive crew.

During his phantasmagoric trial for plagiarism and sexual assault in "Circe," Bloom is identified as Moses twice: first in the anonymous accusation from the gallery (*U*, 15.847–848), "Moses, Moses, king of the jews,/Wiped his arse in the Daily News" (which recalls Bloom's sanitary use of a story by Beaufoy, the literary plaintiff in this scene, in "Calypso," 4.537), and second in his defense attorney's argument, "such familiarities [the sexual assault on Mary Driscoll] . . . being quite permitted in my client's native place, the land of the Pharaoh" (*U*, 15.945–47). The literary accusation involves Bloom's desire to write moral stories, imitations of Beaufoy's that would be better than those sordid items. In the gallery's outcry that desire gets associated sardonically with the prophet's legendary literary achievement, authorship of the original moral story, the Pentateuch. The locale of Bloom's birth is one of many items in the novel symbolizing his yearning for return to the Promised Land, a yearning elaborated throughout the novel as Mosaic. Bloom thinks of a Mideastern Utopia first in "Calypso" (*U*, 4.84–98), and then again several pages later in the pork butcher's, where he reads an advertisement for "the model farm at Kinnereth on the lakeshore of Tiberias" supported by "Moses Montefiore" (*U*, 4.154–55). At the end of "Oxen of the Sun" Lenehan involves Molly in the Exodus symbolism when he describes Bloom's wife as "None of your lean kine, not much" (*U*, 14.1475–76), a reference to the period of prosperity the Hebrews enjoyed in Egypt during Joseph's management of the bounty and famine that precedes Moses' entry into Judaic history. Molly, in Lenehan's reference, is the domestic model farm Bloom dreams about, as she is later in "Ithaca," this time symbolized as the postexilic Canaan and Ithaca (*U*, 17.2229–2236).

Bloom's longing for Canaan appears earlier in "Ithaca," this time in an opposite guise. Seeking happiness in a fanciful plan for escaping Molly, Bloom thinks of flight in terms symbolically linked to the exilic wandering led by Moses. He will travel to far-off places guided at night by a woman's bottom, called a "a bispherical moon," imperfectly and variously revealed through an opened skirt, and following for the remaining hours "a pillar of cloud by day" (the sign leading Israel through the wilderness) (*U*, 17.1995, 1998). These two opposite Mosaic plans for domestic happiness (married and unmarried) have a narrative counterpart in Bloom's memory of another domestic duty—reverence of his father and the faith of his fathers. In "Aeolus," watching a typesetter read backwards, he thinks, "Poor papa with his hagadah book, reading backwards with his finger to me. Pesach. Next year in Jerusalem. Dear, o dear! All that long business about that brought us out of the land of Egypt and into the house of bondage *alleluia*" (*U*, 7.206–9). Bloom has misquoted the psalm, reversing the operative second part, a mistake with extensive conceptual value for the novel. Bloom repeats the mistake in "Nausicaa" when, musing on the superstitions of sea voyagers who wander from their wives through years of ordeal (one more Odyssean motif), he remembers his forefathers' religious observations: "And the tephilim no what's this they call it poor papa's father had on his door to touch. That brought us out of the land of Egypt and into the house of bondage" (*U*, 13.1157–59). Once more, as in the last appearance of the psalm in "Ithaca" at Stephen's departure, Greekjew meets Jewgreek.

Psalm 114 also has political meanings in *Ulysses*, referring of course to Irish enslavement under England. In that context America is cited as the Promised Land to which so many Irish fled. In "Cyclops" the Citizen says of the English, "Ay, they drove out the peasants in hordes. Twenty thousand of them died in the coffin-ships. But those that came to the land of the free remember the land of bondage" (*U*, 12.1371–73). Ireland's struggle for Home Rule, as well as the emigration during the famine, was treated in Mosaic symbols by the Irish themselves long before Joyce used it in his fiction. Daniel O'Connell was called Moses and known as the great liberator during his efforts, as was his successor, Parnell, who acquired the title of "the second Moses." On Christmas Eve 1882 a reporter for *United Ireland* wrote of Parnell and the Irish, "If it be hero worship to follow such a man as trustfully as a Pillar of Fire, the Irish people are not likely to shrink from the imputation."[6] Parnell himself, at the crucial committee meeting in which he was ousted from the almost liberating coalition he had created, spoke of his political efforts in the same terms: "If I am to leave you tonight, I should like to leave you in security. I should like—and it is not an unfair thing of me to ask—that I should come within sight of the promised land" (*CSP*, p. 520). Bloom, who is identified with Parnell's domestic and political tragedy throughout *Ulysses*, especially in "Circe" and "Eumaeus," also shares in this political Mosaic symbolism.

The sacrificial comedy surrounding Bloom's execution had a place in Ireland's national consciousness long before Joyce. The uprisings against Moses in the desert, and the Crucifixion, both symbolically ascribed to Bloom and Parnell, are part of what F. S. L. Lyons in his biography *Charles Stuart Parnell* calls "the myth of the 'extreme'" (*CSP*, p. 610).

> That the myth should have become rooted so quickly and so deeply was due mainly to the second transforming development of those post-Parnellite years, the complex cultural phenomenon sometimes called, with dangerous simplicity, the Irish literary movement. The Parnell tragedy fitted marvelously well with a tradition which went far back into the underground life of Ireland. It has been called a Messianic tradition because, as is common among peoples long held in subjection, it looked for deliverance to the coming of a Messiah or leader. Parnell had seemed to be that leader, but the leader had been sacrificed. Yet, the idea of sacrifice too was implicit in the myth, for from sacrifice came the resurrection from which the true leader might spring. As a modern writer, Herbert Howarth, has well said, Parnell, both in his style and in his fate, had personified the legend. "His aloofness, his very despotism, had made men ready to worship him. His followers invested him with the status of a prophet. Those who hated him most after the divorce proceedings hated him most because they could not bear their prophet to be less than immaculate. The Irish committed the crucial act of killing their prophet, and the guilt, the desire to purify the guilt, the belief that his sacrifice sanctified, the belief that sacrifice assures rebirth, gave them irresistible vigour in the next generation." [*CSP*, pp. 610–11]

As I have already argued in analyzing Bloom's incineration in "Circe," these impulses toward sacrificial purgation of cultural guilt, this quick change from adoration of imperiousness to hatred of it, are applied full force to Poldy in his guise as the great Liberator, the third Moses.

These scattered elements of the analogy are all concentrated in "Aeolus." The Exodus psalm already mentioned is followed in the scene at *The Freeman's Journal* by three prominent Mosaic analogues: the description of Michelangelo's statue by Seymour Bushe, the John F. Taylor speech about the new literary movement, and Stephen's parable about the Vestal Virgins. The Bushe speech, recited by J. J. O'Molloy as proof that eloquence still exists in Ireland, makes Moses a grand symbol of the soul's transfigurations and so gives the Hebrew prophet a central place in Joyce's symbolic presentation of universal experience in Bloom's day. Bushe said of Michelangelo's Moses: "*that stony effigy in frozen music, horned and terrible, of the human form divine, that eternal symbol of wisdom and prophecy which, if aught that the imagination or the hand of sculptor has wrought in marble of soultransfigured and of soultransfiguring deserves to live, deserves to live*" (*U*, 7.768–71). In the narrative this transfiguration of the soul refers to the change from pure retributive Mosaic justice to Roman law with its emphasis on rational demonstration of criminal behavior and legalistic codified retribution. The glorious moral certainty and economy of Mosaic justice finds its real fulfillment in the Roman requirement that *lex talionis* only be applied when guilt is clearly demonstrated by evidence: some such contrast figures in Bushe's forensic praise of Moses, which is used to defend his client, Childs, against charges based merely on circumstantial evidence.

In the symbolic order of *Ulysses* Michelangelo's great figure of wisdom and prophecy, the grand nationalist and lawgiver, is transfigured in Bloom. During Poldy's trial in "Circe" J. J. O'Molloy defends him by citing again the *lex talionis* of Moses argumentatively praised by Bushe: "The Mosaic code has superseded the law of the jungle" (*U*, 15.969–70). Transfigured into John F. Taylor (whose oration on Moses immediately follows O'Molloy's quotation of Bushe in "Aeolus") and then into Bushe, Bloom's lawyer transfigures the description of Michelangelo's statue on Bloom's behalf: "When the angel's book comes to be opened if aught that the pensive bosom has inaugurated of soultransfigured and of soultransfiguring deserves to live I say accord the prisoner at the bar the sacred benefit of the doubt" (*U*, 15.1001–4).

In the novel's conceptual order the transfigured and transfiguring soul of Michelangelo's Moses is one more condensed and oblique symbol of the subject of *Ulysses* at its most grand—life's universal and eternal principle in action, the soul perpetually transfigured by the matter it transfigures. Aristotle formulates that principle in his idea of the soul's capacity as form of forms to become all things; Bruno with the concept that the soul is, always has been, and will be all the things it transforms; and Dante in his dramatic ordering of such transformation as the soul moves toward salvation. In Bushe's speech Joyce claims for his artistic recreation of Moses in Bloom what Bushe, via a character with Joyce's initials, claimed for Michelangelo's sculpture—eternal vitality for artistic presentation "of the human form divine." Such a transfiguration (or incarnation) governs, in various formulations and emphases, Aristotle's, Bruno's, and Dante's understanding of the soul. In the aesthetic order of *Ulysses* that incarnation has its analogue in the constant conjunction of opposites, in the fusion of symbol and story that animates details in the novel, and in the extended metaphors that put these details into a dynamic order. The most prominent extended comparison in *Ulysses* makes Moses a partner to Odysseus in that order.

The Bushe speech casts Bloom in the mature Mosaic role of lawgiver, father of his race's conscience, a pose that Bloom assumes in the narrative through his civic-minded righteousness and his attempt to impart it to Dedalus, and the men in Barney Kiernan's bar. John F. Taylor's speech, which Professor MacHugh quotes to cap O'Molloy's example of high talk, dwells on the youthful Moses who resists authority and later, as an old man of eighty, leads his people into exile and becomes an outcast in order to establish the culture that he eventually stabilized with the Decalogue. The speech has two symbolic meanings in the narrative—it glorifies the Irish cultural revival, specifically the resurrection of Irish (and so refers to Stephen's ambitions ironically), and it glorifies the political ferment which that literary movement shared in, a ferment for Home Rule in which context Moses refers to Parnell (and thereby once more to Bloom). The speech is the centerpiece of the Mosaic analogy in *Ulysses*, aligning Ireland with Israel and England with Egypt on the issues of cultural, military, and religious domination, issues that recur in every chapter of the novel, and which are important concerns for Stephen and Bloom. Stephen links himself to the youthful Moses as a figure of cultural resistance and literary genius at the start of the speech: "Noble words coming. Look out.

Could you try your hand at it yourself" (*U*, 7.836–37). His temperament and his destiny figure prominently in its conclusion.

> —*But, ladies and gentlemen, had the youthful Moses listened
> to and accepted that view of life, had he bowed his head and
> bowed his will and bowed his spirit before that arrogant ad-
> monition he would never have brought the chosen people out
> of their house of bondage, nor followed the pillar of the cloud
> by day. He would never have spoken with the Eternal amid
> lightnings on Sinai's mountaintop nor ever have come down
> with the light of inspiration shining in his countenance and
> bearing in his arms the tables of the law, graven in the lan-
> guage of the outlaw.* [*U*, 7.862–69]

Joyce was asked by Sylvia Beach to record something from *Ulysses* in 1924, and chose this speech, explaining the choice by claiming the passage was the only thing in the novel that could be quoted
out of context, being an oration.[7] No one who has heard the fervor
and heroism in Joyce's recording could doubt there was more in
that choice than an aesthetic consideration (any of the parodies in
"Oxen of the Sun" or "Cyclops" would have done just as well as
self-contained units of rhetorical extravagance). Stephen's satanic
identification with the rebellious Moses (paradoxical in the best
Joycean manner) is preserved in Joyce's declaration for the phono-
graph of his own most cherished ambitions and self-estimation. Son
to Bloom's Odysseus, Dedalus becomes son to Bloom's Moses as
well, symbolically associated with the youthful courage and daring
that resulted in the mature patriarch's wisdom and authority. The
irony here rests in the fact that Stephen and Joyce have dissociated
themselves from the cultural goal Taylor longs for, and that Stephen has just returned from a failed artistic exile that was carried
out in part to liberate Ireland's cultural life. Nonetheless, the Mosaic promise of deliverance for Stephen applies, just as the promise
of Telemachus's eventual success does. Dedalus may not understand this, but Joyce and readers do.

If the son is in the father, the father must be in the son, according
to trinitarian logic, and Stephen's aesthetic of *Hamlet*, both of
which play through *Ulysses* ceaselessly. The law holds in this case,
since the political meanings of the speech, its references to Psalm

114 (the house of bondage) and the exilic wandering (the pillar of cloud) bring Bloom, in whose sphere these symbols move, into Taylor's rhetorical account of the youthful Moses, as does O'Molloy's appearance as John F. Taylor in the scene from "Circe" cited above. Contraries coincide here: the two speeches cited by antagonists in a rhetorical contest in "Aeolus" have one symbolic figure. That figure applies to Stephen and Bloom in opposite ways, symbolizing youthful faith and courageous rebellious struggle, and the mature establishment of binding laws. And there is, of course, leveling comedy. In "Ithaca," Bloom's unwitting prophecy of Throwaway's racetrack victory repeats Moses' mystic reception of the divine laws on Sinai as presented by Taylor: "he [Bloom] had proceeded . . . with the light of inspiration shining in his countenance and bearing in his arms the secret of the race, graven in the language of prediction" (*U*, 17.337–41).

Stephen's connection to Moses as author recurs soon after Taylor's speech, as he takes up the challenge he put to himself to try his hand at creating literature. In an autobiographical review of his literary beginnings, Joyce has Stephen compose a story whose tone and subject match the writer's first collection, *Dubliners*. Silently naming his effort after that book, Stephen composes the story of two aged virgins who travel to Nelson's pillar, eat plums, and spit the pits over the railings into the street below (*U*, 7.921–1059). This is his answer to Myles Crawford's confident request for writing from Stephen, for "something with a bite in it" (*U*, 7.616). Obliging, and sarcastic, Stephen makes eating one of the two events in his story. The symbolic bite emerging from the modest snacking in Dedalus's story is the bite of Joyce's *Dubliners*, where scorn for moral paralysis is delivered in sharp, unclimactic, almost unplotted narratives with enigmatic symbols presenting, very clearly, spiritual decay. The union in this story of narrative and symbol in the term "bite" is one of the more obvious examples Joyce offers of the artistic strategy by which *Ulysses* identifies fact and idea, story and symbol, particular and universal. The Mosaic connection in Stephen's effort comes clear when MacHugh suggests a Latin title for the story, which Stephen rejects in favor of his own title. "No, Stephen said, I call it *A Pisgah Sight of Palestine or the Parable of the Plums*" (*U*, 7.1057–58). Linking Moses to his ecclesiastical double, Christ, according to the figural typology developed in Catholic interpretation of the Bible, Stephen unwittingly associates himself with Bloom once more, since Poldy shares in that typological relation of Christ to Moses through his many comparisons to both. While the parable has meaning only as a literary achievement for Dedalus, it has moral significance for Bloom. That significance comes clear when the Taylor speech and the parable are both repeated in Stephen's last meeting with the elder Moses.

As mentioned earlier, "Ithaca" comically attaches prophecy to Bloom's Mosaic role as liberator when, before the exit from Eccles Street, it describes his unwitting disclosure of the secret of the Gold Cup race. As it turns out, Lyons has played his role as stiff-necked Jew to Bloom's Moses, ignored the prophecy he greedily accepted in "Lotus Eaters," and lost money on the race. Once Lenehan dissuades him from the bet on Throwaway (U, 12.1554–55), Lyons bets on the French horse Maximum 11, which loses (U, 16.1287). Stephen's response to Bloom is the contrary to Bantam's— he seeks nothing and recognizes nothing in the inspired countenance, yet leaves Bloom possessed of the human race's secret, that existence means interchange of souls, vivifying, fatal interchange. Dedalus cannot bet on his own future on the strength of that secret because he does not realize (as Bloom has not all day) that he is carrying it. Unlike Lyons, however, who found true profit falsely in Bloom's speech and forsook it, Stephen, who forsakes the deliberate offer of material benefit Bloom makes, profits from knowledge gained innocently and unconsciously from the older man. The gambler loses, the artist gains.

Bloom benefits not at all from his prophecy to Lyons, and only tangentially from his kindness to Stephen. Throwaway's victory causes him some regret, which he allays by thinking that he has lost nothing through inaction (an observation that he later also applies to his passivity in Molly's romp with Boylan) and "brought a positive gain to others. Light to the gentiles" (U, 17.353–54). This last remark refers to his belated recognition of why Lyons found a tip in remarks about a newspaper (U, 5.531–41). That gentile, ironically enough, gains nothing, because he shunned the light by changing his bet. Once more Bloom comically and without knowledge represents Christ's saving grace, a light shining in darkness that darkness could not comprehend. Dedalus is the gentile Bloom has helped, not Lyons, and the assistance was not material, as

Bloom imagines it might have been to Lyons, and wanted it to be for Stephen, but spiritual in those ways analyzed in the preceding pages.

Bloom, through his kindness to Stephen, reenacts one more event from Moses' life, the prophet's "Pisgah sight of Palestine." Joyce suggests this by having Stephen repeat his Mosaic parable to Bloom just before leaving Eccles Street (*U*, 17.639–40). The title describes, among other things, the distracted imperfect excitement two Dublin women feel overlooking their city from the top of Nelson's pillar. The women are virgins, and their imperfect excitement is sexual—the pillar titillates them, the "one-handled adulterer" Nelson teases them (*U*, 7.1019). Stephen's subtitle for the story, the "Parable of the Plums," also reveals their sexual frustration. The virgins eat the fruit and throw away the seeds, the stones of their plums, just as they ooh and ah over the adulterer and his massive obelisk, without any expectation of real sex themselves, without receiving or hoping to receive any man's stones, pillar, or seed. Like all parables, this one has many meanings, but they all involve some variant on women's sexual connection to men, to stones that produce seeds.

In Bloom's case the Pisgah sight of Palestine is his short experience with Stephen of what being a father to his son Rudy might have meant. The culmination of this provisional fatherhood is Stephen's exit, the Exodus that Bloom, the civic-minded, solicitous advisor, Moses as buffo, has made possible. The infertility in the virgins' Pisgah sight of Palestine also figures in Bloom's identity as Stephen's ghostly father. Rudy's death left Bloom unwilling, though not unable, to impregnate Molly. "Could never like it again after Rudy," he thinks in "Lestrygonians" (*U*, 8.610). Snatching an occasion to befriend a young man, Bloom indicates how bereft Rudy's death has left him for the past ten years. Fathering a son can never be more than temporary, uncalled for adoption in Bloom's case. Having been for a few hours a provisional son to Bloom has improved Dedalus, has given him a future. Bloom's lot is sorrier. Stephen's departure reveals how unlikely any permanent satisfaction of paternal feeling is for Bloom. Joyce identifies the melancholy in Poldy's kindness to Stephen poignantly in "Oxen of the Sun" when he writes: ". . . and now sir Leopold that had of his body no manchild for an heir looked upon him his friend's son and was shut up in sorrow for his forepassed happiness and as sad as he was that him failed a son of such gentle courage (for all accounted him of real parts) so grieved he also in no less measure for young Stephen for that he lived riotously with those wastrels and murdered his goods with whores" (U, 14.271–76). Like Moses, Bloom leads the way to happiness he cannot enter, like Virgil he brings a pilgrim to knowledge he himself cannot attain. Like all fathers of sons, he extends his life into another man's, and in the process loses it, is excluded from its achievements. Stephen drives the point home in the National Library, when, discussing Hamlet and Shakespeare (both doubles for Bloom and Dedalus) he says: "The son unborn mars beauty: born, he brings pain, divides affection, increases care. He is a new male: his growth is his father's decline, his youth his father's envy, his friend his father's enemy" (U, 9.854–57).

The Mosaic analogy applies to Bloom as spouse also: like all husbands, like all men, in Joyce's thinking, Bloom can also have nothing more than a Pisgah sight of Palestine with his wife, since, as he thinks climbing into Molly's bed after Dedalus has left, no man is the first or only man to win any woman, no man lives in the promised land of sexual fidelity where women are concerned (U, 17.2127–31). The imperfection of marriage carries over into its result, offspring. Not only Rudy, but all sons, Ulysses has it, ruin their father's potency. By living, if not by dying, sons leave sires behind as the Jews did Moses, as Dante did Virgil. Because Ulysses is comic there is no prolonged melancholy over this. Bloom feels the "cold of interstellar space" (U, 17.1246) once Stephen leaves, but he ends up happily drifting into childhood adventure fantasies while he falls asleep with his face near the seat of bliss, Molly's adulterous rump. The fantasies are listed in 17.2322–26, the seat of bliss is described as follows:

In what final satisfaction did these antagonistic sentiments and reflections, reduced to their simplest forms, converge?
Satisfaction at the ubiquity in eastern and western terrestrial hemispheres, in all habitable lands and islands explored or unexplored (the land of the midnight sun, the islands of the blessed, the isles of Greece, the land of promise) of adipose anterior and posterior female hemispheres, redolent of milk and honey and of excretory sanguine and seminal warmth,

reminiscent of secular families of curves of amplitude, insusceptible of moods of impression or of contrarieties of expression, expressive of mute immutable mature animality.

[*U*, 17.2227–36]

One point remains—the symbolic link between the *Odyssey* and Exodus Joyce makes by centering his Mosaic analogy for Bloom and Stephen in a chapter entitled "Aeolus." The topic that prevails over literature, journalism, and rhetoric in this chapter, the issue most passionately discussed, is Ireland's political failure to gain independence. The Moses speech of Taylor, the journalistic coup of Ignatius Gallaher recalled by Myles Crawford, the superiority of Greece to Rome harped on by MacHugh, the Passover psalm, and Stephen's parable (indirectly in its title) all refer to the defeated hopes of Irish nationalism most tragically apparent in the betrayal and death of Parnell. Homer's story provides one analogy: just as Odysseus was deprived, on the coast of Ithaca, of his homecoming by the greed and depravity of his crew, which caused them to disobey him and release the winds confined by Aeolus, so driving the ship out to sea again and antagonizing divine power, so Ireland has been deprived of Home Rule, through the hysteria and depravity of Parnell's underlings who revolted against him and thereby ruined the coalition with Gladstone that might have liberated them. Just as Odysseus slept at the tiller, allowing his crew to revolt, so Parnell lapsed morally through his entanglement with Kitty O'Shea, bringing on himself the same destructive force—religious opposition—that oppressed Homer's hero. And as the winds that were erstwhile favorable to Odysseus turned against his hopes, so the rhetoric of public opinion they symbolize in the newspaper chapter turned the Irish hero it created into a victim. Rhetoric and journalism are unreliable authorities in politics, the chapter argues, falsifiers of historical victory and defeat.

Moses, Parnell's symbol in and out of Joyce's fiction, suffers the same rebellion in the desert that the Greek and Irish leaders did from a stiff-necked, treacherous crew, and like Parnell, like Odysseus for most of his journey, Moses cannot enter the Promised Land he strove to gain because of a transgression against divine law (Deut. 34:48–52). Bloom experiences the same frustrated glimpse of domestic serenity and rest as Homer's king does, and reenacts a version of Odysseus' final success. Poldy also suffers a variant of the punishment Parnell earned through sexual licentiousness: he has lost the struggle for Home Rule to Boylan through a sexual error opposite to Parnell's. His comical, ambiguous reversal of that loss— the return to Molly's bed—played out as a Pisgah sight of Palestine, links Bloom's domestic situation to the forestalled satisfaction withheld from Moses. In this last case Bloom's neglect of Jewish ritual, through which he pained his father, and for which he feels remorse in "Ithaca" (U, 17.1893–95), also matches the prophet's neglect, when bringing water from a rock at Meribah, to ceremoniously ascribe the miracle to God, a sin punished in God's withholding from Moses entry to the promised land (Num. 20:1–13). If opposites coalesce comically, they must do so tragically as well, and it is just such a tragicomic tone that governs Bloom's final Mosaic reconciliation with Molly and loss of Stephen in the novel's penultimate chapter.

Victorian Soul-Making

Given Joyce's contempt for the Celtic literary revival that Arnold's Oxford lectures, The Study of Celtic Literature, published in 1867, helped launch, one expects to find the English sage simply ridiculed in Ulysses. And of course he is ridiculed, appearing as a gardener mowing the lawn at Oxford (U, 1.172–74). His contemporary Tennyson is done in with the curt gibe "Lawn Tennyson" (U, 3.492, 9.648), a mordant sarcasm that links the laureate to the eminent analyst of culture. Sniping away like this at the two great English literati of his youth, Joyce displays a powerful and clear antagonism toward British cultural hegemony, and an equally clear contempt for their productions: Arnold works as a menial laborer, and his defense of culture is equated with trimming the grass, maintaining the sheen in the abyss of English snobbism, Oxford; Tennyson is worse, producing rhymes with no more force or meaning than that required for a risibly pallid and precious aristocratic imitation of sport. Arnold's Celtic enthusiasm, present in Ulysses as the literary antiquarianism of the British intruder Haines, has degenerated into effete dangerous patronizing of Ireland's authentic and besieged literary genius (Stephen). After such knowledge, what forgiveness?

What value could a Victorian mandarin offer an Irish exile if not the value of having formulated elaborately and influentially a unified opposition Joyce was also using to construct his shocker—the interdependence of Europe's two original and primary traditions, the Greek one in things intellectual and artistic, the Jewish one in things religious and moral. Bloom was to be a Greekjew in the Edwardian British Empire, with the cultural heroism of those two races comically gleaming in his trivial day, and Arnold's terms of cultural analysis—"Hellenism" and "Hebraism"—had permeated Edwardian Britain. The incorporation of Arnold into *Ulysses* as a prominent spokesman for civilized life seems, in this light, quite predictable, given Joyce's habit of creating fiction by making everyone else's literature and everyone else's ideas grist for his mill, and given his aesthetic principle justifying the plunder—that art could only be made out of preexisting reality and preexisting art.

Saying he used Arnold because Arnold was there is an accurate but incomplete account of the matter, for Arnold was there in a large way, as the most powerful spokesman for civilized humanism in Joyce's culture. Plodding as *Culture and Anarchy* may be rhetorically, soggy and vague as it is intellectually, the work is an enormously urgent statement of those humanistic goals which Joyce cherished, and which he despaired of in Ireland—intellectual spontaneity and range, respect and compassion for the human struggle to resist the spiritually fatal influence of mechanism, moral courage and perseverance in the rectitude of brotherly love that proffers the privileges of civilization to every man. These virtues are all Bloom's portion, and potentially Stephen's, and no one else's in Dublin as Joyce presents the city. Bloom is the one good man for whom Joyce preserved the evil place, and Bloom's goodness owes much to Arnold's conception of value, largely because Bloom is the middle-class alien Arnold hoped most could advance humanistic culture.

As for the political discrepancy: *Culture and Anarchy* is no hymn to English society; it attacks its fundamental assumptions with more civility than Joyce showed his countrymen, but with no less conviction or disgust. Even Arnold's enthusiasm for Celtic literature, based on enthusiasm for Irish artistic dreaminess that Joyce abominated, was set out in terms that directly attacked English social values.[8] An Irishman eagerly asserting the enduring excel-

lence of humanity to redeem his own fallen nation could use
Arnold's terms with no thought of going over to the English enemy,
since those terms, already critical of England, are modern names for
the two mentalities that centuries before had created, and in Joyce's
day still maintained, the cultural standards of all Europe. The intersection of universal laws of being with particular historical circumstances is one of Joyce's subjects in *Ulysses*. Arnold's cultural
analysis suits that topic neatly, because it brings the first principles, the ancient enduring principles of humanistic excellence, to
bear on contemporary life in the empire. Jeffrey Perl has also observed Joyce's response to Arnold in *Ulysses*, and he puts the matter in the broader perspective of the history of ideas of cultural
recovery and historical continuity in his book *The Tradition of Return*, especially in Chapter 6, "Novel and Epic: The Ithaca of
History."[9]

The parallel actions of the archetypical Greek and Jewish heroes
structure *Ulysses* from start to finish. To chart it, this chapter has
referred to all eighteen episodes in the novel, to all its major characters, and a dozen or so minor ones. Aristotle and Bruno offered
models for the soul's universality that Joyce found valuable for creating Bloom's personal experience and the novel's aesthetic design.
Dante also provided aesthetic ideas but gave Joyce something the
philosophers did not—a conception of the soul's operation in society. Arnold's essay, like Dante's epic, insists that the soul realizes
itself only through operating in society among other souls, and
again, as Dante does, it provides a theoretical model for the growth
of culture in individuals and of individuals in culture. The unified
opposition of "Hellenism" and "Hebraism" has its analogy with
the empirical and speculative psychology of Aristotle and Bruno,
where coalescence of contraries under the form of forms is the rule
for particular lives, and in Dante's symbolic narration of a particular life's absorption and creation of cultural values. Defining culture's value, Arnold offers a theory of the soul's dynamic progress
remarkably similar to the theories of Aristotle and Bruno, and the
symbolic journey of Dante: "It is in making endless additions to
itself, in the endless expansion of its powers, in endless growth in
wisdom and beauty, that the spirit of the human race finds its ideal.
To reach this ideal, culture is an indispensable aid, and that is the
true value of culture" (*CA*, p. 476).

Stemming from the extended presentation of Bloom's spiritual progress, the documentary-like reconstruction of Bloom's nation also owes much of its order to Arnold and Dante, especially to Arnold, the comprehensive analyst of British modernity whose terms were paradoxically well suited to Joyce's Irish epic purpose. Not the realism of *Ulysses*, the reconstruction of physical facts and historical details—which Joyce learned from Dante and modern French writers—but the cultural history of the novel, its positioning of Ireland in Europe's modern transfiguration of Hellenism and Hebraism, came to Joyce largely through Arnold's achievement. Because Joyce seems to have thought, along with Pound, that epics contain history, universal history at that, Bloom needs to display in his own person the character of his crisis-ridden nation, where the traditions initiated by Homer and Moses seem hopelessly degraded. And Bloom's story had to be an exile's story, given his superiority to every one of his contemporaries, the story of a good man struggling to survive and mitigate the dangerous force of the bad men he lives with. Moses and Odysseus were the natural choices for universalizing analogues to Bloom's predicament, and mock-heroism the only possibility of resuscitating their ancient force in Poldy, given the degenerate state of his world. Mock-heroism need not be antiheroism, but can be a drastic reduction of the terms in which heroes create themselves. So Arnold's Hellenism and Hebraism, while they do come in for hard ridicule in *Ulysses*, also provide central values that make the novel affirmative. And they provide terms that put *Ulysses* into its historical context as a novel concerned with the deterioration and unsuspected endurance in Edward's empire of Britain's Victorian inheritance from Greece and Israel.

The pleasures and pains of civilization appear in the attempt to reestablish personal order in Homer's epic, as they do in Joyce's enormous parody of it. *Ulysses* insists, in the meticulous superfluity of Bloom's realistic and circumstantial narrative, that this individual life must display all experience, that Bloom's Odyssean struggle to go home is the fundamental impulse in all personal ambition, and in all social ambition. This ambition has its symbolic analogue in the novel's comic recreation of Moses' struggle to create a nation. Although Hellenism and Hebraism require each other, and are in that sense coinciding contraries, although Hellenism's contemplative freedom alone makes Hebraism's rectitude valuable, and vice versa, *Ulysses* begins, in its title, with emphasis on subjugated Hellenism (Latin "Ulysses" instead of the Greek "Odysseus") and maintains that emphasis throughout, displaying Moses as an emanation of Odysseus, as culture is an emanation of individual souls in Arnold's essay. Throughout the book Joyce highlights Bloom's Odyssean role, the Greek face of his Jewish soul, the private source of his public life, the free intellectual origin of binding social norms. Moses and Odysseus are created equal in Bloom's symbolic universality, but Odysseus is created more equal, or to give him the name of Moses' last Greek descendant, Constantinople's Eastern Orthodox patriarch, "first among equals."

conclusion

I have undertaken this long analysis of ideas of the soul in *Ulysses* for two reasons: to discover which ontological principles constitute Bloom's universal day, and to discover what artistic shape they take on, what narrative and symbolic life they give Joyce's fiction. The earliest, and still one of the best, philosophical investigations of the formal structure animating *Ulysses* was carried out by Edmund Wilson in *Axel's Castle* in 1931. Wilson cites Joyce's French predecessors as the originators of literary modernism, distinguishing two styles of artistic construction that he associates with two opposed laws of being. The symbolists, Wilson argues, held that each moment of consciousness is unique, operates under mysterious spiritual authority, and cannot be expressed by direct statement or description, only suggested by evocative symbols or magically recreated by irrationally associated aesthetic effects. Hence the linguistic density and intellectual obscurity of Rimbaud, of Mallarmé. Naturalists, on the other hand, held that all consciousness operates identically under natural laws that can be understood rationally. Consequently, consciousness can be fully presented in objective, accurate narratives structured with the mechanistic logic of cause and effect. Hence the factual representational density of Zola and the Goncourt brothers. In making *Ulysses* a fully naturalistic account of objective, circumstantial reality and a fully symbolic account of inviolably subjective experience, Joyce closed, according to Wilson, the intellectual and artistic gap in modernism, and gave twentieth-century literature a philosophical and imaginative range that it has nowhere else. I cite Wilson here to indicate my debt to his method (finding conceptual value in literary styles and structures) and to say that my own probe into the philosophical unity of *Ulysses* goes farther back in time, and to another place in Joyce's mind, searching out those laws of being that Joyce found in writers from classical Greece, medieval and Renaissance Italy, and Victorian England. The conceptions of opposites unified in the soul that are supplied by these sources are all analogous to the central opposition in Wilson's argument. Considered together, these conceptions define that humanistic intellectual inheritance which enabled Joyce to reconcile the modernist conceptual and stylistic opposition of naturalism and symbolism.

For the modern writers, as Wilson presents them, the conceptual opposition in these styles was between objectivity and subjectivity, the rational and irrational authorities in experience. This ideational opposition enforced a stylistic choice between presenting the unrepeatable particular or the perpetually repeated universal in literature. Aristotle and Bruno indirectly address the modern dichotomy of object and subject, reason and nonreason, when they discuss the soul as a dynamic form which, by uniting the particular and universal, makes every unrepeatable particular the locus for representation of the universal. Their systematic, rational accounts of the universalizing factor in particular subject and object relationships let Joyce out of the deadlocked modernist opposition between naturalism and symbolism. Larding *Ulysses* with analogies, parodies, and symbols whose relation to the narrative is logically derived from Aristotle's form of forms and Bruno's dynamic world-soul, Joyce was able to write everything in all ways at once.

Working with Aristotle's thought as it was modified by Neoplatonism in Aquinas (the same Neoplatonism Bruno elaborates later), Dante also created an epic account of the merger of universal and particular in individual souls, a fully objective statement of the fully subjective experience of one soul that is all souls—hence his relevance to Joyce's union of naturalism and symbolism in *Ulysses*, the book of Bloom as Everyman. And finally, Matthew Arnold, the near contemporary of Joyce whom Wilson omits from the conflict of literary modernity, offered the novelist conceptual terms for analysis of those universal laws governing objective, public experience, the province of naturalism, and the subjective realm, the province of symbolism. Referring to that public experience as culture, and arguing that culture arises from private spiritual impulses in perpetual conflict with each other in individual minds—"Hellenism" and "Hebraism"—Arnold gave Joyce one more theoretical formulation with which to display the soul's capacity to unite contraries, in this case the citizen and his nation. Using the Victorian formulation of unified opposites, Joyce was able to show in Bloom's world the most recent historical presence of those eternal laws of being that govern the novel's artistic design. Wilson starts his literary history from an existential, psychological base, discussing reality in terms of private and public experience. The integration of these oppositions in the existential, psychological dimension of *Ulysses*, its narrative, takes place according to technically sophisticated philosophical principles. The book's symbolic order presents the philosophical topic—ontology, reality conceived as the soul's capacity mutatis mutandis to integrate forms—which generates and contains the psychological one. The dynamic synthesis of opposites in the soul considered as the substantial activity of being in human nature, and—according to the micro- and macrocosm analogy—in the created universe at large: that concept bestows a philosophical order on *Ulysses* and unifies the artistic forms that actualize Bloom's naturalistic and symbolic day.

Ulysses presents humanity as a hologram of the cosmos, one item that manifests the structure, and thereby implicitly the content as well, of all reality. Coincidence of identical contraries (the part and the whole) is the nature of holograms and the fundamental principle in Joyce's fictional one. The corollary laws are all descriptions of how the contraries coalesce; how universality creates particularity, how the one creates the many, how form actualizes matter, which possibility becomes actuality, and so on. The transformation from one state to the other, in which both are preserved, is the vital principle of reality, what Aristotle calls the soul, restricting himself to organisms. Bruno extends that term to all existing things, convinced, as the ancient scientist was not, that all of reality is alive, that every item in it is part of a "rational organism." Working in a theological matrix of psychology, ethics, and cosmology, Dante dramatizes the transformations of this vital principle of reality in his *Commedia*, restricting himself, after the example of Aristotle, to one organism as the first and only rational organism, and therefore the most significant life in worldly reality—the human being. In Dante, as in Bruno and Aristotle, a human being's soul is the substantial activity that locates the human in the cosmos and the cosmos in the human. A form that actualizes itself by incorporating other actualized forms and identifying itself with them, a human soul presents the primary activity of reality—perpetual transformation of contraries one into the other. Just such a

transfiguring incorporation of forms governs both the artistic design and the artistic matter of *Ulysses*, as I have argued in the close
analyses of scenes and details in scenes that make up the bulk of
this study. This is the occasion for one bald statement of that argument, one last account of how Aristotle, Bruno, Dante, and Arnold
figure in Joyce's overdetermined representation of the soul's unity
in *Ulysses*.

Aristotle provides the conceptual foundation for the artistic design of the novel with his argument in *De Anima* that human beings are made real by the activity of their souls, which brings them
into a relationship of identity with other existing things. The soul
has a universal function in each particular organism, thus uniting
objective and subjective reality in all human beings, and it always
operates on matter and in matter the same way, bringing possibility
into actuality and thus reconciling the fundamental opposition in
human experience between mentality and physicality. And finally,
the soul, being the form of the body, is entirely present in each part
of the living organism, although its transfiguring and identifying
functions are actualized variously in the body's various parts. This
understanding of being allowed Joyce to make a particular man universal in *Ulysses*, to make one narrative all narratives, to make
every part of that narrative an element in a symbolic structure that
brings encyclopedic ranges of literary forms into one literary form.
When the narrative of the book is understood as the body and the
symbolism as the soul, these analogies to Aristotle's treatise come
clear.

Bruno contributes to the dynamic universality of *Ulysses*, which
Aristotle largely made possible, primarily the law of association,
the major principle governing narrative and symbolic structures in
the novel. Where Aristotle maintained an ontological distinction
between particulars and generalities, Bruno establishes a mystical
ontological unity, arguing that all is in all by virtue of the world-
soul. He incorporates Aristotle's conception of the soul's growth,
according to which matter limits the forms an individual soul can
actualize, but ends up contradicting it with the idea that the world-
soul is actualized in each individual form, that all reality is thus
present, realized and unrealized, in whatever forms an individual
being takes on or casts off throughout its existence. As all forms are
both distinct and identical, so the potential that forms actualize,

matter, is identical in all its transfigurations. In this conception, Bruno concurs with Aristotle.

He defies his ancient predecessor, however, with the conception that infinite and universal matter is not only the opposite of form, but identical to it, that potentiality is already actuality, and vice versa. In Aristotle's thought a life is nothing more than itself, nothing more than the set of those forms that the soul actualizes in the material realm of one body that perishes. The identity of the soul and external reality comes in perceptual and rational interchange of forms that does not extend to the permanently separate material embodiment of those forms. In Bruno's thought one life is both nothing more than itself, nothing more than the set of forms actualized by the soul, and at the same time everything that it is not, has not yet become, or never was, since one life contains the whole of the world soul, in which are contained all the forms everywhere actualized in the past and present, and all those yet to be actualized in the future. Because form and matter are not just mutually dependent, but ontologically identical to Bruno, every soul is also all matter, formed and unformed. And finally, since every existing item is a soul for Bruno, not only human beings and organisms, but the vast realm of inorganic nature is included in this identity. Anything and everything is both part and whole in the world-soul, which renders all things fully universal and fully particular.

These transformations of Aristotle's identification of the soul and body provide much of the intellectual coherence for Joyce's incessant association of details in the narrative order of *Ulysses*, and in the symbolic one, and for the constant incremental transfiguration of details from one order into the other, and back again. The objective specificity of the narrative, and the kaleidoscopic permutations that generalizing symbolism works there, depict the actions of Bruno's world-soul as well as those of Aristotle's individuating, rational *anima*. The theory of metempsychosis Bloom dwells on is a variant account of the world-soul's transformations across time through many different material embodiments, and it implies, when it is seen in the context of Bruno's thought, that the literary structure embodying Bloom's day is also the literary structure embodying Odysseus's journey, a form substantially active in *Ulysses*, not merely ironically juxtaposed there against the foreign matter of modernity.

And finally, in addition to organizing the associations that integrate the book (repetition and coincidence in the narrative; allusion, parody, etc. in the symbolism), and making Bloom Everyman as well as Noman (a common man, a nobody), the idea that all is in all gives *Ulysses* its cosmic dimension. Aristotle provides no model for the literary representation of the infinity of actuality and its double, possibility. Without making the *Odyssey* into a symbol of transcendental metaphysics and the disembodied soul as the Neoplatonists did, Joyce, working with Bruno's transfiguration of Aristotle, was still able to keep Homer's story a literary image of absolute and infinite being. Humanity is the locus of being in the novel, but not the terminus. Bloom's day tells the tale of humanity and of everything else that is. The laws that unite contraries in *Ulysses*, derived in large part from Bruno's heterodox mysticism, govern being as humanity receives it, and they provide structures for Joyce's symbolic extension of limited human existence into the limitless cosmos and for his narrative reversal of the same procedure. That double action goes on throughout the novel, but it is most clearly at work in the penultimate chapter, "Ithaca," whose subject is the identity of home and exile, of the kitchen at 7 Eccles Street and the boundless created universe, of the maximum and minimum embodiments of the world-soul.

Dante's *Commedia* showed Joyce how a contemporary epic of the soul containing all life in the symbolic depiction of one man's crisis and recovery, constructed with an epic of antiquity as a controlling metaphor, could be written. Just as Dante exceeds the confines of Virgil's *Aeneid*, elaborating the political and moral heroism of that work with conceptions that arose long after its completion (conceptions drawn largely from the complex merger of Christian and pagan philosophy called Scholasticism), so Joyce exceeds Homer's epic, locating in his modern continuation of Odysseus's journey ideas of the soul foreign to it. The poetics by which Dante was able to incorporate other texts into his own as sustained and local analogies to elements of the pilgrim's experience, and the literary technique of polysemous narration of the soul's progress from error to happiness that resulted from those poetics, make up Joyce's most significant inheritance from Dante.

Because the soul travels in two opposed dimensions on earth, struggling to bring impermanent physical reality to a state of spiritual perfection, the representation of that struggle, as Dante saw it, needed to be multidimensional. Hence, the theoretical formulation, in the letter to Can Grande, of the polysemous allegory governing the poem. The crucial issue in that letter is symbolism's emanation from narrative, the indelible literal origin of all figurative signification in fiction, or, to put the matter in philosophical terms, the soul's inextricable connection to the body in Aristotle's thought, the irreducible particularity in which the world-soul's universality always appears in Bruno's thought. The literal dimension, like matter, which is substantially potential, sustains and organizes a vast number of figurative significations, becomes the ground for actualizing progressively more general forms in Dante's epic. In the narrative this principle that formal amplification starts from an irreducible material origin shows up in the autobiographical claims of the fiction: Dante's own personal choices in the world of the quick presented to him in Florence have led him to an enforced Odyssey through the afterlife, during which he confronts all the damning and redeeming choices of the soul arranged hierarchically in the three kingdoms he moves through. One soul's choice reveals the full range of all souls' choices in the fiction of the epic, just as one symbolic form, the journey, is elaborated in the figurative order of the epic until it becomes an encyclopedic account of every medieval intellectual discipline's development of classical and Christian tradition, and of every literary form preserved in that vast historical partnership of opposites. It is hard not to think that Dante did not perceive his epic presentation of the soul's destiny as a literary form of forms, a poem representing, in a manner, all that is, especially when his veneration of Aristotle is considered.

It is not hard to see Joyce's epic imitation of such polysemous depiction of the soul in *Ulysses*, where Bloom's crisis and recovery reveal the full range of human experience in a symbolic literary form that incorporates every intellectual discipline in Joyce's world. Functional texts (wills, contracts, insurance policies, bills, newspaper articles and advertisements, library fines, etc.) from modern Ireland as well as artistic texts, including the repertoire of popular and classical song, from every development of English literature, and many other literatures (Greek, Italian, Spanish, French, American, German, to name the most prominent) crowd into *Ulysses* to make it a universal history of verbal art forms even more copious than

Dante's, which does not absorb popular texts at all. Dante's insistence on locating a universalizing multiplicity of forms and meanings in the literal level recurs in Joyce's inweaving throughout *Ulysses* of allusions, parodies, and the like into the realistic circumstances of June 16, 1904. There no symbol merely suggests extended meaning for fictional details (as the symbolism of Ibsen's *The Master Builder* does, for instance), but systematically projects those details—the color of Bloom's suit and Stephen's for one—into an intellectually coherent order that presents the soul's power to unify contraries. In Dante's allegory a literary form tells human beings all the most vital truth of their souls' experience, which is the most important truth in reality. In Dante's case, one controlling metaphor in that truth-telling comes from Exodus, as the poem and the Can Grande letter make clear, and one from the *Aeneid*. In his modern Irish epic, Joyce uses the same biblical analogy and quotes the same psalm that appears in Dante's poem and letter. His other controlling metaphor is the Greek classic that organizes much of Virgil's poem, and hence Dante's—the *Odyssey*.

Like Dante, Joyce values intellectual analysis and erotic devotion more highly than other mundane experiences of the soul, and he makes his narrative primarily the occasion for intellectual analysis of a crisis and recovery in the protagonist's erotic devotion. The difference comes, of course, in the objects of that analysis and desire. In Dante's poem all the soul's transfigurations eventually bring it to rest in the unified serene being of Being (unless the soul is damned), to the moving stillness where desire and satisfaction are coinciding contraries—God. In Joyce's book the soul's transfigurations have no such rest because God has been ignored in favor of worldly imperfection. For Bloom, for all of us as Joyce saw it, experience complicates itself without resolution, and desire ends inevitably in frustration, in provisional sating at best. All is in all outside the created universe to Dante's mind, and the soul learns and participates in the reality of this law of being only in the empyrean, where it is blessed. All is in all in every item of the created universe, beyond which nothing is, to Joyce's mind, and the soul participates in that reality, with or without knowledge, in all places at all times. Dante's portrayal of the soul's struggle to be ends in a vision where reception of ultimate Being ineffably exceeds all powers of human expression. Joyce's similar portrayal of the laws of being ends in an intersection of contraries, in the hour when night starts to be day. This symbolic finale implies that: the end of being is not ineffable, but immanent in the order of mundane life; that spiritual striving is not for transcendental perfection but toward secular happiness, which is a matter of perpetually evanescent merging of conflicting oppositions; and finally, that erotic pursuit and intellectual analysis, the soul's largest purchase on being, locate human beings by dislocating them, and bring them into reality by keeping them longing for it.

Matthew Arnold's conception of the unification of oppositions in the cultural progress of man's spirit was the modern British version of the soul's complex unity that Joyce chose to add to the classical, medieval, and renaisssance formulations. Arnold's ethical analysis of individuals and their political relations provides terms for figurative magnification of Bloom and his world that operate as Dante's allegorical, Aristotle's psychological, and Bruno's ontological analyses of the soul do—with a theory of contraries coinciding. Arnold is by far the least of these minds, and the one who contributed least to Joyce's philosophical ambitions. He belongs in their company more as an agent who expedites Joyce's refashioning of their thought into a universal history of the soul than he does as an original force.

For Aristotle, Bruno, and Dante, all experience centers in the soul, which is conceived by each of them as the customhouse of reality as far as humanity is concerned, the place where all being begins and ends for human beings. Each one of them ascribes infinity to the soul (Aristotle more sketchily than the others), which is fitting, since infinity is all middle. Aristotle's conception of the soul's centrality comes in his perception of it as a ratio through which forms are dynamically interchanged and assimilated, an ontological as well as ethical mean; Bruno's comes in the idea that any particular embodiment of the world-soul is the center of the world-soul's universal creativity; and Dante's comes in an allegorical narrative that takes a man at mid-life through every reality the soul can actualize, an epic journey that relies extensively on Aristotle's thinking. *Ulysses*, absorbing and transfiguring the thought of these three, also presents the soul, embodied in Bloom, as the fulcrum of all reality's forces, the origin and end of all being's material forms insofar as they relate to humanity. Bloom's book presents the soul's infinity by beginning *in medias res*, staying there at all points, and ending there, substituting worldly circumstances for Dante's salvation, and blending Pisgah into Homer's Ithaca.

Odysseus's crisis does not end in Joyce's telling of it, but operates throughout as the controlling symbol for the constant interchange of being's permanent law and history's particular and ephemeral actualities. "This and that, this is that" are the rules governing all experience in the novel, and all critical analysis of it. The narrative embodiment of that law is Bloom's constant intellectual and emotional adjustment to changing circumstances. In the book's formal structure that law wraps all realistic details into symbolic ones, and vice versa, making Bloom's journey a literary image of Bruno's idea that in the soul, which is in all things, all is in all. In its drabbest details—Stephen's thinking Eve had no navel, Bloom's thinking Greek goddesses have no anus, Bloom and Boylan's sharing one tailor and one profession—in its emphatic controlling metaphors—that Bloom is Odysseus and Moses, that Ireland is Greece and Israel—*Ulysses* displays the permanent, universal reality of the soul when it displays contraries coinciding. Reading *Ulysses* as an epic of the soul accounts for the book's form, its matter, and locates Joyce in the company of those philosophical artists in the Christian tradition who thought of humanity as the center of being. Aristotle, Bruno, Dante, and Arnold enabled Joyce to make *Ulysses* a symbol of unified and universal being, to make Bloom an image of the soul —an image, in an Irish manner, of all that is.

notes

INTRODUCTION

1. Joyce, "Drama and Life," in *Critical Writings*, pp. 40, 45 (hereafter cited as *CW*).

2. For a detailed history of this critical debate see Lamberton, *Homer the Theologian*.

3. Johnson, "Preface to Shakespeare," in *Selected Prose*, p. 240.

4. Georges Borach, "Conversations with James Joyce," in *Portraits of the Artist in Exile*, ed. Potts, p. 69, and Budgen, *James Joyce and the Making of Ulysses*, pp. 16–18.

CHAPTER ONE

1. Joyce, *Letters*, 2:28, 35, 38 (hereafter cited as *L1* or *L2*).

2. Borach, "Conversations with James Joyce," in *Portraits of the Artist in Exile*, ed. Potts, p. 71.

3. Brief mention of the importance of Aristotle's antiidealistic idea of the soul to Joyce's conception of *Ulysses* can be found in Ellmann's *Ulysses on the Liffey*, pp. 12–18. The point is also made in Perl's *Tradition of Return*, p. 181.

4. To date there has been no detailed critical account of the presence of ideas of the soul from *De Anima* in *Ulysses*. When the term "soul" is used as a term for critical analysis at all it is usually loosely synonymous with some permanent quality of mentality or personality. Epstein's "James Joyce and the Body" in *A Starchamber Quiry*, pp. 75–82, exemplifies this critical habit. In Epstein's essay the word "soul" is used as equivalent to the deepest part of the unconscious mind, the medium in which mind and body are united. The idea has a rough analogy to Aristotle's case, but no dependence on it, as Epstein develops his argument. Analyzing very well the appearance of Lipoti Virag in "Circe," Epstein first argues that Joyce locates fear of death and eros in this "soul" and then presents the conjuction of these two impulses as the source of linguistic creativity. Epstein's argument is plausible and important, but the use of the term "soul" is misleading, especially considering Joyce's expertise in the Aristotelian definition of the soul, which is explicitly presented repeatedly, and often prominently, in *Ulysses*.

5. Aristotle, *De Anima*, p. 69 (hereafter cited as *A*).

6. Joyce, *Ulysses*, 2.67–76 (hereafter cited as *U*).

7. Smith, *History of Mysticism*, pp. 51, 70.

8. Alighieri, *Inferno*, 4.42 (hereafter cited as *Inf*).

9. Gifford, *Ulysses Annotated*, 3.8–9n (hereafter cited as *G*). The reference is to the note for lines eight through nine of episode three. Gifford's annotations are all keyed to the episode and line numbers of Gabler's edition of *Ulysses*.

10. For further investigation of the Neoplatonic tradition of interpreting the *Odyssey* as an occult presentation of the soul's sojourn in the world of matter, which Joyce mocks and revises in *Ulysses*, see Lamberton, *Homer the Theologian*.

11. Senn, "Book of Many Turns" in *Joyce's Dislocutions*, p. 131.

CHAPTER TWO

1. Joyce, *My Brother's Keeper*, p. 132. Other citations of Bruno's personal significance to Joyce are Ellmann, *James Joyce*, pp. 61, 93, 144, 151, 154, 249 (hereafter cited as *E*); Tindall, *James Joyce: His Way of Interpreting*, p. 172; Potts, ed., *Portraits of the Artist in Exile*, p. 172.

2. Gose, *Transformation Process in Joyce's Ulysses*. This book does refer to Joyce's use of Bruno in *Finnegans Wake*, but it concentrates primarily on *Ulysses* and is, in fact, the most extensive and intelligent previous study of the subject.

3. Bruno, *Cause, Principle, and Unity*, p. 80 (hereafter cited as *C*).

4. Blake, "Auguries of Innocence," in *William Blake's Writings*, 2:1312.

5. Blake, *Marriage of Heaven and Hell*, in *William Blake's Writings*, 1:88.

6. Mention of the importance to Joyce of Bruno's ideas of the coincidence of contraries, the universality of particulars, and the extension, via Bruno, of Joyce's Aristotelian materialism can be found in Ellmann, *Ulysses on the Liffey*, pp. 53–56. Treatment of Aristotle and Bruno in relation to Joyce can also be found in Brivic, *Joyce the Creator*, pp. 44–54. Brivic concentrates primarily on these thinkers' conceptions of God as they provide models for Joyce's conception of himself as creator-god. Aristotle is represented by *Metaphysics* and *Poetics*, with a mention of *De Anima* on p. 64. Bruno's *Cause, Principle, and Unity* is mentioned briefly to indicate his dissatisfaction with Aristotle's incapacity to understand the coincidence of contraries.

7. Joyce, *Portrait of the Artist*, p. 249 (hereafter cited as *P*).

8. Pater, *The Renaissance*, p. 130; Wilde, *Salome*; Yeats, *Oxford Book of Modern Verse*, p. 1. An excellent analysis of the sources of the femme fatale in *A Portrait of the Artist as a Young Man* appears in Gifford, *Joyce Annotated*, pp. 257–66. The figure shows up in Stephen's villanelle "Are you not weary" in Chapter 5 of *P*, pp. 217–24.

9. Senn, "The Rhythm of Ulysses," in *Joyce's Dislocutions*, p. 197.

10. Many scholars have come to grief trying to track down every connection between all the symbolic elements of *Ulysses*. Senn, in "Weaving and Unweaving," in *Joyce's Dislocutions*, pp. 45–70, offers a necessary and eloquent caveat against this procedure by accurate and provocative analysis of the limitations of the symbolic orders in *Ulysses*, of the loose ends Joyce left dangling between the systematic analogies he enmeshed throughout the novel. Except to imply that Joyce's unweaving of the symbolic structures is a narrative principle for representing the limited knowledge possible in any one reading of *Ulysses*, Senn provides scant conclusions about the meaning of these gaps in the structure of the book. Seen in the light of Bruno's conception of the infinite variability of the soul's transformations through time and space in the material world, the limited coherence of the analogical overlays displays a philosophically coherent literary structure. Read against Bruno, the weaving and unweaving that Senn traces are literary forms that present the soul's power to implicate and explicate, constantly, all universals from particulars, and vice versa.

11. Herring, *Joyce's Ulysses Notesheets*; Litz, *Art of James Joyce*.

12. Joyce, *Finnegans Wake*, p. 20 (hereafter cited as *FW*).

13. Aristotle, *Poetics*, p. 35. The standard citation is *Poetics*, viii, 9.

9. What we have said already makes it further clear that a poet's object is not to tell what actually happened but what could or would happen either probably or inevitably. The difference between a historian and a poet is not that one writes in prose and the other in verse—indeed the writings of Herodotus could be put into verse and yet would still be a kind of history, whether written in metre or not. The real difference is this, that one tells what happened and the other what might happen. For this reason poetry is something more scientific [philosophical] and serious than history, because poetry tends to give general truths while history gives particular facts.

14. Ibid.

15. Brivic, *Joyce the Creator*. Brivic's book is the most extensive and intelligent discussion of the persistent metaphor for the artist in Joyce's work, that of creator-god.

CHAPTER THREE

1. Alighieri, "On Eloquence in the Vernacular," in *Literary Criticism*, p. 15 (hereafter cited as *LCD*).

2. de Bruyne, *Etudes d'esthétique medievale*; Smalley, *Study of the Bible*.

3. Tindall, "Dante and Mrs. Bloom," in *James Joyce: His Way of Interpreting*, pp. 85–92. Tindall's essay is one of the earliest connections of

Dante to Joyce's novel. The most comprehensive recent work on the subject is Reynolds, *Joyce and Dante.*

4. See also Alighieri, *Paradiso* 24–26 (hereafter cited as *Par*).

5. Joyce, *Ulysses* (New York: Random House, 1961), p. xii.

6. Alighieri, *Purgatorio* 27, p. 299 (hereafter cited as *Pur*).

7. Reynolds, *Joyce and Dante*, p. 76. Reynolds cites here the importance of this line from Virgil to Dante ("Wherefore I crown and mitre you over yourself") for Joyce's development of the theme of the necessity and difficulty of organic maturity in a successful artist.

8. St. Augustine of Hippo, *Expositions*, pp. 275–91.

9. Gilbert, *James Joyce's Ulysses*, p. 369.

10. Ibid., p. 369.

11. Reynolds, *Joyce and Dante*, pp. 122–28. Reynolds's discussion of the Exodus psalm concentrates on Stephen's initiation through lustration rites into a secularized artistic priesthood.

12. See Reynolds, *Joyce and Dante*, pp. 35–44, for Reynolds's discussion of Bloom's status as Virgil, a spiritually paternal figure to Stephen's artistic immaturity.

13. Ibid., pp. 180–81.

14. See Chapter 3 of Reynolds's book for a lengthy analysis of the secularization of Dante's religious symbols for love in *Ulysses*.

CHAPTER FOUR

1. Arnold, "Culture and Anarchy" in *Portable Matthew Arnold*, p. 472 (hereafter cited as *CA*).

2. For a full account of sexuality in Joyce's major fiction, see Brown, *James Joyce and Sexuality*. Joyce's thinking about homosexuality is reviewed in this work on pp. 78–84.

3. Raleigh, *Chronicle of Leopold and Molly Bloom*. The following facts are collected here from Raleigh's book, and placed together for convenience.

Bloom's Addresses

Poldy is born in 1866 in May, probably on the sixth, at 52 Clanbrassil Street, where he lives until 1881, when he is fifteen. From then until he is twenty-one there is a six-year period for which no address can be assigned him. He cannot be at Clanbrassil Street because his parents have purchased the Queen's Hotel in Ennis, Clare, by 1886, the year they both die. Late adolescence is a dangerous time to have no home (interestingly enough for the connection of Bloom to Dedalus, it is exactly during that period that Stephen also leaves home, never to return), and Joyce makes no effort to establish any substitute familial stability, domestic or otherwise, for Bloom in these risky years. By

1888 he has married Molly and lives on Pleasant Street with her until 1892, except for a brief stint somewhere in those four years on Arbutus Place. From 1892 till the spring of 1893 they live at Lombard Street West, after which they move to Raymond Terrace, where they stay for less than a year until moving again, this time to the City Arms Hotel. During the year they stay there (until 1894) the Blooms' marital happiness collapses, Rudy dies, and carnal knowledge between them enters that state of dimness in which it remains for ten years. In 1895 the hapless pair experience their worst time, "on the rocks" at Holles Street, where they stay until 1897 when they move to Ontario Terrace, where they remain until 1898. The years from 1899 to 1903 have no accountable address. This second blank space in Bloom's residential history vanishes by 1904 when he and Molly are at 7 Eccles Street, the final quarters recorded for Poldy in the novel, the place he brings Dedalus home to in "Ithaca," the place where the novel closes in "Penelope."

Bloom's Employment History

At fifteen in 1881, he is working as a door-to-door salesman of trinkets for his father. Until 1888 he has no steady job, but is variously employed as a packager in Kellet's mail house, a traveling salesman, and some kind of political assistant to Alderman John Hooper and the solicitor Valentine Dillon. From 1889 till 1893 he works, presumably as a salesman, for Wisdom Hely, stationer. Sometime in 1893, for unspecified reasons, he leaves that job and gets employed by Joe Cuffe, a cattleman, as an actuary, a job from which he is dismissed in 1894, when Wisdom Hely rehires him, this time in part as a debt collector. He has no job in 1895, but works again in 1896 for an insurance company, Drimmies, until 1898. Sometime between then and 1904 he secures his job as ad-canvasser for *The Freeman's Journal*, which he tenuously holds down on the day *Ulysses* is in progress. He has also worked, in an unspecified capacity, at an unspecified time, for *Thom's Directory* in Dublin. In twenty-three years Bloom has had ten jobs, none of them for more than four years, and for some of that time he has been out of work all together; for some of it Joyce specifies no economic situation at all.

4. Eliot, "Burbank With A Baedeker: Bleistein With A Cigar" in *T. S. Eliot, Collected Poems, 1909–1935*, p. 24.

5. For an extended interpretation of *Ulysses* based on Bloom's sexual scheming to involve Stephen in a triangle with Molly, see Empson, "The Ultimate Novel," pp. 217–59. Empson's argument that Stephen will eventually capitulate to Bloom's plot is not convincing, but he does pay more serious attention to the whole problem of Bloom's sexual connection to Stephen than any critic before him.

6. Lyons, *Charles Stewart Parnell*, p. 238 (hereafter cited as *CSP*).

7. The story is told, with commentary corroborating my analysis, in Beach's *Shakespeare and Company*, pp. 170–73. The recording is available on the Caedmon label, # TC1340.

8. Seamus Deane's essay, "Arnold, Burke and the Celts," in *Celtic Revivals*, gives an excellent account of the place Arnold's literary history had in Irish and British political life in the last third of the nineteenth century.

> Even now it is difficult to overestimate the importance of Arnold's Oxford Lectures, *The Study of Celtic Literature*. . . . Of course, every virtue of the Celt was matched by a vice of the British bourgeois; everything the philistine middle classes of England needed, the Celt could supply. (The reverse was also true.) The dreamy, imaginative Celt, unblessed by the Greek sense of form, at home in wild landscapes far from the metropolitan centres of modern social and political life, could cure anxious Europe of the woes inherent in Progress.
>
> [Deane, p. 25]

It is precisely this image of the softly noble Irish savage that Joyce laughs out of existence in *Ulysses*, and precisely "the Greek sense of form" that he sought to enact in Irish life by making his novel out of Homer, and by having his hero live with a clear sense of the other Greek virtue Arnold lionized, the scientific spirit of free rational inquiry.

9. Perl, *Tradition of Return*.

bibliography

ARISTOTLE

Aristotle. *The Basic Works of Aristotle.* Edited by Richard McKeon. New York: Random House, 1941.
_____. *De Anima.* Translated by W. S. Hett. Cambridge: Harvard University Press, Loeb Classical Library, 1975.
_____. *Poetics.* Translated by Hamilton Fyfe. Cambridge: Harvard University Press, 1927.
_____. *The Works of Aristotle Translated Into English.* Edited by W. D. Ross. 12 vols. Oxford: Oxford University Press, 1908–52.
Jaeger, Werner. *Aristotle: Fundamentals of the History of His Development.* Translated by Richard Robinson. 2d ed. Oxford: Oxford University Press, 1948.
Kiernan, Thomas. *Aristotle Dictionary.* Introduction by Theodore James. New York: Philosophical Library, 1962.
Lloyd, G. E. R. *Aristotle: The Growth and Structure of His Thought.* Cambridge: Cambridge University Press, 1968.
Ross, W. D. *Aristotle.* 6th ed. Oxford: Oxford University Press, 1955.

MATTHEW ARNOLD

Arnold, Matthew. "Culture and Anarchy." In *The Portable Matthew Arnold*, edited by Lionel Trilling. New York: Viking Press, 1949.

BRUNO

Bruno, Giordano. *Jordani Bruni Opera latine conscripta, publicus sumptibus edita.* Edited by F. Fiorentino, F. Tocco, H. Vittelli, V. Imbriani, and C. M. Tallarigo. 3 vols. in 8 pts. Naples and Florence, 1879–91.
_____. *Le Opere di Giordano Bruno, ristampate da Paolo de Lagarde.* 2 vols. Göttingen, 1888. The standard Italian edition of Bruno in Joyce's early life.
_____. *The Ash Wednesday Supper: La Cena de le Ceneri.* Translated with an Introduction and Notes by Stanley L. Jaki. Paris and The Hague: Mouton, 1975.

_____. "Concerning the Cause, Principle, and One." In *The Infinite in Giordano Bruno*, edited by Sidney Thomas Greenburg, pp. 79–197. New York: King's Crown Press, 1950.

_____. *The Expulsion of the Triumphant Beast*. Translated with an Introduction and Notes by Arthur D. Imerti. New Brunswick: Rutgers University Press, 1964.

_____. *Five Dialogues by Giordano Bruno: Cause, Principle, and Unity*. Translated with an Introduction by Jack Lindsay. Westport, Conn.: Greenwood Press, 1976.

_____. *Giordano Bruno's "The Heroic Frenzies."* Translated with an Introduction and Notes by Paul Memmo, Jr. Chapel Hill: University of North Carolina Press, 1965.

_____. *The Heroic Enthusiasts*. Translated by L. Williams. London: 1887.

_____. "On The Infinite Universe and Worlds." In *Giordano Bruno: His Life and Thought*, edited by Dorothea Waley Singer, pp. 102–16. New York: Henry Schumann, 1950.

McIntyre, J. Lewis. *Giordano Bruno*. London: Macmillan and Co., 1903.

Michel, Paul Henri. *The Cosmology of Giordano Bruno*. Translated by R. E. W. Maddison. Paris: Hermann; London: Methuen; Ithaca: Cornell University Press, 1973.

Nelson, John Charles. *The Renaissance Theory of Love: The Context of Giordano Bruno's "Eroici Furori."* New York: Columbia University Press, 1958.

Salvestrini, V. *Bibliografia delle opere di Giordano Bruno, e degli scritta ad esso attinenti*. Pisa, 1926.

Singer, Dorothea Waley. *Giordano Bruno: His Life and Thought*. With annotated translation of his work, "On the Infinite Universe and Worlds." New York: Henry Schumann, 1950.

Yates, Frances A. *Giordano Bruno and the Hermetic Tradition*. Chicago: University of Chicago Press, 1964.

DANTE

Alighieri, Dante. *La Divina Commedia*. Edited by Eugenio Camerini. Biblioteca Classica Economica. Milan: E. Sonzogno, 1904.

_____. *The Divine Comedy*. Translated with commentary by Charles S. Singleton. 6 vols. Bollingen Series 80. Princeton: Princeton University Press, 1970.

_____. *The Literary Criticism of Dante Alighieri*. Translated and edited by Robert S. Haller. Lincoln: University of Nebraska Press, 1973.

Singleton, Charles S. *Commedia: Elements of Structure*, Vol. 1 of *Dante Studies*. Baltimore: Johns Hopkins University Press, 1954.

_____. *Journey to Beatrice*, Vol. 2 of *Dante Studies*. Baltimore: Johns Hopkins University Press, 1958.

Bibliography

WORKS BY JAMES JOYCE

Joyce, James. *The Critical Writings of James Joyce*. Edited by Ellsworth Mason and Richard Ellmann. New York: Viking Press, 1964.
_____. *Dubliners*. New York: Viking Press, 1967.
_____. *Finnegans Wake*. New York: Viking Press, 1939.
_____. *A Portrait of the Artist as a Young Man*. Edited by Chester G. Anderson. New York: Viking Press, 1968.
_____. *Ulysses*. New York: Random House, 1961.
_____. *Ulysses*. New York: Random House, 1986. The Corrected Text, edited by Hans Walter Gabler, with Wolfhard Steppe and Claus Melchior.

BIBLIOGRAPHIES OF JOYCE CRITICISM

Cohn, Alan M. Current and Supplemental Checklists appearing regularly in *James Joyce Quarterly* since 1964.
Deming, Robert H. *A Bibliography of James Joyce Studies*. 2d ed., rev. and enl. Boston: G. K. Hall and Co., 1977.
Rice, Thomas Jackson. *James Joyce: A Guide to Research*. New York and London: Garland, 1982.
Stanley, Thomas. "James Joyce." In *Anglo-Irish Literature: A Review of Research*, edited by Richard J. Finneran. New York: MLA, 1976.

BIOGRAPHIES OF JOYCE, MEMOIRS, AND CORRESPONDENCE

Beach, Sylvia. *Shakespeare and Company*. New York: Harcourt, Brace, 1959.
Ellmann, Richard. *James Joyce*. New York: Oxford University Press, 1982.
Gorman, Herbert. *James Joyce*. New York: Farrar and Rinehart, 1939.
Joyce, James. *Letters of James Joyce*. Edited by Richard Ellmann. 3 vols. New York: Viking Press, 1966.
Joyce, Stanislaus. *The Dublin Diary of Stanislaus Joyce*. Edited by George Harris Healey. Ithaca: Cornell University Press, 1972.
_____. *My Brother's Keeper*. Edited by Richard Ellmann. London: Faber and Faber, 1958.
Potts, Willard, ed. *Portraits of the Artist in Exile: Recollections of James Joyce by Europeans*. Seattle and London: University of Washington Press, 1979.

GENERAL STUDIES OF JOYCE'S WORKS

Books

Adams, Robert Martin. *James Joyce: Common Sense and Beyond.* New York: Random House, 1967.
_____. *Surface and Symbol.* New York: Oxford University Press, 1967.
Benstock, Bernard and Shari. *Who's He When He's at Home: A James Joyce Directory.* Urbana: University of Illinois Press, 1980.
Bowen, Zack, and Carens, James F., eds. *A Companion to Joyce Studies.* Westport, Conn.: Greenwood Press, 1984.
Brivic, Sheldon. *Joyce the Creator.* Madison: University of Wisconsin Press, 1985.
Brown, Richard. *James Joyce and Sexuality.* Cambridge: Cambridge University Press, 1985.
Cixous, Hélène. *The Exile of James Joyce.* Translated from the French by Sally J. Purcell. New York: David Lewis, 1972.
Deming, Robert, ed. *James Joyce: The Critical Heritage.* 2 vols. London: Routledge, Kegan Paul, 1970.
Epstein, E. L., ed. *A Starchamber Quiry.* New York: Methuen, 1983.
Gifford, Don. *Joyce Annotated: Notes for Dubliners and A Portrait of the Artist as a Young Man.* Berkeley: University of California Press, 1982.
Givens, Seon. *James Joyce: Two Decades of Criticism.* Rev. ed. New York: Vanguard Press, 1963.
Gross, John J. *James Joyce.* New York: Viking Press, 1970.
Herr, Cheryl. *Joyce's Anatomy of Culture.* Urbana and Chicago: University of Illinois Press, 1986.
Kenner, Hugh. *Dublin's Joyce.* Bloomington: Indiana University Press, 1956.
Levin, Harry. *James Joyce: A Critical Introduction.* Norfolk: New Directions Books, 1941.
Litz, A. Walton. *The Art of James Joyce.* New York: Oxford University Press, 1968.
Magalaner, Marvin, and Kain, Richard M. *Joyce: The Man, The Work, The Reputation.* New York: New York University Press, 1959.
Moseley, Virginia. *Joyce and the Bible.* DeKalb: Northern Illinois University Press, 1968.
Peake, C. H. *James Joyce: The Citizen and the Artist.* London: Edward Arnold, 1977.
Schutte, William. *Joyce and Shakespeare: A Study in the Meaning of Ulysses.* New Haven: Yale University Press, 1957.
Senn, Fritz. *Joyce's Dislocutions: Essays on Reading as Translation.* Edited by John Paul Riquelme. Baltimore: Johns Hopkins University Press, 1984.
Tindall, William York. *James Joyce: His Way of Interpreting The Modern*

World. New York: Scribners, 1950.

———. *Reader's Guide to James Joyce.* New York: Noonday Press, 1959.

General Books on Ulysses

Budgen, Frank. *James Joyce and the Making of Ulysses.* 1934. Reprint. Bloomington: Indiana University Press, 1964.

Ellmann, Richard. *Ulysses on the Liffey.* London: Faber and Faber, 1972.

Gifford, Don, with Seidman, Robert J. *Ulysses Annotated: Notes for Joyce's Ulysses.* Berkeley: University of California Press, 1988.

Gilbert, Stuart. *James Joyce's Ulysses.* London: Faber and Faber, 1930.

Gose, Eliot P., Jr. *The Transformation Process in Joyce's Ulysses.* Toronto: University of Toronto Press, 1980.

Groden, Michael. *Ulysses in Progress.* Princeton: Princeton University Press, 1977.

Herring, Phillip. *Joyce's Ulysses Notesheets in the British Museum.* Charlottesville: University of Virginia Press, 1972.

Kain, Richard M. *Fabulous Voyager: James Joyce's Ulysses.* Chicago: University of Chicago Press, 1959.

Kenner, Hugh. *Flaubert, Beckett, and Joyce: The Stoic Comedians.* London: W. H. Allan, 1964.

———. *Joyce's Voices.* Berkeley: University of California Press, 1977.

———. *Ulysses.* London: George Allen and Unwin, 1980.

Perl, Jeffrey M. *The Tradition of Return: The Implicit History of Modern Literature.* Princeton: Princeton University Press, 1984.

Raleigh, John Henry. *The Chronicle of Leopold and Molly Bloom.* Berkeley: University of California Press, 1977.

Reynolds, Mary. *Joyce and Dante: The Shaping Imagination.* Princeton: Princeton University Press, 1976.

Staley, Thomas R., and Benstock, Bernard, eds. *Approaches to Ulysses: Ten Essays.* Pittsburgh: University of Pittsburgh Press, 1970.

Sultan, Stanley. *The Argument of Ulysses.* Columbus: Ohio State University Press, 1964.

Thornton, Weldon. *Allusions in Ulysses.* Chapel Hill: University of North Carolina Press, 1968.

Wilson, Edmund. *Axel's Castle.* New York: Scribners, 1931.

Articles on Ulysses

Blackmur, R. P. "The Jew in Search of a Son." *Virginia Quarterly Review* (Winter 1948).

Donoghue, Denis. "Joyce's Method of Philosophical Fiction." *James Joyce Quarterly* (Fall 1967):9–21.

Bibliography

Eliot, T. S. "*Ulysses,* Order and Myth." *Dial* 75 (November 1923):480–83.
Empson, William. "The Theme of *Ulysses.*" *Kenyon Review* (Winter 1956):26–52.
_____. "The Ultimate Novel." In *Using Biography.* London: Chatto & Windus, Hogarth Press, 1984.
Frank, Joseph. "Spatial Form in Modern Literature." *Sewanee Review* 53 (April 1945):223–35.
Raleigh, John Henry. "Bloom as Modern Epic Hero." *Critical Inquiry* 3 (Spring 1977):583–98.

SOME RELIGIOUS, LITERARY, AND HISTORICAL CONTEXTS FOR *ULYSSES*

St. Augustine of Hippo. *Expositions on the Book of Psalms.* Translated by Rev. H. M. Wilkins. Oxford: Oxford University Press, 1853.
Blake, William. *William Blake's Writings.* Edited by G. E. Bentley. Oxford: Clarendon Press, 1978.
Deane, Seamus. *Celtic Revivals: Essays in Modern Irish Literature 1880–1980.* London: Faber and Faber, 1985.
de Bruyne, Edgar. *Etudes d'esthétique medievale.* Bruges: Tempel, 1946.
Eliot, T. S. *T.S. Eliot, Collected Poems, 1909–1935.* New York: Harcourt, Brace, and World, 1971.
Johnson, Samuel. *Samuel Johnson: Rasselas, Poems, and Selected Prose.* Edited by Bertrand H. Bronson. New York: Holt, Rinehart, and Winston, 1958.
Lamberton, Robert. *Homer the Theologian.* Berkeley: University of California Press, 1986.
Lyons, F. S. L., *Charles Stewart Parnell.* New York: Oxford University Press, 1977.
Pater, Walter. *The Renaissance.* London: Macmillan and Co., 1897.
Smalley, Beryl. *The Study of the Bible in the Middle Ages.* Notre Dame: University of Notre Dame Press, 1964.
Smith, M. *An Introduction to the History of Mysticism.* London: 1939.
Wilde, Oscar. *Salome.* London: Melmoth and Co., 1904.
Yeats, William Butler, ed. *The Oxford Book of Modern Verse.* Oxford: Oxford University Press, 1936.

index

Virgil, xiii, xiv, 96, 99, 205; as literary character, 31, 97, 105, 112, 113–14, 193; *Aeneid*, 96–97, 205, 207

Wilde, Oscar, 61, 64, 142; *Salome*, 62; *The Picture of Dorian Gray*, 142
Wilson, Edmund: *Axel's Castle*, 200–201
Wordsworth, William, 88

Yeats, William Butler, 15, 37–38, 61–64; "Who Goes with Fergus," 15, 38; *The Oxford Book of Modern Verse*, 62

Zenn, Fritz, 36, 66–67
Zola, Émile, 27, 200